THE POETRY OF THE
AENEID

THE POETRY OF THE
AENEID

FOUR STUDIES IN
IMAGINATIVE UNITY AND DESIGN

Michael C. J. Putnam

HARVARD UNIVERSITY PRESS

CAMBRIDGE, MASSACHUSETTS

1965

64705

Distributed in Great Britain by Oxford University Press, London

Publication of this book has been aided by a grant from
the Ford Foundation

Library of Congress Catalog Card Number 65-12787

Printed in the United States of America

FOR MY MOTHER AND FATHER

PREFACE

I⊤ is possible to give to any great poet a variety of valid interpretations, and any generation, by applying its own critical theories, will attempt to discover in an author what most appeals to or has bearing upon the age and its concerns. This is usually what previous generations have neglected or considered of secondary import. Strangely enough, instead of being the first, the poets of classical antiquity are all too often the last to receive attention in terms of the most recent developments in critical methodology.

Virgil has not suffered as some other Latin authors have, for from the time of the completion of the *Aeneid* in 19 B.C., the year of his death, to the present day, his fellow poets have found in him a constant source of inspiration. And, in spite of an occasional unsteady voice of dissent, there is little sign that this popularity is on the wane, even at a time when the shorter products of a lyric muse, more personal and therefore supposedly more spontaneous, are held in higher repute than the grander, more measured dimensions of epic. Above all, the traditions of Virgilian scholarship are long and affectionate.

In this respect recent generations can be particularly proud. The present volume, like all works written in the twentieth century devoted to understanding the meaning of the *Aeneid*, stems in large part from the great reappraisal of Virgil's art offered by Richard Heinze in *Virgils epische Technik*, published in 1902. It is Heinze who first set as a specific goal the search for the original elements in the poetry of the *Aeneid*. By detailed examination of the text, primarily in terms of the inherited patterns of epic structure and the variations of the Aeneas legends available to Virgil, Heinze discussed the poet's particular methods of composition and such special topics as plot construction and character development.

More recent essays, such as those of Cartault and Prescott, dealing in greater detail with matters of style, have been more or less dependent on Heinze's accomplishment. In Viktor Pöschl's *Die Dichtkunst Virgils* (1950) Virgil received another highly sympathetic treatment in which the development of personality throughout the epic was defined within the framework of certain imagistic patterns which inform the poem as a whole. Pöschl's work shows that as far as imaginative achievement is concerned Virgil is no Christian moralizer or slavish imitator of Homer, but is a poet of power and originality whose basically pessimistic personality creates a work of art in which the essential theme is the ultimate triumph of violence and death over any idealistic and reasoned pursuits. Those who hear in Aeneas and his progress a mighty paean of praise for the peace and prosperity of Augustan Rome do the force of much of Virgil's poetry the greatest disservice.

But Pöschl did not extend his insights by offering a detailed investigation of any single book of the epic, though this is a logical corollary to his volume. And since the appearance of his work, only a few articles have been published which concentrated attention upon the poetry of certain books, and these usually were written with attention limited to one specific pattern, theme, or group of lines.

Perhaps even more important, neither Heinze nor Pöschl, in their search for originality, specifically discussed Virgil's use of language or analyzed, in particular, the power that individual metaphors and patterns of verbal similarity can infuse into a given book or even into the total epic. Indeed, if one major development of recent literary criticism deserves more stress than any other, it is the importance of seeking for unity in dealing with a work of the creative imagination. Especially in the case of Virgil, the search for and analysis of poetic design must begin with an examination of those subtle variations and repetitions of metaphor and image by which action and structure are defined and unified.

I offer here, in attempting to fill this need, interpretations of four books of the *Aeneid*, treating them first in terms of their own unique qualities, as entities held together by special verbal designs, and then as parts of a larger whole which is strikingly unified not only by repetition of key words and lines but by one or two symbols which take a special place in the total design.

An examination such as this, based primarily on the poetic devices which unify a text, also forces what is original in Virgil constantly and inevitably to the forefront of discussion. Originality in epic can only be sought properly within the fabric of the poet's heritage, since the writer of epic depends not only on new developments of language and style but on the modification of inherited plot construction as well. A poet of Virgil's stature gains rather than suffers when passages in which he is clearly deriving his material from other authors are juxtaposed with their sources of inspiration. Indeed there is no classical poet more carefully conscious of his literary inheritance than Virgil, and not infrequently his genius is seen to best advantage at moments when he is molding past achievements, of others and even of himself, to his present purpose. For this reason, then, the story of Aeneas' adventures begins to assume its own special place when viewed, as this book does on occasion, in the broader perspective of other treatments of heroic endeavor, especially the *Iliad* and the *Odyssey*. Finally, by appeal to other works of Virgil, in particular the *Georgics*, a clearer impression is often gained of the meaning of some of the most important passages of the *Aeneid*.

It is not my purpose to deal here with technical matters such as style and meter. Rather my primary intent is to examine certain of the poet's characteristic means of composition and essential ideas as seen through his use of words.

I utilize, moreover, a critical method which may offer evidence that Virgil's imagination, in the act of creation, transcends any superficial reliance upon numerical or even tonal balances within individual books of his epic or within any larger divisions which the critic cares to define in the epic as a whole.

We may partition the *Aeneid* in many ways, and analogies between one section and another will certainly do our appreciation of the poet no harm. But pressed beyond a certain limit they must fail. In particular, there are many reasons why Virgil should not be treated as a Homer reincarnate, not least because Homer's shaping artistry triumphs through the balances used by any mnemonic technique and within the conventions of exacting harmony which ruled the Geometric Age. Virgil's poetic sophistication lies elsewhere.

It is not difficult to discover examples where concern for the niceties of external arrangement tends to neglect richer poetic meaning. The fifth book of the *Aeneid*, it has been proposed, has close similarities to Book VIII, and taken together they frame what in a literal sense might be called the middle third of the poem. But the relationship of V to Book III and especially to Book VI is of primary importance. Book IX, to offer another example, begins a pattern in the life of Turnus which leads inevitably to XII. But though this parallelism seems to round off the last four books into a whole, Book IX bears even more striking imaginative links with Book II.

The many further examples which could be adduced seem to me to offer evidence which runs counter to the recent thesis propounded by several American and European scholars who search for numerical proportions as the basis of Virgil's method of composition. Rather I suggest that the reader of Virgil should put aside any attempt to impose a calculated symmetry on the poem and search not for some deeper proportion or more hidden harmony but for the unifying imaginative patterns discernible in any masterpiece. If happily such analysis leads to a further integration of one book with another, we may rejoice, but pattern is something which should be discovered as an end, not imposed as a means of critical evaluation.

I have chosen to limit my discussion to only four books from the twelve which comprise the epic, and each of these has a chapter to itself. Nevertheless, these four, though themselves my primary concern, all have links with nearly every other segment of the poem. Different books, especially IV and VI, might seem to offer better examples for more positive and productive discussion. But, in spite of the fact that much in them remains yet to be clarified, they have been the most frequently treated parts of the *Aeneid*. It seems a better course, therefore, to allow them to play what may be termed a secondary but no less vital role in the general presentation. We cannot, for instance, attempt to interpret Aeneas' journey up the Tiber without constant mention of his previous wandering in the world of the dead. Moreover, the story of Turnus' death gains much of its power from the many reminiscences the poet suggests of Dido's tragedy as described in Book IV.

In tracing here imagistic strands peculiar to individual books, I hope that, even without undue emphasis, certain salient images will stand out from the total design. In spite of the diverse episodes into which the hero's changing world is partitioned, there is a marvelous symbolic unity to the poem. One illustration will suffice for the moment. Early in my analysis of Book II a special connection is made between the wooden horse and the seastorm which nearly destroys Aeneas as the epic opens. Nevertheless, the full potentiality of this violent outburst, with nature roused against mankind through the intervention of divinity, is not realized until the very moment of Turnus' death, as Aeneas now gains a final triumph through the tacit agreement, not the opposition, of Juno.

My goal in examining such relationships is to offer further proof of the brilliance of Virgil's mind at work, weaving a texture which unifies not only single books but the total epic as well. To propose that in this imaginative integrity lies perhaps his greatest achievement is my chief excuse for another volume on Virgil's poetic artistry.

Any attempt, however sympathetic and careful, to delineate or clarify a poet's special, often private, symbolism, is subject to many hazards. I am not unaware of the difficulties of moving over a terrain wherein the already subtle boundary-line which separates critic from creator grows dimmer still. Some will complain, only rightly, that certain points have been carried too far and that others have been left untouched. My final analysis of Book XII, itself springing directly from analysis of imagery, is a case in point.

The meaning of the clash between Aeneas and Turnus, which brings the poem to a violent and seemingly inconclusive end, has long been a subject of debate. Why, one tends to ask, does Virgil, if he wishes his poem as a whole to stand as praise of Augustus, conclude in a tone of such gloom and sudden bitterness that the only afterglow reflects an image of Aeneas' personal spite, not the glory that remains for Rome?

In the final books and especially in the last, Virgil is forced to have his hero play a double role, since, though Aeneas remains to some extent the ideal embodiment of future Rome as envisioned by his father Anchises in Book VI, he now becomes as well the actual instrument whereby this destiny is imposed. Spiritual dream can only be created by physical force which must here be defined either ideally as that heroism which rids the world of destructive elements or, more realistically, as the clash of individual with individual which has little apparent purpose other than the display of brute violence. Though the end of the *Aeneid* can be defended on the surface in terms of dramatic necessity, nevertheless the killing of Turnus demonstrates not a willingness on the part of Aeneas to reconcile opposing elements into a creative harmony, as suggested by Anchises, but rather the opposite, an adherence to a type of personal vendetta which had in previous moments put so many obstacles in the path of his own destiny.

I do not feel that this in any way betokens a change in the thinking of the poet. Concerning his own feelings of admiration and awe in the face of Roman might and accomplishment there can be little debate. His doubts about the manner of this achievement are a different matter, however, and Book XII was the most forceful and conclusive place for their expression. The *Aeneid*, and especially its last book, must not be interpreted as a political tract in praise of Augustus or as a program for him to follow in the future but rather as a profound meditation on the necessities of historical development as seen through the eyes of a poet. The poem's final pages do not offer evidence of a sudden alteration in political philosophy on Virgil's part. Instead they show the poet coming to grips with reality at last, contemplating the exigencies demanded by rule and realizing the violations of personal integrity which necessarily follow in the wake of empire. Book XII is an inevitable and forceful reaction to this realization.

In sum, the results of this present analysis of Book XII show Virgil, through his use of words, attributing to Aeneas emotions and motives which he had hitherto denied but which, in the hands of his antagonists, had been the chief cause of trial and suffering to him in the past. There are few hints in the action of Book XII of any greatness of character in Aeneas and no mention whatever of the future brilliance of Rome, save in the idealistic utterances of Jupiter at the end, predicting a future harmony to which his own sudden violence against Turnus gives an immediate lie. For whatever reason (and the reactions of a poet must never be weighed purely in the perspective of history), Virgil seems to say here, if we judge correctly, that Aeneas — and through him Augustus — can never fulfill in fact the ideal conditions of empire, where force and freedom must be fused into a fortunate amalgam.

It is little wonder, then, that the poetry which accompanies Virgil's revelation is some of his finest and that here, as brilliantly as anywhere, his imagination functions in splendid collaboration with his ideas. Here, above all, repetition of past images and conscious renewal of past associations cast special light on the poet's thoughts.

To those who feel at the end of Book XII the final triumph of good over evil, and hence assume (what the poet never says) that a golden age is just around the corner, this interpretation will be a matter of debate, and such it should be, for this work — indeed any work which presumes to explore the poetic mind — can at best be merely suggestive, never definitive. Full acceptance of content or method would be unusual, almost inappropriate, if only because the appeal of a sensitive poet will vary from person to person. My chief desire in this book is simply to review and re-evaluate certain special qualities of a great author and to propose by tentative example new methods for approaching this greatness again.

Since one of the book's chief critical methods consists in striving to show how one context can help explain another through the poet's use of repetition, the Latin text has been quoted liberally, often at length. For the sake of the reader's ease, smaller quotations have been kept to a minimum, and only when the poet lays particular stress on a metaphor have Latin words or phrases been quoted within a sentence. The translations are my own and aim more for a literal rendering of the text than for any further realization of poetic effect. At certain instances when one English word must suffice to replace a poetic ambiguity or especially rich metaphor in the Latin, the subsequent analysis in the text will usually offer some further clarification.

My debt to the great mass of earlier Virgilian scholarship, including commentaries, biographies, and critical essays, however inadequately expressed in the notes, will be readily apparent throughout the text. I have tried to cite recent criticism at relevant moments, yet hopefully without overburdening the reader.

It is a pleasure to acknowledge the aid I have received. My greatest debt is to three friends, Professor and Mrs. C. H. Whitman and Professor J. P. Elder. Had I not been privileged to enjoy for many years the encouragement of their insights and share their enthusiasm for Virgil, this book would not have been written. At different stages of composition the manuscript was read and emended by Professors C. L. Babcock and W. V. Clausen. I have also benefited from the criticisms of two anonymous readers provided by the Harvard University Press. Members of my family, especially Mrs. Michael A. Post, have been most helpful. Finally I must thank my editor at the Harvard University Press, Miss M. Kathleen Ahern, for her courtesy and care. The responsibility for the faults and infelicities which remain is, of course, my own.

The book was finished at the American Academy in Rome during the summer of 1963. I must thank the trustees of the Academy for their award of a Rome Prize Fellowship and President Barnaby C. Keeney of Brown University for giving me a leave of absence to accept this grant. The President and Fellows of Harvard College have given permission to reprint, as chapter 2, a revised version of an article which originally appeared in the Harvard Studies in Classical Philology 66 (1962) under the title "Unity and Design in *Aeneid* V."

MICHAEL C. J. PUTNAM

Petersham, Massachusetts
August 13, 1964

CONTENTS

THE POETRY OF THE

AENEID

I'MADNESS AND FLIGHT

ADHERING to a pattern Virgil often followed, the second book of the *Aeneid* possesses three main divisions,[1] of which the first could well be entitled the tale of Sinon and the wooden horse. Its action, for the most part, takes place outside Troy's walls, but it reaches a triumphant peak of excitement when the horse bursts through the gates, without benefit of military support, and the men, hidden in its teeming belly, spring forth in turn to the destruction of the night-enshrouded city. The book's second segment describes the ensuing battle, beginning in the darkened streets and leading, with Virgil's typical fondness for focusing every action on one central place or figure, to the palace of Priam and ultimately to the death of the aged king himself. In the third and final section, Aeneas escapes to his father's house and persuades him, with the help of propitious omens, that retreat is necessary. While the family is leaving the sinking inferno of the past, Creusa, the wife of Aeneas, loses her way, and he returns to the city in search of her. Though his quest fails, this event in itself has auspicious overtones, for her spirit appears to him and prophesies the kingdom and royal bride that will ultimately be his.

The movement from symbolic introduction to a period of action, revelation, and then withdrawal, could also serve as a skeletal outline for other books of the *Aeneid*, especially VI and VIII, the theme of a later chapter. The first several hundred lines of Book VI, for example, offer a summary instance of how the in-

3

terplay of figure and symbol announces poetic motifs which subsequent action vivifies and elaborates. There the clash between
the two main figures, one who wants to experience death to
learn of the future, both immediate and distant, the other who
knows the future and has no choice but to live associated with
the world of the dead, is clarified by the two symbols with which
the Sibyl forces Aeneas to associate himself before he can journey
to his father — the corpse of Misenus and the living-dead golden
bough. This interplay between life and death, past and future,
symbolized in the bough, creates the challenge of the whole
voyage upon which the two are about to embark, as mortality
and emotion begin to yield before the progress of history.

The opening of Book II follows a similar pattern. It does not
present the calm before the storm, but the first loud thunderclaps
of a fury soon to be more fully revealed. It is the time when the
strands are stretched upon which the developing intricacies of
the book's poetic texture will be woven. The various parts of the
book complement and contrast, yet the effect of motifs fixed in
these initial lines extends beyond momentary questions of tone
to the establishment of a more general unity within the book. In
II, however, there is a special concinnity to the individual por-
tions of the book as well. If we look only at the external action
of the first part, for instance, we find a beautiful circular quality,
over and above more subtle imagistic patterns.

As Aeneas begins the recital of his tragic story for Dido, night
has long since descended from the heavens and the stars urge
sleep. Suddenly, however, as the narrative proceeds, we are no
longer at Carthage, but confronting the enormous bulk of the
wooden horse, with Laocoön charging down from the citadel
in a futile attempt to expose its fraud. Then Sinon appears —
because he is Greek the object of as much doubt to the Trojans
as the horse, and equally false. But his lying tale, having deceived
his captors, urges belief that the horse brings the blessing of the
gods upon the city, not potential destruction. Sinon is the voice

of the horse, and their fortunes change in unison. As if to lend further credence to his fiction, twin snakes make a sudden and spectacular appearance, swimming over the sea from Tenedos (where only the reader knows that the Greeks lie in wait), and devour Laocoön and his sons, ostensibly because he dared to challenge the horse. The snakes flee to the citadel, whence Laocoön had first rushed to give his unheeded warning, and to the shrine of Athena, who, as we know from Aeneas' opening description, was the protectress of the horse. The beast, initially the object of skepticism and distrust, now makes triumphant entry into the city, and Virgil completes his plot's circular course in terms of natural description as it had begun, for the horse releases its deadly burden as sleep grips the Trojans in fast embrace.

Such a summary does little to elucidate the magnificent interplay between symbol and action as the snakes and the horse become focal images in this dialogue between Laocoön and Sinon, the one seeking to expose, the other to deceive and then destroy. To clarify this poetic design we must examine with care Virgil's mind at work on first one strand and then another of the imagistic texture, now separated, now woven together. We turn first, as does Aeneas, to the wooden horse (lines 13–20):

> . . . Fracti bello fatisque repulsi
> ductores Danaum tot iam labentibus annis
> instar montis equum divina Palladis arte
> aedificant, sectaque intexunt abiete costas;
> votum pro reditu simulant; ea fama vagatur.
> huc delecta virum sortiti corpora furtim
> includunt caeco lateri penitusque cavernas
> ingentis uterumque armato milite complent.

Broken by war and driven back by the fates, the leaders of the Greeks, after the passage of so many years, build with Pallas' divine art a horse of mountainous size, weaving its ribs with planks of fir. They pretend it is an offering for their return (this rumor goes abroad). Here into its dark side they covertly lock a select body of men chosen by lot, and fill up its huge caverns and belly deep inside with armed soldiery.

Three distinct metaphors are suggested here, to which the poet refers with variations and additions in the subsequent lines. First, the horse is an animal and possesses ribs, side, and belly. Moreover, though made of wood and seemingly dead, it deceives paradoxically in this as in so many aspects of its appearance and is actually very much alive.[2] These same images, evoked from the animal nature of the beast, can also be applied to a ship inside whose spacious hold a deadly cargo has been stowed.[3] Finally, to expand further the hyperbolic quality of the horse, it is as huge as a mountain within whose dark side and cavernous interior soldiers can be hidden with stealth and safety. Indeed, as the people stare at it in amazement and wonder, it is the animal's size that the poet stresses. So huge and tall is it, Laocoön suggests in his speech of warning — ironically attributing to it features only a live creature could possess — that it could look down upon the walls and upon the very houses of the people (line 47),

inspectura domos venturaque desuper urbi . . .

about to gaze into our homes and plunge upon the city from above.[4]

Here, too, Virgil accentuates its hollowness, for in drawing attention to the cavernous lurking-places of its belly (*cavas uteri latebras,* line 38), the poet develops through his images the same ambiguity of beast, ship, and mountain and stresses once again the situation of those enclosed within it (*inclusi,* line 45, echoing *includunt,* line 19).

This towering object seems to Laocoön the perfect place for hiding. His speech (lines 42–49) merely reveals this supposed gift for the fraud that it really is.[5] In no way to be trusted, it appears to Laocoön as the ideal war machine wherein the wily Greeks could lurk unnoticed. In hope of proving his point and revealing the hidden deceit, Laocoön throws his spear at the horse (lines 50–53):

sic fatus validis ingentem viribus hastam
in latus inque feri curvam compagibus alvum

6

contorsit. stetit illa tremens, uteroque recusso
insonuere cavae gemitumque dedere cavernae.

When he had said this, he hurled his huge spear with mighty strength
into the side of the beast and the curved frame of the belly. There it
halted, quivering, and, as the womb was struck, the hollow cave rumbled
and gave forth a groan.

Once more the previous metaphors reappear. Like the monster
that it is, the beast has flanks and a womb. Like a cargo vessel,
it possesses sides, a belly, and a hold, and the joints which keep
a vessel's sides together. At the same time, the words *latus* and
cavae cavernae recall the deep mountainous hollow mentioned
in line 19, from which now issues forth the groan that would
have betrayed the animal's life, had fate allowed.

After Laocoön's failure, attention changes briefly from the
horse to Sinon, but once he has been accepted and Laocoön, the
horse's challenger, slain, the way is open for the beast's grand
entry into Troy (lines 234–40):

dividimus muros et moenia pandimus urbis.
accingunt omnes operi pedibusque rotarum
subiciunt lapsus, et stuppea vincula collo
intendunt: scandit fatalis machina muros
feta armis. pueri circum innuptaeque puellae
sacra canunt funemque manu contingere gaudent:
illa subit mediaeque minans inlabitur urbi.

We breach the walls and lay open the bastions of the city. All gird themselves for the task and put gliding wheels under [the horse's] feet and
stretch hempen bonds about its neck. The deadly machine climbs the
walls, pregnant with arms. Around it boys and unwedded maids sing
holy songs and delight in touching the rope with their hands. It moves
on and glides menacingly into the midst of the city.

It glides in like a ship, pulled on slippery wheels, yet it seems
ominously able to climb under its own power, pregnant not as
an ordinary animal, but with the potentiality of armed might.
It is indeed a monster in both senses of the word as it treads a
path up to the citadel to join the company of the ravenous snakes,
for under the guise of a huge towering beast it portends the down-

7

fall of Troy. The walls had not long been opened, the horse had scarcely made its festive way to the city's heart, when, under cover of a benign darkness, Sinon broaches its swollen belly to let forth the hidden Greeks (lines 257–60): [6]

> . . . fatisque deum defensus iniquis
> inclusos utero Danaos et pinea furtim
> laxat claustra Sinon. illos patefactus ad auras
> reddit equus, laetique cavo se robore promunt . . .

Protected by the unjust will of the gods, Sinon stealthily undoes the bars of pine and releases the Greeks enclosed in the belly. The opened horse restores them to the outside air and happily they issue forth from the hollow wood.

From the moment when the horse was first described in lines 13–20 — and the many repetitions in these lines clearly recall the initial description — the action has made a complete reversal. In the initial lines we read of the Greeks, broken in war and driven back by the fates. Now, after the horse's festive reception, the poet in cogent irony alters the same words and describes Sinon, father of Troy's doom, as defended by the gods' will. And as Virgil makes final use of the latent metaphors of ship, mountain, and life preserved within what appears dead, the horse makes its way without force up onto the citadel of the enemy, and its violent brood escapes joyfully into the night air to combine with allies waiting outside to bring ruin upon the city.[7]

The pattern of metaphor traced above is not the only one of importance used in relating the adventures of the wooden horse. We will return to another presently. It is worth taking time, however, to examine in passing how Virgil seems to have adopted a similar interaction of image and event to depict another moment whose intensity depends, as does the adventure of the horse, on violence suppressed and then released. I refer to the sea storm in Book I, caused by Aeolus at the behest of Juno, who wishes to rid herself forever of the hated remnants of Troy.[8] The chosen exponents of this madness are the winds whom Aeolus has in his charge. Toward their mountain home Juno makes her vengeful way (lines 50–63):

> Talia flammato secum dea corde volutans
> nimborum in patriam, loca feta furentibus Austris,
> Aeoliam venit. hic vasto rex Aeolus antro
> luctantis ventos tempestatesque sonoras
> imperio premit ac vinclis et carcere frenat.
> illi indignantes magno cum murmure montis
> circum claustra fremunt; celsa sedet Aeolus arce
> sceptra tenens mollitque animos et temperat iras;
> ni faciat, maria ac terras caelumque profundum
> quippe ferant rapidi secum verrantque per auras.
> sed pater omnipotens speluncis abdidit atris
> hoc metuens molemque et montis insuper altos
> imposuit, regemque dedit qui foedere certo
> et premere et laxas sciret dare iussus habenas.

Pondering such things in her fiery heart, the goddess came to Aeolia, land of storms, a place pregnant with raging winds. Here in a vast cave King Aeolus presses under his sway the vying winds and sounding storms, and bridles them with chains in a prison. Maddened, they roar with mighty groans around the mountain's barriers. Aeolus sits with scepter in hand on a high citadel, soothing their spirits and calming their wrath. Did he not, they would surely bear wildly off with them the seas, lands, and heaven's depths, and sweep them through the air. But, fearing this, the almighty father hid them in a dark cave and placed over them this mass of lofty mountain and gave them a king who, under fixed agreement, would know upon command when to tighten, when to slacken, the reins.

Literally, these creatures are spirits of the air. They whistle with sounding breezes and vie with each other, gale for gale. But to extend his meaning beyond the superficial aspects of the description, Virgil seizes upon the metaphor of horses, which he gradually develops as the scene unfolds. The winds roar like animals (*fremunt*, line 56), and, though they challenge each other, Aeolus soothes and calms their troubled spirits as a charioteer his team. He curbs (*premit*) this strength and bridles them in (*frenat*), but he likewise knows when to give as well as when to tighten hold on his reins. And when Juno shouts her command (line 69),

9

"incute vim ventis summersasque obrue puppis . . ."

"Strike force into the winds and overwhelm the sinking ships,"

she aptly adds the notion of "whipping" to the simile the poet has suggested in the previous lines.[9]

At the same time these winds, though interpreted metaphorically as horses, partake to a certain extent of the characteristics of human beings. They are, after all, figures fraught with potential destruction, and the poet can best portray their reactions by allowing them a certain modicum of ordinary feelings. They are inhabitants of a small political state — their fatherland in fact — with Aeolus as king, the man who holds the scepter of power and the royal command. The law of Aeolus is in turn that of the prison. Aeolus is the charioteer of horses rife with power and at the same time keeper of the prison where the forces of revolution are held in check. If the mountain cracks or the prison door is left open, these creatures of violence will be let loose to wreak destruction wherever opportunity allows.

They can be expected to respond to any request with the passion and anger which it is the duty of Aeolus to suppress. As a result, they naturally chafe against their lot. It comes, then, as no surprise that when the whole episode is nearly concluded and Neptune has stilled the waters and chastised the unruly winds and their guardian who has disobeyed him, the poet compares them to a seditious mob calmed by a man weighted with *pietas*, indeed the very god of the sea (I, 148–54):

> ac veluti magno in populo cum saepe coorta est
> seditio saevitque animis ignobile vulgus;
> iamque faces et saxa volant, furor arma ministrat;
> tum, pietate gravem ac meritis si forte virum quem
> conspexere, silent arrectisque auribus astant;
> ille regit dictis animos et pectora mulcet:
> sic cunctus pelagi cecidit fragor . . .

Just as often in a great nation when a revolution arises and the meaner folk rage spiritedly, and now torches and rocks fly about (madness lends them arms), then if by chance they see a man of noble character and achievement, they grow silent and stand by with ears alert. He rules their wrath with his words and soothes their hearts. Thus fell the whole roar of the ocean . . .

Though these revolutionaries are also possessed of spirits which are soon quieted,[10] the simile at first appears out of place, or at least unusual, since it compares supposedly inanimate nature to the world of mankind. But throughout his account of the winds and their doings, Virgil treats them metaphorically either as horses or as a foolish mob, part beast, part brutish man, easily misled into wreaking havoc. Since the emotional fury of Juno finds tangible outlet in Aeolus and his forces, the chief contrast arising from the whole episode is that between the characters of Aeolus and Neptune, the one impelled by base motives to misuse his royal power, the other filled with piety, capable of quieting the mob once it is out of hand.[11]

There are several other metaphors and ambiguities which help unite this complex cluster of images of winds, horses, and potentially raging forces. Like human beings, they are tied down by chains to keep them confined in their prison. But the word the poet uses for their cage, *carcer*, may also mean the place from which a horserace commences, the bars behind which the horses wait only to burst forth at a given signal. In fact, more than half of its occurrences in Virgil pertain to racing while in only one instance can its meaning be restricted to that of "prison."[12] Moreover, the word *claustrum* (line 56), which often signifies the bolts that shut a prison's door, can stand as well for the bounds that mark a racecourse or, all but synonymous with *carcer*, for the bars that restrain the horses before the commencement of a race.[13]

Thus, in brief, the opening lines of Book I find the raging winds described in terms of horses ready to dash at a given signal and of a mob murmuring against authority — inanimate creatures depicted through metaphorical ambiguity first in terms of the animal world and then finally of the human.

We must look also at the way the poet describes their habitat. It is a deep cavern (*vasto antro*) hidden under dark rocks, in scope as large as a mountain or enormous rocky mass. Its hollowness is further implied by the phrase *feta furentibus Austris*. The huge cavern is pregnant, teeming with roaring violence. By this hyperbolic elaboration of the weight needed to hem in the winds as well as by the series of images which suggest potentiality and awesome power suppressed and ready to spring forth, the reader is fully prepared for the birth of violence which occurs when Aeolus drives his spear against the mountainside (I, 81–83):

> Haec ubi dicta, cavum conversa cuspide montem
> impulit in latus: ac venti velut agmine facto,
> qua data porta, ruunt et terras turbine perflant.

With these words, he turned his spear-point toward the hollow mountain and thrust it into its side. The winds, as in armed array, rush out where the way was opened and blow with gusts over the lands.

The imagery of humankind combines with the destructive power already suggested to create the thought of an army on the march, rushing forth in array from its gates against the waiting foe.[14]

It is possible that in describing this birth of violence the poet once more has horses in mind. I suggest that he may be thinking specifically of their origin, which he ascribes in *Georgic* I (lines 12–14) to Neptune's striking the ground with his trident:

> . . . tuque o, cui prima frementem
> fudit equum magno tellus percussa tridenti,
> Neptune . . .

And you, Neptune, for whom the land, first struck by your mighty trident, gave forth the neighing horse.

Lucan takes note of the same event in *De Bello Civili* VI, 395–98. Referring to Thessaly, he says

> Hac tellure feri micuerunt semina Martis.
> primus ab aequorea percussis cuspide saxis
> Thessalicus sonipes, bellis feralibus omen,
> exiluit, primus chalybem frenosque momordit . . .

In this land the seeds of fierce Mars burst forth. First the Thessalian steed, of thundering foot, omen of dreadful war, leapt forth when the rocks were struck by the sea-god's spear; first it champed the bit and reins.

The exact location of this event, which Virgil leaves rather vague, Lucan narrows specifically to rocks. On the other hand, the object which performs the action, though described by Lucan only as a spear of the sea (*aequorea cuspis*), Virgil identifies clearly as the very trident of the sea-god. Yet it is a *cuspis* which Aeolus wields to release the winds, and in line 139 their cavernous dwelling is said to consist of enormous rocks.

Though a *cuspis* usually means only the end of a spear, the wording of Neptune's reprimand to Aeolus in line 138 —

> non illi imperium pelagi saevumque tridentem . . .

not his the power over the sea, not his the fierce trident —

sounds as if Neptune were reproving him for usurping the powers of the trident, something the sea-god reserved exclusively for himself. Yet the trident not only has associations with water but is also closely connected with the birth of horses, an event for which we have seen Virgil specifically commend Neptune. Aeolus may lord it over the winds, endowed with the menace of violent beasts, only when they are, so to speak, unborn. To Neptune alone remains the power to authorize the consequences of their release.[15]

But this moment of release is central in other respects, for through his imagery the poet may be subtly suggesting to his reader a comparison with the opening of Book II, with the very time when Laocoön, for a reason totally opposite to that of Aeolus, tries a similar gesture against the wooden horse and fails in the attempt. The lines, 50–56, have been quoted in part above, but deserve reiteration here:

> sic fatus validis ingentem viribus hastam
> in latus inque feri curvam compagibus alvum
> contorsit. stetit illa tremens, uteroque recusso

insonuere cavae gemitumque dedere cavernae.
et, si fata deum, si mens non laeva fuisset,
impulerat ferro Argolicas foedare latebras,
Troiaque nunc staret, Priamique arx alta maneres.

When he had said this he hurled his huge spear with mighty strength into the side of the beast and the curved frame of the belly. There it halted, quivering, and, as the womb was struck, the hollow cave rumbled and gave forth a groan. And had the will of the gods, had our mind not been perverse, he had forced us to defile the Greek hiding-place with iron, and Troy would now stand, and you, lofty citadel of Priam, would remain.

Laocoön's action is futile, because it is fated neither for him to prove his point successfully nor for the horse yet to reveal its armed brood. With this reservation, the images the poet utilizes at each moment remain quite similar. The parallels reveal a special pattern Virgil's mind tended to follow when describing potential violence, at first suppressed and then in operation.[16]

One or two echoes between these two events, which initiate Books I and II, will suffice for illustration. The use of the verb *laxat* at II, 259, recalls two phrases in Book I, one in which Aeolus is said to hold the reins of power tight or loose (*laxas*) and another in which the sides of one of the ships caught in the storm are depicted gaping *laxis compagibus*, with loosened joints (a phrase which in itself recalls the construction of the horse).[17] The warriors have been caged within the horse like the winds inside their mountain prison, and, in each instance, bars (*claustra*) are used as instruments of construction or restraint, hinting at the release of violence should they be put aside.[18] To reinforce such external parallels, and as fitting accompaniment to the attributes of enormous scope and hollowness common to both the horse and Aeolus' mountain domain, Virgil uses the image of pregnancy as an added announcement of potentiality. Almost the first thing we hear of the cave of the winds is that it is a place teeming with raging winds (*feta furentibus Austris*), and this detail is equally applicable, because of its partially animal nature, to the wooden horse, pregnant with arms (*feta armis*).

And when the birth of violence finally occurs, the poet does not cease to infuse the power of the first passage into the second. If the real winds were treated metaphorically as steeds, the brood of the wooden horse draws to itself the image of winds. The first moment Aeneas realizes that ruin has come upon his city Virgil enlivens with a simile comparing this destruction to a flame sped by raging winds (*furentibus Austris*), the same phrase applied to the domain of Aeolus, *feta furentibus Austris*. With a sure touch he adds immediately lines which could take the reader's thoughts directly to the storm the winds create in Book I. In fact, with due regard for the changes which a new setting demands, II, 313 —

> exoritur clamorque virum clangorque tubarum

the shouting of men arises, the shrieking of trumpets —

closely parallels I, 87 —

> insequitur clamorque virum stridorque rudentum

there follows the shouting of men, the creaking of ropes.

The simile serves thereby as a splendid introduction to the havoc the men, escaped from the horse's belly, are about to create in the city as it lies buried in sleep.

Moreover, at the very moment when the twin sons of Atreus are first shown going about their work in Troy's flaming hell, Virgil adds another simile which equates this violence with winds and their companion horses (II, 414–19):

> undique collecti invadunt, acerrimus Aiax
> et gemini Atridae Dolopumque exercitus omnis;
> adversi rupto ceu quondam turbine venti
> confligunt, Zephyrusque Notusque et laetus Eois
> Eurus equis; stridunt silvae saevitque tridenti
> spumeus atque imo Nereus ciet aequora fundo.

Drawn together on all sides they rush in — fierce Ajax, the two sons of Atreus and the whole army of the Greeks — just as, when a storm has burst, winds clash together in enmity, West and South, and East happy in his orient steeds. The woods shriek and Nereus deep in foam rages with his trident and stirs up the waters from the lowest depths.

We need look only to I, 84–86, to find two of the same company about a common ruinous purpose:

> incubuere mari totumque a sedibus imis
> una Eurusque Notusque ruunt creberque procellis
> Africus et vastos volvunt ad litora fluctus: . . .

They swoop down upon the sea and overwhelm it all from its lowest depths, East wind and South together, and Southwest, thick with blasts, and roll vast billows toward the shore.

Finally, when Aeneas' mother allows him to see that the divinities of Troy are themselves aiding in its overthrow, we catch a glimpse of the great Neptune at work ruining the city of his own building (II, 610–12):

> Neptunus muros magnoque emota tridenti
> fundamenta quatit totamque a sedibus urbem
> eruit.

Neptune shakes the walls and the foundations, upturned by his mighty trident, and overwhelms the whole city from its base.

No winds or horse, but now the very god, who can impart destructive power to each, is himself the destroyer.

Both these realms of violence, of mountain and horse, winds and destructive Greeks, fit closely into a pattern of madness, suppressed and released, which we will trace on other occasions. Virgil himself offers us a summary of this theme, crucial to any understanding of his imagination, with the special concision he reserves for lines of the greatest significance, in the symbolic figure of *Furor*, whom Jupiter describes at the conclusion of his prophetic speech to Venus in Book I.

Venus, concerned for her son's safety after the sudden storm roused by Juno, and anxious, too, about her own power and honor among the gods, had inquired of her father about the future. His reply looks far beyond the passing trials of Aeneas to the grandeur that would be Rome under Augustus, when rough ages would become smooth and war be put aside. He concludes his speech as follows (I, 292–96):

> cana Fides et Vesta, Remo cum fratre Quirinus
> iura dabunt; dirae ferro et compagibus artis
> claudentur Belli portae; Furor impius intus
> saeva sedens super arma et centum vinctus aënis
> post tergum nodis fremet horridus ore cruento.

Hoary Faith and Vesta, Romulus with his brother Remus, shall give laws. The gates of War, grim with tight fastenings of iron, shall be closed, and unholy Wrath, sitting within upon fierce arms, bound with a hundred brazen knots behind his back, shall roar dreadfully from his bloody mouth.

Here, in brief and symbolic compass, we have the outline elaborated in both winds and horse, the enclosure shut tight with heavy bars. And in it is this creature, Wrath (*Furor*) raging to get out, roaring like the winds and possessing weapons, like the Greeks inside their horse. The thing is part beast (*fremet ore cruento* is a phrase Virgil applies only to animals or to men who possess their qualities), yet seems at least to have hands which can be pinioned behind its back.

The wooden horse is not the only object in Book II which possesses the attributes of *Furor*. When we first meet Sinon, he too is in the same abject position, with his hands tied behind his back (*manus . . . post terga revinctum*, line 57). Since his release and acceptance is the first sign of that madness which culminates in the opening of the horse, we must examine closely the way in which the poet describes his adventures, connects them with the destruction of Laocoön, and vivifies with further imaginative detail the triumphant progress of the wooden horse.

Sinon, whose name in itself suggests the slippery qualities of the snake, is the voice of the horse. The book's first cycle of dramatic action begins with the horse almost wounded, and hence revealed, by Laocoön. A moment after his failure Sinon enters, bound and, according to his lying tale, having barely escaped death at the hands of Ulysses. The movement ends, however, with Laocoön mangled and Sinon triumphant in the releasing of the horse. After Sinon proves himself, the monster, too, is gradually accepted. The emotional division comes in the third segment of Sinon's feigned rhetoric when, by his fictitious hints, he has raised the Trojan credulity to the point of frenzied inquiry. The relaxing of his bonds, ironically by the doomed Priam himself, is paralleled first in the opening of the gates of Troy, so that the people can enter and observe the beast. But this soon leads, through the instigation of Sinon, to the entrance of the horse into the city and then to the actual broaching of the animal's belly.

The wiles of the Greeks, which Laocoön had so strongly stressed, though centered upon the horse, are absorbed by Sinon. One suspects, moreover, that the Pelasgian guile (*arte Pelasga*, lines 106 and 152), by means of which the clever spy gains the trust of the Trojans, is closely associated with the *divina Palladis ars*, the divine and clever craft of the goddess responsible for the building of the horse. The people crowd around the fettered Sinon (initial mistrust soon yields to mere curiosity) as they had approached Minerva's monster. And he, with well-feigned terror, proceeds to take his stand, with the self-confidence of a man whose life depends on his wit, and to look around (*circumspexit*, line 68), almost mimicking Laocoön's prediction that the horse would soon look down upon their very houses (*inspectura domos*).

After his initial cry of woe, the Trojans react just as he might have calculated (lines 73–74):

> quo gemitu conversi animi compressus et omnis
> impetus.

With his sigh their animosity is put to flight and all their violence stifled.

The reader thinks back only a few lines to the groan which had issued from the monster's belly under the blow of Laocoön. But irony wins the day, for though Sinon's cry echoes, in a sense, the cry of the wounded horse, the challenge offered by Laocoön to the horse, transferred to the Trojan people in their first reaction to Sinon, is now curbed. Even the possibility of acceptance arises, and as this culminates in a total metamorphosis of animosity into generous reception on the part of the Trojans, Sinon, too, changes accordingly and prepares to expose the horse's cargo, not to bring death, as Laocoön had expected with his blow, but deadly life.

The fortunes of Sinon, bound closely to those of the horse, are also tied to the fate of Laocoön, and, as the star of the one rises, the other's falls with equal rapidity. Laocoön is the first to apply violence to the horse. Not long after, Sinon pretends to have been ready for death when, according to his fictitious tale, he was ordained to be a propitiatory human sacrifice to assure the Greeks a safe return. But it is Laocoön, victim of the Greeks, who dared oppose the fate of Troy and the beast, omen of its collapse. Sinon, with prophetic awareness, anticipates the imminent onslaught of the devouring serpents when he suggests (lines 189–91)

> nam si vestra manus violasset dona Minervae,
> tum magnum exitium (quod di prius omen in ipsum
> convertant!) Priami imperio Phrygibusque futurum; . . .

For if your hand had violated the gift of Minerva, then utter destruction — may the gods sooner turn that augury against Calchas himself — would befall Priam's kingdom and the Phrygians.

Death awaits anyone who violates Minerva's offering.

The doom of Laocoön is the doom of all Troy, and as the snakes, seeking the protection of Minerva, make their way up onto the citadel we remember not only that this is the location on which the horse will soon be placed, but that it was from here that Laocoön rushed in his futile attempt to reveal the plot.

The drama of the first segment of the book could be briefly summarized as the replacement of Laocoön by Sinon and his portentous instruments, the snakes and the horse — the symbolic triumph of Greece over Troy preceding the actual ruin. It is the figure of Sinon who facilitates the transition.

As I have mentioned above, there is a special cyclic unity about these preliminary episodes, as the depth of the night at Carthage blends into the nocturnal destruction of Troy and nature in turn frames Laocoön's challenge and death. The accompanying poetic motifs also culminate and enfold, as an expanding imagery enhances the narrative detail. We have examined the skill with which Virgil delineates the episode of the horse's triumph. Of almost equal importance to the poetic structure is the imagery of snakes which the poet subtly develops so as to reach a climax in the twin creatures who strangle Laocoön and seem to typify the surreptitious side of the lurking Greeks as the horse typifies their pent-up fury.

But we note, too, that the horse possesses this quality of stealth emphasized as the poet draws for effect upon the language which accompanies Sinon and his snakes. After Sinon has relieved the horse of its burden, the snakes also seem to have fulfilled their chief role, though subsequent pages will show that the imagery which accompanies them is used frequently by the poet long after they have fulfilled their mission. At the moment we might begin by observing how symbol and reality become one in the virtually human purpose behind their deadly intent. To trace the full power of Virgil's poetic technique we must not only return once again to the book's opening lines, but must look outside the *Aeneid*, to the third *Georgic*, for the genesis of one of Virgil's finest achievements.

The first fact that we learn about the twin snakes is that they make their onslaught from Tenedos, and this detail takes the reader's mind back to the lines which follow immediately upon the first introduction of the wooden horse (II, 21–22):

> est in conspectu Tenedos, notissima fama
> insula, dives opum Priami dum regna manebant, . . .

There is in sight Tenedos, an island well-known in fame, rich in resource, while the kingdom of Priam stood.

One line alone (24) is devoted to what the Greeks are doing there:

> huc se provecti deserto in litore condunt.

Sailing hither they bury themselves on the deserted shore.

The verb *condo* has a distinctly sinister side. Witness Juno's ironic reaction to the Trojan arrival at Tiber mouth: *"optato conduntur Thybridis alveo"* (VII, 303), "They are buried in the belly of the Tiber for which they longed." The same word reappears at II, 401, where a sudden turn of fortune forces the Greeks to seek once more the protection of the horse's paunch and bury themselves in the belly they knew so well (*nota conduntur in alvo*). In II, 24, the connotations suggest only that which is momentarily hidden and lying in wait.

The concept of hidden deception is now transferred to the curved belly of the horse, the *latebrae* (lines 38 and 55), or hiding-places, in which the Greeks lurk. Laocoön himself uses a version of this same image when he suggests that some trickery lies hidden (*latet*, line 48) in the horse. But soon the figure of Sinon appears on the scene, adding another and still grander dimension of duplicity and deceit. His own words of false recollection support the poet's plan, for twice of late Sinon had been forced to cower in the darkness of retreat, he claims, once when Ulysses had procured the death of his friend Palamedes (line 92) —

> adflictus vitam in tenebris luctuque trahebam

I dragged on my troubled life in darkness and grief —

and more recently when he had escaped from his supposed role as a human sacrifice (lines 134–36):

> eripui, fateor, leto me et vincula rupi
> limosoque lacu per noctem obscurus in ulva
> delitui, dum vela darent, si forte dedissent.

I snatched myself from death, I confess, and broke my bonds, and in a marshy lake I lurked, hidden in the sedge throughout the night until they should set sail, if by chance they would.

The verb *delitesco*, though it inherits the root of *lateo*, has a revelatory importance since its only other appearance in Virgil occurs during a passage in the third *Georgic* toward which the poet's mind often turned as he wrote *Aeneid* II. Poisonous snakes, harmful to field and fold, is the theme. First the viper (lines 416–17):

> saepe sub immotis praesepibus aut mala tactu
> vipera delituit caelumque exterrita fugit . . .

Often under unclean sheds lurked a viper, dreadful to the touch, which fled frightened from the air above.

This is Sinon's role for the moment, lurking yet dangerous. Then there is the water snake which the poet describes at even greater length in *Georgic* III. Swollen with wrath, it remains hidden in its watery coverts until drought and heat force it onto the land (lines 432–34):

> postquam exusta palus, terraeque ardore dehiscunt,
> exsilit in siccum, et flammantia lumina torquens
> saevit agris asperque siti atque exterritus aestu.

After the swamp is dried up and the earth gapes from heat, it leaps onto the dry land and, rolling its flaming eyes, it rages in the fields, fierce from thirst and maddened with the heat.

And in the last five lines of his description the poet changes image but not idea (lines 435–39):

> ne mihi tum mollis sub divo carpere somnos
> neu dorso nemoris libeat iacuisse per herbas,
> cum positis novus exuviis nitidusque iuventa
> volvitur, aut catulos tectis aut ova relinquens,
> arduus ad solem, et linguis micat ore trisulcis.

May it not be my desire then to snatch soft sleep under the open sky or to lie in the grass on a wooded slope when, fresh with slough cast off and gleaming with youth, it rolls along, leaving its young or eggs at home, and, blazing toward the sun, it darts from its mouth a three-forked tongue.

In the winter time, the serpent remains happily hidden, cherishing its young. But when the season arises to slough off its coil, then is the time to beware as it leaps forth into the sunlight with youth renewed.

The horse serves for a while as the ideal hiding-place (*latebrae* is a word Virgil twice applies in the *Georgics* to the dens of snakes).[19] Sinon, too, lurks for a while like a serpent. But once his hands have been released and his fiction creates trust in the horse, the time is ripe for the Greeks to strike. The attack is threefold and begins symbolically with the death of Laocoön, for as he is performing sacrifice in his role as priest of Neptune (lines 203–5):

> ecce autem gemini a Tenedo tranquilla per alta
> (horresco referens) immensis orbibus angues
> incumbunt pelago pariterque ad litora tendunt; . . .

But behold twin snakes from Tenedos swim through the ocean's calm depths with enormous coils — I shudder as I retell it — and make their way together toward the shore.

The hidden snakes lurking on Tenedos, whose stealth and duplicity are inherent in the character of Sinon, take initial revenge on the attempted revealer of the horse's deception.[20] Like the water snake in *Georgic* III, they leap up onto the land, bloody, their eyes flashing fire. Their intent is immediately apparent as they make straight for Laocoön (*Laocoonta petunt*). First, they devour his sons; then he, too, struggles in vain (lines 220–27):

> ille simul manibus tendit divellere nodos
> perfusus sanie vittas atroque veneno,
> clamores simul horrendos ad sidera tollit:
> qualis mugitus, fugit cum saucius aram
> taurus et incertam excussit cervice securim.
> at gemini lapsu delubra ad summa dracones
> effugiunt saevaeque petunt Tritonidis arcem,
> sub pedibusque deae clipeique sub orbe teguntur.

His fillets covered with gore and dark poison, he struggles to tear off the knots with his hands and at the same time he raises dreadful cries to the heavens like the bellowings of a wounded bull who has fled from the altar and shaken from his neck an ill-aimed ax. But the two serpents take flight, gliding to the shrines on high. They make for the citadel of cruel Minerva and are protected under the feet of the goddess and the circle of her shield.

He who shortly before had offered a bull in due sacrifice to Neptune, the god about to partake in the destruction of his own city, is now himself the first symbolic sacrificial victim, and the snakes are the precursors of the floodtide of madness, as they strangle him to death. His offering, in this prophetic twilight, is soon expanded into the demise of all Troy and its aged king, in the second part of the book. And with grand massacre yielding once again to individual private suffering, Laocoön's death also looks to the death of Creusa at the book's conclusion, when at last Aeneas' emotional attachment to Troy must be relinquished and denied.

Any possible allegorical connection between the twin snakes and the twin sons of Atreus does not become explicit until the destructive pair is first mentioned in line 415. There is, however, a clear and important link between the serpents, the horse, and the forces on Tenedos who come to join their newly escaped comrades (lines 254–56):

> et iam Argiva phalanx instructis navibus ibat
> a Tenedo tacitae per amica silentia lunae
> litora nota petens, . . .

And now the Greek force, with ships arrayed, goes from Tenedos under the friendly quiet of the silent moon, seeking the well-known shore.

The snakes had the destruction of Laocoön as their specific goal. The Greeks who now arrive from their hiding place on Tenedos are like the snakes, brought forth at last into the open. The poet, however, reinterprets his symbol on a much larger scale, for they now seek all Troy as their province.

This whole complex of lines displays Virgil's subtle yet masterful use of imagery to enhance the drama of the moment.[21] The word *lapsus*, for instance, we have seen used to describe the gliding motion of the snakes as they climb up to the citadel, their work done. Not long after, the Trojans put slippery wheels, (*rotarum lapsus*) under the horse so it, too, can glide, with serpentine deceit, into the city.[22] And with the passage of but a few hours the men inside the horse, themselves absorbing the attributes of snakes, are said to glide down the rope lowered from the beasts belly (*demissum lapsi per funem*).

And Sinon's own characteristics, too, color the words. One of the snakes wriggles its huge back (*sinuatque immensa volumine terga*). And, after a glimpse at the serpent's horrible deed, fear creeps into the Trojans' trembling hearts (*insinuat pavor*), like Sinon and the snakes into their city.

Finally, Virgil, following his usual procedure, utilizes the same metaphors in his depiction of the natural setting which accompanies these events. Just before Sinon broaches the horse we are told (lines 250–53):

> Vertitur interea caelum et ruit Oceano nox,
> involvens umbra magna terramque polumque
> Myrmidonumque dolos; fusi per moenia Teucri
> conticuere; sopor fessos complectitur artus.

Meanwhile the sky revolves and night rushes from the ocean, surrounding with deep shade the earth, the heavens, and the wiles of the Greeks. Throughout the fortress-town the Trojans [lie] stretched in silence as slumber embraces their tired limbs.

Here both the words *involvens* and *complectitur* metaphorically reflect the moment not long past when the snakes strangle Laocoön and hence anticipate the onslaught of the full Greek armament, which is at that very moment making silent way from Tenedos. Even clearer is the imagery the poet uses a few lines later to introduce Aeneas' dream of Hector (lines 268–69):

> Tempus erat quo prima quies mortalibus aegris
> incipit et dono divum gratissima serpit.

It was the hour in which peace first comes to failing mortals and creeps in most sweetly, a gift of the gods.

As sleep glides in, it brings death in its wake.

With equal validity, then, these images look forward to the coming debacle. The word *ruit*, for instance, occurs several times later and the verb *verto* is repeated at one of the most graphic moments of Aeneas' narrative (lines 624–25):

> Tum vero omne mihi visum considere in ignis
> Ilium et ex imo verti Neptunia Troia . . .

Then indeed all Ilium seemed to me to collapse in flames and Neptune's Troy to be overturned from its foundation.

The all-encompassing motif of this opening pageant is the idea of violence suppressed and then coming to the surface. In the second segment of the book this madness comes fully into its own. We have noted above how the imagery of winds, on the rampage at last, is taken over from the first part to play a vital role in the catastrophe of Troy's dark night. The potentiality of the snake imagery is not discarded either. It recurs at two important moments.

The first is the episode of Androgeos, introduced with vivid irony by the same phrase used first to bring Laocoön to our attention as he arrives accompanied by a great crowd (*magna comitante caterva*). Androgeos is a Greek who has through mischance fallen upon a band of Trojans led by Aeneas (lines 377–82):

> . . . sensit medios delapsus in hostis.
> obstipuit retroque pedem cum voce repressit.
> improvisum aspris veluti qui sentibus anguem
> pressit humi nitens trepidusque repente refugit
> attollentem iras et caerula colla tumentem,
> haud secus Androgeos visu tremefactus abibat.

He sensed that he had slipped into the midst of the enemy. He stood aghast, and in silence drew his foot back. Like a man who, treading on the ground, has stepped upon a serpent, unseen amid rough brambles, in sudden fear flies from it as it rises in wrath, swelling its dark neck: thus Androgeos retreated, terrified at the sight.

For a brief space of time, as they gain a fleeting victory, the Trojans seem to incorporate the capacity of the hateful snakes. We even find the Trojan Coroebus glorying in this sudden success (*successu exsultans*, line 386) in a manner not far different from that of Sinon, *insultans* (line 330), leaping about like the horse which he had successfully brought into the city.[23]

It is a passing victory, and at its second reappearance the snake imagery has reverted to its rightful owners. Pyrrhus, the merciless son of Achilles, on vengeance bent, gains this poetic honor (lines 469–75):

> Vestibulum ante ipsum primoque in limine Pyrrhus
> exsultat telis et luce coruscus aëna;
> qualis ubi in lucem coluber mala gramina pastus,
> frigida sub terra tumidum quem bruma tegebat,
> nunc, positis novus exuviis nitidusque iuventa,
> lubrica convolvit sublato pectore terga
> arduus ad solem, et linguis micat ore trisulcis.

Before the very entrance and on the first threshold, Pyrrhus, shining in brazen light, revels in arms — as a water snake nourished on poisonous herbs whom cold winter has protected, swollen beneath the earth, now comes into the light with slough cast off and gleaming with youth. He rolls his slippery body with chest upraised, blazing toward the sun and darting from his mouth a three-forked tongue.

It will be immediately apparent that the better part of the simile's last three lines comes from the section in *Georgic* III devoted to the poisonous water snake and quoted extensively above. Here at last the latent violence of the snake imagery bursts forth in all its new brilliance. It has been symbolized before in the snakes' conquest of Laocoön. But the death of Laocoön has a double significance when it announces the fall of Troy. First, as the enemy of the horse's fated progress, Laocoön must die, sacrificed to a higher, more destructive power. Secondly, as he and his sons perish in the monsters' strangling grip, we cannot help seeing in the episode a vision of the future, for it anticipates the power of the serpents openly at work in their strongest human manifestation. The madness of Pyrrhus, slaughtering first Polites and then his father, the aged King Priam, creates the focal episode of the book's second section, to which we now turn.

The second part of Book II also has a circular design of its own. It begins with Aeneas' dream of Hector (lines 289–90) —

> "heu fuge, nate dea, teque his" ait "eripe flammis.
> hostis habet muros; ruit alto a culmine Troia . . ."

"Alas, flee, goddess-born, and snatch yourself from these flames," he cries. "The enemy holds the walls; Troy collapses from its lofty summit." —

and concludes with the appearance of Venus, who reiterates Hector's demand that Aeneas escape while he is still able (lines 619–20):

> "eripe, nate, fugam finemque impone labori.
> nusquam abero et tutum patrio te limine sistam."

"Take flight, my child, and put an end to trial. Never will I desert you, but will place you safely on your father's threshold."

As in Book VI Aeneas, through the offices of the Sibyl, turns from contemplating the dread tortures of those already damned in Tartarus to looking at the bright future found in the Elysian fields, so Venus now takes his attention away from the death of Troy and the madness of war which accompanies it and urges him to think of his family and ponder the necessity of escape to a promised land.

The intervening lines depict the horrors of battle in what is undoubtedly the darkest, most mysterious, scene of fighting in the *Aeneid* (lines 314–17):

> arma amens capio; nec sat rationis in armis,
> sed glomerare manum bello et concurrere in arcem
> cum sociis ardent animi; furor iraque mentem
> praecipitat, pulchrumque mori succurrit in armis.

Out of my mind I seize arms; there is little purpose in weapons, but my heart burns to gather a band for battle and to rush with my comrades to the citadel. Madness and anger drive my mind headlong. The beauty of dying in arms strengthens me.

Aeneas' own rage reaches a climax at the moment in which he plans the murder of Helen (*furiata mente ferebar*: line 588). But no sooner has the thought struck him than his mother appears. *Pura per noctem in luce refulsit*, she gleamed clear as light through the darkness (line 590). Never before was she so brilliant before his eyes.

The episode is of crucial importance. Expressed through imagery, it can be visualized in terms of a contrast between light and dark, between the splendor of Venus' sudden appearance and the gloom of Aeneas' previous road through the shadows of death, *obscura nocte per umbram*. Venus proceeds to withdraw this veil of human passion from the eyes of her son (lines 604–6):

> "aspice (namque omnem, quae nunc obducta tuenti
> mortalis hebetat visus tibi et umida circum
> caligat, nubem eripiam . . .)."

"Behold, for I shall snatch away all the cloud which, drawn before your eyes, dulls your mortal vision and in darkness shrouds your sight."

And from the new vantage point she offers he can view the meaning of his own rage as the gods themselves take furious joy in Troy's demise.[24] Hence, through the wisdom of his mother as she recalls to him the manifold attraction of love and fate which must now impel him to create, not to demolish, Aeneas makes the transition from deep involvement in useless violence to commitment to family and future.

But Aeneas' attempt to defend his dying homeland had not been meager in the time which separated his withdrawal from his father's house (and consequent realization that he must for a while give himself over to war) from the moment when Venus commands that he leave this ruined world behind. Virgil visualizes his hero's actions in two parts, a walk through the city toward the central palace and the death of the aged king himself, to which Aeneas is witness.

This journey in the city, amidst the horror and hell of flames and carnage, has one noteworthy episode, the Trojan exchange of arms with the Greek dead, bringing at first a passing victory which forces the Greeks to retreat back to shore and the wooden horse, but ultimately a tragic massacre of Trojan by Trojan. Virgil begins now the second part of the pattern of triple division which he follows again in Books VI and VIII, where a symbolic introduction leads to a period of trial and action, and this in turn gives place to another episode, involving retreat and prophecy of future events.

As far as establishing the imagistic structure of their respective books is concerned, Laocoön, Sinon, and the monstrous horse have much in common with the Sibyl, the corpse of Misenus, and the magical bough. But the parallel between the subsequent episodes in both II and VI, between the beginning of Troy's dying hour and the moment when Aeneas and the Sibyl plunge into the world of the dead, is not merely skeletal. Whatever the order of composition, it is well to reflect, especially when attempting to arrive at a critique of Book II, that at these two moments the same imagistic design seems to have suggested itself to the poet. One or two similarities of imagery are especially evocative.

Take, for instance, Aeneas' speech of exhortation, before they rush into battle, to the young men he has drawn together as a result of Panthus' sad news (lines 347–54):

> quos ubi confertos audere in proelia vidi,
> incipio super his: "iuvenes, fortissima frustra
> pectora, si vobis audendi extrema cupido
> certa sequi, quae sit rebus fortuna videtis;
> excessere omnes adytis arisque relictis
> di quibus imperium hoc steterat; succurritis urbi
> incensae: moriamur et in media arma ruamus.
> una salus victis nullam sperare salutem."

When I saw them drawn together and eager for battle, I say to them: "Youths, hearts vainly valiant, if it is your fixed desire to follow me in my last adventure, you see what fate is left to our cause. All the gods, in

whose hands this empire rested, have withdrawn, their shrines and altars
deserted. You aid a city in flames. Let us meet death and rush into the
midst of arms. The one safety for the conquered is to hope for none."

In considering his words we could well think of two moments in
the Sibyl's conversation with Aeneas. The first comes at VI,
133ff, where she announces what must be done beforehand if
such passion (*tanta cupido*) grips him to indulge in the mad effort of a visit to the underworld. The second occurs at the moment of descent. I quote for illustration the end of the Sibyl's cry
and the opening lines of the deathly journey itself (VI, 261–72):

> "nunc animis opus, Aenea, nunc pectore firmo."
> tantum effata furens antro se immisit aperto;
> ille ducem haud timidis vadentem passibus aequat.
>   Di, quibus imperium est animarum, umbraeque silentes
> et Chaos et Phlegethon, loca nocte tacentia late,
> sit mihi fas audita loqui, sit numine vestro
> pandere res alta terra et caligine mersas.
>   Ibant obscuri sola sub nocte per umbram
> perque domos Ditis vacuas et inania regna:
> quale per incertam lunam sub luce maligna
> est iter in silvis, ubi caelum condidit umbra
> Iuppiter, et rebus nox abstulit atra colorem.

"Now you need courage, Aeneas, now a strong heart." Speaking only this,
she plunged raging into the open cave. He, with fearless steps, keeps
pace with his advancing guide.
   O gods, whose dominion is over spirits, and you, silent shades; and
you, Chaos and Phlegethon, wide, silent wastes of darkness, allow me
to tell what I have heard. Allow me, by your divine approval, to reveal
things covered deep in earth and gloom.
   They went enveloped in the lonely darkness through the shadows
and through the empty houses and vacant realms of Dis, as on a road
through woods under the baleful light of a hazy moon when Jupiter
has plunged the sky in shadows and dark night has taken away color
from the world.

It is startling in itself that the very phrase through which the
poet appeals to the gods of the nether world for support as he
embarks on the ensuing narrative, *di quibus imperium*, should
be used by Aeneas in Book II as he notes the departure of Troy's

protective deities. Nor can the similarity of setting be dismissed, for immediately after Aeneas' call to arms Virgil adds the following simile (II, 355–60):

> . . . inde, lupi ceu
> raptores atra in nebula, quos improba ventris
> exegit caecos rabies catulique relicti
> faucibus exspectant siccis, per tela, per hostis
> vadimus haud dubiam in mortem mediaque tenemus
> urbis iter; nox atra cava circumvolat umbra.

From there, like predatory wolves in black mist, whom hunger's lawless rage drives blindly forth and whose whelps left behind await their return with dry throats, we make our way amid weapons and foes into certain death and hold a course toward the city's center. Black night sweeps around us with its hollow shadow.

As Aeneas, like a ravening wolf, makes his way into the private hell of Troy's fall, Virgil prepares the reader for his longer, more fateful, journey through the land of death into the very jaws of Orcus.

And in Aeneas' thoughts, as he treads a path through the corpses which lie strewn about, a vision of death seems to pervade all things (lines 368–69) —

> . . . crudelis ubique
> luctus, ubique pavor et plurima mortis imago.

Everywhere is cruel grief, everywhere fear and death's constant presence.

But these specters, which haunt destruction's dream, stalk with equal menace before the gates of hell (VI, 273–77):

> vestibulum ante ipsum primis in faucibus Orci
> Luctus et ultrices posuere cubilia Curae,
> pallentesque habitant Morbi tristisque Senectus,
> et Metus et malesuada Fames ac turpis Egestas,
> terribiles visu formae, Letumque Labosque . . .

Before the very entrance, on the first threshold of Orcus, Grief and avenging Cares have made their beds. Pale Diseases dwell there and bitter Age, Fear and ill-counseling Hunger and ugly Poverty, shapes terrible to see, and Death and Suffering.

As Aeneas and his companions roam about in the night's dark shadow (*obscura nocte per umbram*, II, 420), it is only in preparation for the later, grander confrontation with the spirit of death itself in all its forms as he and the Sibyl begin their journey, dark in death's dark land, *obscuri sola sub nocte per umbram.*

But the center of this inferno and the goal of Aeneas' march is the palace of Priam where the fighting is most intense. Even there the Trojans in order to protect must destroy (lines 445–47):

> Dardanidae contra turris ac tota domorum
> culmina convellunt; his se, quando ultima cernunt,
> extrema iam in morte parant defendere telis . . .

Opposite, the Trojans tear down towers and whole roofs of houses. With these as weapons, when they see the end is near, they prepare to defend themselves now at the very moment of death.

Aeneas, too, tears off one of the largest towers and hurls it at the enemy (lines 460–67):

> turrim in praecipiti stantem summisque sub astra
> eductam tectis, unde omnis Troia videri
> et Danaum solitae naves et Achaica castra,
> adgressi ferro circum, qua summa labantis
> iuncturas tabulata dabant, convellimus altis
> sedibus impulimusque; ea lapsa repente ruinam
> cum sonitu trahit et Danaum super agmina late
> incidit.

There was a tower standing on the edge and rising heavenwards from the housetops, whence all Troy could be seen and the ships of the Greeks and the Achaean camp. Assailing this round about with iron, where its highest stories offered feeble joints, we tore it up from its lofty foundation and hurled it. Crashing down, it brings sudden ruin with its collapse and falls far and wide over the Greek ranks.

He is no longer creating a hell. Yet he finds himself, as it were, within it, offering defense against those who would ravage the palace with impunity.

The intruder is Pyrrhus whom Virgil introduces with a key line (469–70):

Vestibulum ante ipsum primoque in limine Pyrrhus
exsultat telis et luce coruscus aëna; . . .

Before the very entrance and on the first threshold, Pyrrhus revels in
arms, shining in brazen light.

These initial words, we recall, Virgil uses to present Aeneas' first
glimpse of the personified trials and troubles who make their
home before the very entrance to Hades (VI, 273–74). But instead of grief or fear, old age or the sleep of death, or even death-
dealing war which Aeneas sees on the underworld's opposing
threshold (*mortiferumque adverso in limine Bellum*), we find at
the palace gate Pyrrhus, the reborn snake, in whom is concentrated all the violence and thirst for revenge which the Greeks
possessed.

Violence is on the loose and, in ironic contrast to the book's
opening section, must seek escape for its energy by breaking into
the object of its hatred (II, 479–88):

> ipse inter primos correpta dura bipenni
> limina perrumpit postisque a cardine vellit
> aeratos; iamque excisa trabe firma cavavit
> robora et ingentem lato dedit ore fenestram.
> apparet domus intus et atria longa patescunt;
> apparent Priami et veterum penetralia regum,
> armatosque vident stantis in limine primo.
>   At domus interior gemitu miseroque tumultu
> miscetur, penitusque cavae plangoribus aedes
> femineis ululant; ferit aurea sidera clamor.

He [Pyrrhus] himself among the first, wielding a double-headed ax,
breaks through the heavy gateway and wrenches the brass doors from
their hinges. And now, cutting through a panel, he hollows out a way
through the solid oak and makes a window huge with wide mouth. The
house within lies open, the long halls gape wide. The inner chambers of
Priam and the kings of old are revealed and they see armed warriors
standing on the first threshold.

But inside the house, grief and piteous shouts are mingled and, deep
within, the hollow chambers echo with the cries of women. The din
strikes the golden stars.

There are several details in this description which could remind
the reader of the wooden horse. When the palace re-echoes from

its depths with women's wails, we recall the beast's huge hollow filled deep with armed might:

> . . . penitusque cavernas
> ingentis uterumque armato milite complent.

They fill up its huge caverns and belly deep inside with armed soldiery.

The last phrase, too, recurs as the Greeks force their entrance into the palace (lines 494–95):

> fit via vi; rumpunt aditus primosque trucidant
> immissi Danai et late loca milite complent.

Force makes a way. Once let in, the Greeks break through the entrance-ways, cut down the first guards and fill up the place far and wide with soldiers.

But the bars here (*claustra*, line 491) are not like those released by Sinon in the horse's paunch. Now they are the collapsing doors of Priam's palace which offer only the last sad resistance to the floodtide of wrath.

As a later chapter will demonstrate in some detail, this complex of actions, the hurling of the tower, forced entrance, and revelation, possesses much in common with Virgil's description in Book VIII of Hercules' passage into the cave of the monster Cacus. There, in order to expose the beast in its lair, he must tear up the high crag which overhangs it (lines 237–42):

> dexter in adversum nitens concussit et imis
> avulsam solvit radicibus, inde repente
> impulit; impulsu quo maximus intonat aether,
> dissultant ripae refluitque exterritus amnis.
> at specus et Caci detecta apparuit ingens
> regia, et umbrosae penitus patuere cavernae, . . .

Straining against it from the right, he struck it and tore it up, wrenched free from its deep roots; then suddenly he hurled it. At this thrust the mighty heaven thunders, the banks leap apart, the river in fear stays its current. But the cave, huge home of Cacus, stands clear and uncovered, and the shadowy caverns within lie exposed.

This cave, according to the poet's imagistic exposition, is also a type of hell, for as the interior stands open, Virgil adds a simile comparing its black hole to the nether regions and the monster himself to the shades who tremble at the sudden burst of light.

In Book II the scene now shifts from violence on the outside to the interior court itself, within which, again like the entrance to the underworld, stands an old ash tree, overshadowing the altar and offering scant protection for the aged king and his family. As Priam girds futile arms about his feeble limbs, Pyrrhus rushes in pursuing Polites, kills him at his father's feet and then, after dragging the old man up onto the altar, slaughters him in turn (lines 550–58):

> . . . hoc dicens altaria ad ipsa trementem
> traxit et in multo lapsantem sanguine nati,
> implicuitque comam laeva, dextraque coruscum
> extulit ac lateri capulo tenus abdidit ensem.
> haec finis Priami fatorum, hic exitus illum
> sorte tulit Troiam incensam et prolapsa videntem
> Pergama, tot quondam populis terrisque superbum
> regnatorem Asiae. iacet ingens litore truncus,
> avulsumque umeris caput et sine nomine corpus.

Saying this, he dragged the old man, trembling and slipping in the streaming blood of his son, to the very altar and, grasping his hair in his left hand, with his right he drew forth his gleaming sword and buried it in his side up to the hilt. This was the end of Priam's fortune, this the fate destined for him, as he saw Troy burned and Pergamum in ruin; he, once proud ruler over so many peoples and lands of Asia. He lies upon the shore, a huge trunk with head torn from shoulders, a corpse without a name.

At first glance such a moment might seem, in the light of the parallels suggested above, to be the death of the ruler of this hell. Virgil uses the same initial phraseology when describing Hercules' abduction of hell's guardian in VI, 395–96:

> Tartareum ille manu custodem in vincla petivit
> ipsius a solio regis traxitque trementem; . . .

He sought by force to put into chains the guardian of Tartarus and dragged him trembling from the very throne of the king.

But the cumulative effect is far different, for the inferno's violent center turns out to be only a pitiful old man. And when Pyrrhus grabs him by the hair and pulls him toward the altar, trembling and slipping in the blood of his son, the poet invites his reader to recall the death of Laocoön. For, as he offered sacrifice, the twin snakes grasped in deadly embrace (*implicat* appears both in lines 215 and 552) first his sons and then himself, coming helplessly to their aid. If the sacrifice of Laocoön is no more than a symbolic precursor of the debacle to come, the death of Priam at the very altars announces its conclusion. And his collapse at the hands of Pyrrhus, the serpent rejuvenated, seems to the spectator Aeneas to signify Troy's final collapse.

But the last ghastly picture of Priam's corpse, a trunk with head torn from the shoulders, lends to his death a further special significance in the life of Aeneas. The image of "rending" is a cumulative one here. We have seen it in many lines quoted above, as Aeneas and his comrades tear off the palace turrets to heave on the enemy, as Pyrrhus wrenches the doors from their hinges, or when Priam notices the threshold torn from his tottering house (*convulsa limina*, lines 507–8). The image now centers on the body of the old king, who is himself a figure for his ruined city. This same type of symbol will not be unknown to Aeneas at many crucial moments in the adventures which lie ahead. In dwelling on the passing of Troy and the necessity of departure, we think, among many examples, of Palinurus' mutilated boat, with part of the poop wrenched off, or of the rending of the golden bough, demanded by the Sibyl if Aeneas is to put the past finally behind him in favor of the historical future of Rome.

As he witnesses this sad event, Aeneas thinks of his father and family and, though he ponders for a moment the killing of Helen, it is this need for protecting his own which Venus now urges upon her son as she reveals to him the role of the gods in Troy's downfall. To conclude this section of the book Virgil adds a simile of unsurpassed distinction and power (lines 624–33):

Tum vero omne mihi visum considere in ignis
Ilium et ex imo verti Neptunia Troia;
ac veluti summis antiquam in montibus ornum
cum ferro accisam crebrisque bipennibus instant
eruere agricolae certatim; illa usque minatur
et tremefacta comam concusso vertice nutat,
vulneribus donec paulatim evicta supremum
congemuit traxitque iugis avulsa ruinam.
descendo ac ducente deo flammam inter et hostis
expedior: dant tela locum flammaeque recedunt.

Then indeed all Ilium seemed to me to collapse in flames and Neptune's
Troy to be overturned from its foundation, just as when farmers vie with
each other to bring down an aged ash tree amid mountain peaks, they
gird it with iron and attack it with many an ax blow. Ever it threatens,
and the trembling foliage nods on its stricken crest until, little by little
overcome by wounds, it groans for the last time and, torn from the ridges,
drags destruction in its path. I descend and, under the direction of the
god, make my way between fire and foes. The weapons give place and
the flames withdraw.

The initial impulse for the simile must be found in the lines
which immediately precede it, in which the poet describes the
roles of various deities in forcing Troy's fall. The position of the
tree on the mountain-top (*summis in montibus*) adds not only to
the hyperbolic effect of its crash but specifically points to the
position Athena takes to preside over the end of Troy from the
city's heights (*summas arces*, line 615). Moreover, when we
read of the ash struck by iron (*ferro accisam*), we think back but
a few lines, if in sound alone, to Juno *ferro accincta* (line 614),
girt with steel and lending a helpful hand to her destructive col-
leagues. Likewise the verb *eruo* is applied both to Neptune, in
the preceding description, and to the farmers as they go about
their work. But the gods are not the only ones involved here, for
the *bipennis*, or double ax, is the instrument we recall was used
by Pyrrhus to smash his way into Priam's palace. *Instat vi patria*
— he attacks with the power his father Achilles had, the poet says
of Pyrrhus in line 491, a phrase which gains further force from
the reappearance of its verb in line 627.

But it is not so much the destroyer as the destroyed which moved the poet's fancy. The old tree seems by design to be almost human. Quivering, it nods its stricken head and groans under the redoubled blows. We think of the dying city and the groans which issued from the palace halls. But above all we recall once again the wounds which inflicted death upon the old king himself. By his hair Pyrrhus had drawn him, trembling like the tree, to a bloody demise upon the altar (the noun *coma* and verb *traho* appear prominently at each moment). Similarly, when we read of the ruin which results when the tree is torn from the ridge, *iugis avulsa*, we consider again not only the desolate city, where now appear only piles of scattered rubble and rocks torn from rocks (*disiectas moles avulsaque saxis / saxa*) but also the huge trunk of Priam, desolate on the shore, with head torn from its shoulders, *avulsumque umeris caput*.

And with this vision, Aeneas turns away from the past to bring help to his family and attempt the hazardous escape from Troy's dying embers.

But to convince Anchises of the necessity of departure is not an easy task. The aged Trojan wants to die with his city and his king, even at the risk of lying unburied. Light is the loss of burial, he claims. As Aeneas turns to put on his arms again, his wife now prays to be allowed to die with him. But the gods intervene at the moment of her despairing cry (lines 679–84):

> Talia vociferans gemitu tectum omne replebat,
> cum subitum dictuque oritur mirabile monstrum.
> namque manus inter maestorumque ora parentum
> ecce levis summo de vertice visus Iuli
> fundere lumen apex, tactuque innoxia mollis
> lambere flamma comas et circum tempora pasci.

Crying thus, she filled the whole house with her groans when, amazing to tell, a sudden omen appears. For, among the hands and faces of his sad elders, behold the topmost crest of Iulus' head appears to pour forth a subtle flame, and the fire, harmless to the touch, seems to lick his soft locks and feed about his temples.

At this important instant, when a favorable omen must force

Anchises to put credence in the future, Virgil's imagination reverts to one of the two violent omens which introduced the downfall of Troy, the twin snakes. As the flames lick about the head of Iulus we recall the very same gesture on the part of the serpents (line 211):

> sibila lambebant linguis vibrantibus ora.

They licked their hissing mouths with quivering tongues.

And in a flash each turns to devour the unfortunate trio and feeds with its jaws upon their hapless limbs (*miseros morsu depascitur artus*, line 215). In the omen seen upon Iulus' head, the same image is used of the fire which, however, licks at his hair without hurt and feeds harmlessly on his brow. The viper in the third *Georgic*, which lurked under the sheepfolds, we remember, was harmful to the touch (*mala tactu*). The lapping flame here is harmless and innocent (*tactuque innoxia*). Virgil turns imaginatively back to one of the more violent moments which preceded the destruction of Troy and adapts almost the same words to a new prodigy which is now thoroughly beneficent, as Aeneas starts to put Troy's smoldering ruins behind him in preparation for a creative future.

In response to Anchises' request for further confirmation, Jupiter sends a second omen (lines 692–97):

> Vix ea fatus erat senior, subitoque fragore
> intonuit laevum, et de caelo lapsa per umbras
> stella facem ducens multa cum luce cucurrit.
> illam summa super labentem culmina tecti
> cernimus Idaea claram se condere silva
> signantemque vias . . .

The old man had scarcely spoken these words when, with sudden crash, it thundered on the left, and a star, falling from heaven through the shadows, ran its course, drawing after it a trail filled with light. Gliding brightly over the heights of the rooftop, we watch it bury itself in the forest of Ida, showing us the way.

Here, too, the metaphor inherent in *lapsa* and *labentem* reminds the reader of the snakes, of the horse as it glides quietly into the city, and indeed of the collapse of Troy itself. But the image is now kindly and creative and wipes away all doubt from the mind of Anchises. Aeneas shoulders the burden of his father, clasps his son by the hand, and begins to make his way toward the new day which will fulfill the prophecy of the comet's gleam, as it sails behind the forest of Ida.

Since the saving signs of flame and star lent conviction to Aeneas' plans, Anchises agrees to withdraw from Troy and, with this decision, the last and perhaps the most gripping section of the narrative commences. The book's ominous opening offered, with superb interplay of character and symbol, the setting of the whole. There followed immediately the actual creation and flourishing triumph of the Greeks' destructive conflagration, poetically initiated by Aeneas' walk toward the center of the city (and the conflicts encountered during its course) and concluded only with the assault on Priam's palace and the death of the aged king himself. Thereupon Aeneas, as we have seen, retreated to his father's house at the instance of Venus. It is from there that the drama of escape from this hell takes its start.

There is no better example of Virgil's mind at work than in these lines; no better illustration of the patterns toward which his imagination naturally turned, given a certain set of circumstances. Since in the subsequent narrative the chief event is Aeneas' loss of his wife, Creusa, Virgil, not unexpectedly, seems to turn back to his own account of the tragic story of Orpheus and Eurydice, found at the end of the fourth *Georgic*. I shall make constant reference in the pages which follow to this tale of the near victory of love and poetry over the powers of hell. Whether the poet echoes his own thoughts consciously or not matters little; the parallels are clear and salient.

Aeneas gives the order of departure with seeming care, but one detail in the recital of events receives emphasis through repetition. He raises his father to his shoulders and leads his son by the hand. But his wish for Creusa is that she should follow their footsteps from afar (*longe servet vestigia coniunx*, line 711). And as the journey begins she dutifully obeys (*pone subit coniunx*, line 725). *Pone* is notable as the word used in *Georgic* IV, line 487, to describe the distance Eurydice keeps behind Orpheus at the behest of Proserpina, as they make their way out of hell. This prophetic note is momentarily dropped in order to develop the atmosphere of death from which all hope to escape. We are borne through places of darkness (*ferimur per opaca locorum*, line 725), Aeneas describes it, anticipating many occasions in Book VI — for instance, line 633 — where hero and guide are walking with like pace through the darkness of the roads (*pariter gressi per opaca viarum*).

But the connection of escape from the land of death with specific reference to the story of Orpheus and Eurydice gains point from the lines which follow. Aeneas approaches the city gates and seems momentarily to have completed his journey (lines 730–31):

> Iamque propinquabam portis omnemque videbar
> evasisse viam . . .

And now I approached the gates and seemed to have come all the way.

Similar phraseology is used by Virgil at an equally crucial moment in *Georgic* IV (line 485) as Orpheus nearly regains the world above:

> iamque pedem referens casus evaserat omnis . . .

And now retracing his steps he had escaped all misfortune . . .

And we recall the Sibyl's warning concerning the prime difficulty in breaking free from Hades (*A.* VI, 128–29).

> sed revocare gradum superasque evadere ad auras
> hoc opus, hic labor est.

But to retrace one's path, to make one's way out into the air above, this is the task, this the trial.

It is at this instant that both Orpheus and Aeneas (in Book II) fail, and though Aeneas errs because he is careless and forgets to keep a careful watch, Orpheus because the madness of his passion forces him to cast his eyes back, the imagistic parallels are worthy of consideration. Aeneas asks himself the reason for Creusa's loss (lines 738–43):

> heu misero coniunx fatone erepta Creusa
> substitit, erravitne via seu lassa resedit,
> incertum; nec post oculis est reddita nostris.
> nec prius amissam respexi animumve reflexi
> quam tumulum antiquae Cereris sedemque sacratam
> venimus . . .

Alas, it is uncertain whether my wife Creusa halted, snatched away by a cruel fate, or whether she wandered from the path or sat down in weariness. Never thereafter was she restored to our eyes. Nor did I look behind for my lost wife or turn my attention back before we came to the mound and holy temple of ancient Ceres.

Creusa is the one who stops whereas in the other case it is Orpheus (*restitit*: G. IV, 490). And, as noted above, it is Aeneas who does not look back (*nec respexi*), unlike Orpheus who causes his beloved's downfall by just such an action (*respexit*: G. IV, 491). Beyond these obvious distinctions the episodes are markedly similar. Neither Eurydice nor Creusa can ever be returned to her lover (*reddita*: G. IV, 486; A. II, 740), and each in her own pitiful way must yield before the cruelty of fate (*miser*: G. IV, 494; A. II, 738).

During the account of *Georgic* IV the two lovers are about to escape all possible dangers (*casus omnis*, line 485), in the path of such a journey, as they near the world above. It is a like danger which, as we have seen, Aeneas feels he must encounter again (*casus renovare omnis*) as he prepares to return into the hell of Troy in search of Creusa. Though the perils may be specifically of a military nature, as he seeks once more the darkened thresholds (*obscura limina*) and retraces his steps through the night (*per noctem*), we are reminded of nothing more than Aeneas and the Sibyl making their way into the lower world (VI, 268–69):

> ibant obscuri sola sub nocte per umbram
> perque domos Ditis vacuas et inania regna: . . .

They went enveloped in the lonely darkness through the shadows and through the empty houses and vacant realms of Dis.

The women and children clustered near the spoils collected by the Greeks, whom Aeneas is forced to look upon in the hands of the enemy, conjure up an impression not unlike the picture which Virgil borrows in *Aeneid* VI, 306–8, from the fourth *Georgic*, of the dead souls waiting patiently to cross the Styx.

Aeneas' next actions also refer the reader once more directly to Orpheus (II, 768–70):

> ausus quin etiam voces iactare per umbram
> implevi clamore vias, maestusque Creusam
> nequiquam ingeminans iterumque iterumque vocavi.

Nay I even dared to hurl shouts through the darkness and I filled the roads with my voice. Redoubling in sadness my vain cries, I called on Creusa again and again.

This would seem remarkably like the head of Orpheus floating down the Hebrus crying for Eurydice did not the shade of Creusa suddenly appear, to the terror of Aeneas. Her opening words to him (lines 776–77) —

> "quid tantum insano iuvat indulgere dolori,
> o dulcis coniunx?"

"Why do you take pleasure in giving way to such mad grief, my sweet husband?" —

are an excellent example of the subtle art of the Virgilian repetition, of the power one context can exert on another through allusion. *Dulcis coniunx* comes from *Georgic* IV, 465 (the only other appearance of the words so combined in Virgil), where Orpheus first bewails Eurydice's loss. But line 776 is partially reflected also in VI, 135, where the Sibyl outlines what must first be done if Aeneas really means to carry out his foolhardy mission to visit the underworld; if, in fact, it would please him to give himself over to this mad enterprise (*insano iuvat indulgere labori*). The difference lies between the trial of descending to talk with one's father and grief at the loss of one's wife, while roaming about in a hell of destruction. It is a difference not of kind but of degree, for Virgil's mind was following the same outline in the creation of all three episodes.

Finally, there is the gesture of parting, which also exhibits unity of treatment amid contrast of detail, for here at last, in the case of Aeneas, the impersonal necessity of adherence to destiny begins to take precedence over any ties of affection apparent in the Orpheus legend. Orpheus' grief was unceasing, and it is to prevent just such a reaction on the part of Aeneas that Creusa's ghost appears and wishes him godspeed on the journey ahead. Once more the parallels are noteworthy. Both creatures disappear into thin air (*tenuis in auras*: G. IV 499–500; A. II, 791), leaving their loved ones wishing to say many things (*multa volentem dicere*: G. IV, 501–2; A. II, 790–91) and desiring in vain to embrace. But Creusa's role is to dispel grief, not prolong it. It is not without design that lines 792–94, wherein the poet depicts Aeneas' final departure from his wife, are repeated at the meeting of Anchises and his son in VI, 700–2, for Aeneas now returns to his companions with some notion that the clock cannot be turned back, that he must not expect to experience anew emotions connected with the past; that, in fact, Troy's fall is merely the first step in the relentless and deepening involvement of the hero with his destiny. He escapes from his first hell with the vague knowledge of what he must do, but with as yet no tangible evidence that his course is correct. The journey to the actual underworld will provide this evidence.

Virgil lays stress on the step Aeneas is about to take by compressing into one line (795) the transition from the meeting with Creusa to the waiting exiles:

sic demum socios consumpta nocte reviso.

Thus, at last, after the night had run its course, I return to my companions.

It is a line on which his mind dwelt at certain later moments of crisis. Take, for instance, the briefly worded description of Aeneas' desertion of Dido to return to his ship (IV, 395–96):

multa gemens magnoque animum labefactus amore
iussa tamen divum exsequitur classemque revisit.

Sighing deeply, his heart shaken by his mighty love, nevertheless he follows out the orders of the god and returns to the fleet.

Equal in terseness and perhaps even closer in mood is the swift account of the hero's departure from the underworld through the gates of ivory to rejoin his companions (VI, 897–99):

his ibi tum natum Anchises unaque Sibyllam
prosequitur dictis portaque emittit eburna;
ille viam secat ad navis sociosque revisit.

Then with these words Anchises accompanies his son and the Sibyl and sends them out of the ivory gate. Aeneas makes his way to the ships and rejoins his companions.

The brave new world is more imminent now and the hero more aware of the particular type of suffering and triumph allotted him, but the emotional treatment of the moment of parting from Creusa is more strongly emphasized (along with the more symbolic death of Priam) because it is the first of many instances in which the present is torn from a hero who would willingly live undisturbed, but upon whom the future is constantly forced.

Even according to the Sibyl it requires only physical effort, however grievous, for son to visit father in hell. But at the end of Book II Aeneas submits to a combination of passion and grief, and it is from this that he is purged as he leaves Creusa and Troy. Once more, on a level far higher now than mere narrative coincidence, Aeneas is akin to Orpheus. The very tension between human and divine, between mortal love and immortal poetic creativity, forms the tragedy of Orpheus who loses both because he favors one too much. The hell of Troy, and the presence of Creusa therein, offer in subtle conjunction an attraction for all that is human in Aeneas, for his passionate devotion to his city and love for his lost wife. Aeneas yields for a while to their magnetic power. He does return into the doomed city and at later moments of extreme pessimism wishes for nothing more than the ability to re-establish Troy. But the omens had proved the necessity of departure and hinted vaguely at some more august destiny, which Creusa spells out with greater clarity, namely, what to Aeneas should now seem, and will ultimately prove to be, the immortal aspect of his life — what poetry was to Orpheus. But this very intangibility exercises small charm when compared to the loss of city and wife. Hence Aeneas, like Orpheus, must return to hell.

The withdrawal, however, is far different, mostly due to the appearance of Creusa, who chides him for his present involvement and reinforces the necessity of adherence to a future of greater validity. Because of this, as Virgil alters his own paradigm, Aeneas succeeds where Orpheus fails and, in rejoining his companions, proposes commitment to an ideal, however insubstantial, whatever trials may ensue.

The implication is not that all personal emotions are cast suddenly aside. Virgil is more careful with his hero than to do this. In each of the three books that follow we find Aeneas unwillingly associated with a death which betokens further diminishing of past emotional attachments and increased devotion to an ideal which draws constantly nearer. The many parallels between darkening Troy and the underworld, between Creusa and Anchises, show that Book VI, too, is another partial appeal to emotion. But by the end of that book Aeneas realizes that the difficulties involved in following the dictates of fate and establishing the Roman race must take precedence over any personal griefs. It is on a fated journey that Aeneas goes in VI, beckoned by ghostly appearance, bent not on a violent or seductive harrowing of hell but on a need simply for deeper knowledge of the ideal hinted at first in Book II, but never tangibly described.

Aeneas leaves his father through the gate of ivory for several reasons. The Sibyl warned that the descent to hell was easy (*facilis descensus*), the rest fraught with difficulties. We must not expect for Aeneas the *facilis exitus* which the gate of horn provides. But there is a more important reason. Aeneas remains human, neither true dream nor shade, a man suddenly metamorphosized without the need of Lethe into the primogenitor of the Roman race, ancestor of the line Anchises parades before him, whose progress now, from Tiber mouth on, is Rome's beginning. This change is the last purgation of Troy as it is the true foundation of Rome. The very tensions which betoken this transition — the death of the past leading to renewal of life via initiation into the progress of the future, the elimination of emotional attachment in favor of the broader prospect of history — help define the greatness of *Aeneid* VI, but only in relation to a journey which began with the first withdrawal from the silent ashes of Troy.

Once Virgil has established a pattern of imaginative procedure, it is likely that it will appear again, perhaps more than once again, however disguised the semblance. Since many of the themes developed in Book II seem to have recurred to the poet as he created Book IX, I append a brief discussion of it here. Such an analysis will be offered, as in the case of the following chapter, in defense of the strikingly Virgilian qualities of the narrative, the originality of which has occasionally been called into question.

Book IX consists, in the main, of two episodes. One records the prowess of Turnus, seeking and gaining entrance into the Trojan camp and finally forced to retreat, saved from death only by the absolving waters of the Tiber. The second, inserted in the first like a play within a play, is the famous episode of Nisus and

Euryalus, who volunteer to bring news of the Trojan peril to Aeneas at Pallanteum and, after slaughtering their way boldly through the darkened camp of the Rutulians, meet their doom at the hands of a newly arriving squadron of Volscians.

This minor adventure, to which we first turn, is often treated as another acknowledgement on Virgil's part of his indebtedness to Homer, a Latinization, as it were, of the story of Dolon in *Iliad* X, which tells how a Trojan spy attempted to make his way into the Greek forces and what befell him there.[25] If the plot of the story is partially of Homeric inspiration, the imaginative details are thoroughly Virgil's own.

Virgil's description of the setting of the Rutulian camp is of primary importance. One item in the picture is stressed four times, the vulnerability of the enemy, gradually yielding to drunken sleep. First we are told (lines 164–67):

> discurrunt variantque vices, fusique per herbam
> indulgent vino et vertunt crateras aënos.
> conlucent ignes, noctem custodia ducit
> insomnem ludo.

They rush about and share their duties in turn. Stretched on the grass they enjoy wine and overturn the brass mixing-bowls. The fires gleam while the guards spend a sleepless night gaming.

Then Nisus, urging his friend on to high adventure, notes that (lines 189–90):

> "lumina rara micant, somno vinoque soluti
> procubuere, silent late loca . . ."

"Occasional lights gleam forth and they take their rest, overcome by sleep and wine. Far and wide the place grows silent."

It remains the turn of Euryalus, defending their prospective mission before the Trojan elders, to observe (lines 236–37):

> ". . . Rutuli somno vinoque soluti
> conticuere . . ."

"The Rutulians, overcome by sleep and wine, grow quiet."

And, as the exploit begins, the narration once more emphasizes the enemy's position (lines 316–17):

> passim somno vinoque per herbam
> corpora fusa vident, arrectos litore currus . . .

Everywhere they see bodies stretched through the grass in drunken sleep and chariots tilted on the shore.

In many respects these details present a strange combination and elaboration of the way the poet describes the moment when the Greeks enter Troy (II, 252–53):

> . . . fusi per moenia Teucri
> conticuere; sopor fessos complectitur artus.

Throughout the city the Trojans grew quiet, stretched out in sleep. Slumber embraces their tired limbs.

This fact the attacking enemy also notes as (line 265)

> invadunt urbem somno vinoque sepultam . . .

they invade the city buried in sleep and wine.

There is the same ominous silence in both instances, and each, too, gains point by comparison with the actual hell of Book VI. When Nisus states that the place is silent far and wide, we cannot help recalling the poet's own chilling description of Chaos and Phlegethon as places silent in darkness far and wide. A hell not unlike that which the Greeks fashioned out of Troy or that Aeneas experienced to visit his father is now to be re-created by Nisus and Euryalus in the carnage they bring as they make their way through the Rutulian camp. The desire which first seizes the pair (*cupido*, line 185) is a variation of that yearning which the Sibyl notices in Aeneas' initial urgency to confront the shades (VI, 133) and which appears later in Palinurus' wild longing to cross the Styx (VI, 373).[26] And when Nisus announces that he has in mind to enter upon something great (*aliquid . . . invadere magnum*), the reader reaches beyond the metaphor to the actual commencement of the journey. "*Invade viam*," — "begin the journey" — the Sibyl said to Aeneas about to enter the under-world.

This leads directly to the moment of departure (IX, 314–16):

> Egressi superant fossas noctisque per umbram
> castra inimica petunt, multis tamen ante futuri
> exitio.

Going out they surmount the ditches and seek the enemy camp through the shadow of night, fated yet to be the doom of many.

If the phrase *noctisque per umbram* recalls Aeneas and the Sibyl setting out in the lonely darkness through the shadows (*sola sub nocte per umbram*), the strength of the two verbs *superant* and *petunt* looks to a similar moment in Book II, foreshadowing impending violence, symbolically conveyed in the destruction of Laocoön by the twin snakes and literally by the advent of the Greeks. The huge serpents tower over the waves (*superant undas*: II, 207), as they soon are to be depicted devouring the priest of Neptune, towering over him with head and lofty necks (*superant capite et cervicibus altis*: II, 219). They specifically seek out a single foe (*Laocoonta petunt*: II, 213); the forces of the twin Atridae prey on all of Troy (*litora nota petens*: II, 256). Nisus and Euryalus plot a kindred course with results not unlike Aeneas' walk through the carnage of Troy to Priam's palace, and his journey through the underworld, the Sibyl by his side.[27] Here, however, it is the parallel with Book II which is most forceful, for this is not only an entrance into hell but the very creation of hell itself, such as the Greeks and their prototypes, the twin snakes, had made of Troy.

Several details are worth noting in this journey of destruction. There is a particularly gruesome moment during the slaughter of Remus (IX, 332–33):

> tum caput ipsi aufert domino truncumque relinquit
> sanguine singultantem . . .

Then he cut off the head of their master and left the trunk spouting blood.

This moment flashes vividly before the mind of the reader, if only for the parallels it provides in the death of Priam, whose trunk without a name lay headless on the shore. But the frightening rage of the pair could not be better conveyed than by the simile of lines 339–42, applied to Euryalus:

> impastus ceu plena leo per ovilia turbans
> (suadet enim vesana fames) manditque trahitque
> molle pecus mutumque metu, fremit ore cruento:
> nec minor Euryali caedes . . .

As an unfed lion, raging through the filled sheepholds (for mad hunger presses him on), mangles and tears the tender flock, dumb with fear, and roars with bloody mouth: no less was the slaughter of Euryalus.

I will return later to the setting of wild animal and sheepfold. Here I wish to call attention only to the last three words of the simile which have an evocative quality paralleled only rarely in Virgil, *fremit ore cruento*. It is the phrase we have seen the poet use of *impius Furor* in Book I — violence imprisoned and chafing at its bonds. The poet applies it as well to Turnus in XII, 8, where he is depicted as a lion, still raging, though wounded. Here, too, violence is on the loose. Euryalus, we learn immediately, rages about all blazing (*incensus et ipse / perfurit*), rampaging through the sleeping camp like the winds from their cave in Book I and the Greeks from the horse in II. Indeed it is for all of these that *impius Furor* stands as imposing symbol.

Suppression comes swiftly. The way amid the Rutulians is soon completed, but at the expense of what Nisus knows to have been too much lust for slaughter (*nimia caede atque cupidine*). The emblem of this other, heedless *cupido* seems to be the helmet of Messapus which the departing Euryalus dons (the poet has mentioned earlier in the book the attractiveness of crimson plumes) and which sends off the glimmers noticed by the arriving Volcens and his men. It is at this moment, as in Book II, that the great change in the narrative occurs. Volcens commands the pair to halt. They choose not to obey and decide instead (lines 378–80)

> . . . celerare fugam in silvas et fidere nocti.
> obiciunt equites sese ad divortia nota
> hinc atque hinc, omnemque abitum custode coronant.

. . . to hasten their flight into the woods and trust in night. On this side and that, horsemen bar the well-known junctions and surround every exit with guards.

This darkness of the woods, they think, could serve as a shield. Instead, the forest becomes a gigantic prison, a place of death in fact, in which Nisus and Euryalus are entrapped. This forest could well signify the woods of the doomed, like those through which Aeneas must pass in Book VI. They certainly typify as sudden an alteration in the tale of Nisus and Euryalus as the change from rampaging Greeks to escaping Trojans in II. But there is no such happy outcome here.

Virgil's phraseology leaves little doubt concerning his intent. Euryalus, blinded by darkness and overburdened with booty, loses his way from fear (*fallitque timor regione viarum*, line 385). This happens to be the same setting in which Aeneas lost Creusa. As he says: "I withdrew from the way of the streets I knew" (*nota excedo regione viarum*: II, 737). Nisus does break clear, however (lines 386–89):

> Nisus abit; iamque imprudens evaserat hostis
> atque locos qui post Albae de nomine dicti
> Albani (tum rex stabula alta Latinus habebat),
> ut stetit et frustra absentem respexit amicum . . .

Nisus got away, and now, heedless, had escaped the enemy to places later called Alban from the name Alba (at that time King Latinus used them for his stately stalls) when he halted and looked back in vain for his absent friend.

Once more the evocative quality of the words is hard to dismiss, for they relate this context, as we might now expect, not only to Aeneas' plight in II but also to the adventures of Orpheus and Eurydice. Take the verb *evado*, for instance. We noted above its use in II, 731, and drew a comparison with *Georgic* IV, 485, and *Aeneid* VI, 128. The same is true of the word *stetit*, here used in

53

its purest form, but appearing as *restitit* in *Georgic* IV, 490, *substitit* in *Aeneid* II, 739. And, as often in Virgil, it is juxtaposed to the verb *respicio*. Orpheus, by looking back, forced Hades irrevocably on his beloved. Aeneas turned around too late, to find that his unwitting carelessness had caused Creusa's death. Both he and Nisus, however, decide immediately upon a return into the environment of death, an alternative not open to Orpheus (IX, 390–93):

> "Euryale infelix, qua te regione reliqui?
> quave sequar?" rursus perplexum iter omne revolvens
> fallacis silvae simul et vestigia retro
> observata legit dumisque silentibus errat.

"Unfortunate Euryalus, in what place did I leave you? Or where shall I follow?" Turning back again along the whole tangled path through the deceiving woods, he scans his own clear footsteps and wanders amid the silent thickets.

Here Virgil seems clearly to be reflecting once more on the context of Book II, not merely in the common resolution to endure yet again all difficulties in renewed search for someone lost, but in the very imagery itself. These are Aeneas' own words in II, 752–55:

> principio muros obscuraque limina portae,
> qua gressum extuleram, repeto et vestigia retro
> observata sequor per noctem et lumine lustro:
> horror ubique animo, simul ipsa silentia terrent.

At the start I seek again the walls and the dark thresholds of the gate, whence I had made my way out. I follow back my own clear steps through the night and scan them with my eye. Dread everywhere fills my heart; the very quiet as well offers terror.

The same dreamlike aura of deathly silence which surrounds the description of Aeneas' walk back into Troy, as his voice reverberates among the deserted streets, and the initial moments of the journey through the underworld, through the woods of initiation, transition, and potential danger works its magic here.

But when Nisus has retraced his wandering path, back to

the heart of the forest where Euryalus has been caught, all becomes noise and tumult once more as the powers of destruction
draw the two friends back together and encompass their ruin.
There is the same note of helpless frustration when the band
seizes Euryalus (line 398) —

> oppressum rapit et conantem plurima frustra.

Overpowered, it dragged him away, struggling violently but in vain. —

as in the cries of Aeneas bidding a final farewell to Creusa, and
in Orpheus' wishing to say many things to Eurydice, but without success. The poet reacts to the plight of Orpheus and of
Nisus with a series of questions. Orpheus asks (G. IV, 504)

> quid faceret? quo se rapta bis coniuge ferret?

What should he do, whither betake himself, now that his wife has been
twice torn from him?

Nisus, too, asks (lines 399–400)

> quid faciat? qua vi iuvenem, quibus audeat armis
> eripere?

What should he do? With what effort, what arms, might he dare to
snatch the youth away?

Death can be the only result, immediate for Nisus, soon in the
case of Orpheus. Nisus resists in vain, and the enemy rush in
upon the stricken pair like hunters approaching for the kill
and complete their slaughter.[28]

Hence, in much briefer scale, Virgil adheres to the pattern
he had set himself in *Aeneid* II, itself partially modeled on
Georgic IV, embracing first a period of destructive violence
followed by an attempted escape in which only Aeneas is successful.

Likewise, as we have noted, the tale of Nisus and Euryalus is
not without its parallels to *Aeneid* VI, among them the pattern
of journey, real and symbolic. The initial section is straight-
forward enough. Nisus states firmly that the way will not mis-

lead (*nec nos via fallet euntis*, line 243), and, as they begin their carnage, he promises to guide his friend along a wide path (*lato te limite ducam*, line 323). All goes well until they leave the camp, and the helmet of Euryalus betrays them as they turn on a road to the left (*laevo flectentis limite*). As already observed, the helmet may be said to stand as a symbol of their impending doom, and the reasons behind it (lines 373-74):

> et galea Euryalum sublustri noctis in umbra
> prodidit immemorem radiisque adversa refulsit.

And the helmet betrayed heedless Euryalus in the dimly lit shadows of night and flashed back glimmers of light.

The description is reminiscent of previous signs and omens, especially the golden bough of Book VI to depict which Virgil is also searching for striking words to express a hidden gleam of light amid surrounding blackness. (*Sublustris* is as rare as *discolor*, an adjective applied to the bough's special contrasting hue.) The direction the pair takes — now deliberately to the left — is also of symbolic value, for if we apply the pattern of *Aeneid* VI to this small segment of Book IX, as the verbal echoes seem to suggest, Nisus and Euryalus have, at this crucial moment when the helmet gives off its ill-fated light, reached the place where the road through the underworld divides in two.

If we look specifically at Book VI for a moment, the previous way for Aeneas had been a review of the past, conjured up by the appearances of Palinurus, Dido, and Deiphobus (lines 337-534). At the point where the road divides (first mentioned by the Sibyl at line 540) would come for the ordinary mortal an evaluation of his past in the light of his worth for the future, be it for Tartarus or Elysium. Aeneas, alive but following the route of the dead, must turn now to the right because in this direction lie the fields of the blessed where he is to meet his father, but not before the Sibyl has explained in detail the tortures of the damned to balance the subsequent account of the joys offered to the eternally happy. For Aeneas this is the moment of real renunciation (death is an irrelevant term in this context), as he turns his eyes to the future after re-experiencing the past through clashes with the three characters who might most readily summarize it.

It is worth mention in passing that Aeneas' detached interest in Tartarus receives a special and by now familiar form. Take, for example, the verbs *respicit* (VI, 548), as Aeneas turns to look back at the sufferings of the guilty, and *constitit* (VI, 559), as he stands in observation. We have analyzed their various appearances in *Aeneid* II and IX and in *Georgic* IV. One other instance should be mentioned, the opening of Book V (lines 3–4), as we find Aeneas

> moenia respiciens, quae iam infelicis Elissae
> conclucent flammis.

looking back at the walls which now gleam with the flames of unfortunate Dido.

There is the same insistence on the walls aflame as in the description of Tartarus, the same curious wonder on the part of Aeneas, strangely aloof for one who was ultimately the fire's cause. Dido makes for herself a private flaming Tartarus through the madness of her passion, and Aeneas, sailing away on the waves of fate, correct, upright, and emotionless, can look as coolly on Dido's blazing pyre as he can on the varied tortures of Tartarus, once more pursuing the right road to his meeting with destiny.

Nisus and Euryalus choose the path to the left. Perhaps a turn to the right would have meant the safety of Rome and the happy fulfillment of their mission to find Aeneas. The possibility is neither held out nor mentioned. We are only told of certain death in the malignant maze of the obscure wood. Virgil does not press a moral, as he does in the case of those condemned to Tartarus. But *furor* and *cupido*, madness and lust, stand out in the narrative as concepts to which the pair were excessively addicted. We have seen Aeneas almost yield to *furor* in Book II and attempt to slay Helen, only to be rescued by his mother who gleamed with a clear light in the darkness (*pura per noctem in luce refulsit*). This is a helpful light, clear and true, and in this respect contrasts with the glimmering flash from the helmet of Euryalus (which also *refulsit*) and with the gloaming surrounding the bough as it too gleams, *refulsit*, amid the trees.

But the helmet, because Euryalus deliberately donned it as they left the Rutulian camp, could well stand for his *cupido* and hence condemns rather than saves. Aeneas, in II, sheltered from madness by his mother, passes to his father's house and thence to freedom. Book VI, with its highly spiritual, more detached journey of enlightenment, exposes him to his own past and seems to grant him little choice between good and evil in the future. His fate leads him in a direct path from Elysium to Rome. Nisus and Euryalus, forced to destroy, yield to a *cupido* beyond necessity which demands death. Virgil has condensed and further realized his own paradigm.

Woods have a special symbolic value in the *Aeneid*, as in many another masterpiece. In Book I, for instance, after the terrifying introductory passage of the storm, the hero decided he must explore, must take the next step in his own growth which destiny has provided. And as he walks along, ignorant both of place and purpose, he meets his mother (I, 314):

> cui mater media sese tulit obvia silva . . .

And across his path in the middle of the woods his mother confronted him.

Once more, as in II, through her own person, and in VI, through both doves and bough, it is Venus who helps bridge the transitional period and leads her son through a time of doubt and trial to the point where he can quite literally surmount an opposing hill and view Dido's Carthage.

The *silvae* of Book VI are more portentous still. In his note on the phrase *tenent media omnia silvae* (VI, 131), Servius remarks, with his propensity for indulging in allegory:

> causam reddit cur non facilis sit animarum regressus, quia omnia polluta et inquinata sunt: nam per silvas tenebras et lustra significat, in quibus feritas et libido dominantur.

He gives the reason why the return of spirits is not easy, since everything is polluted and stained: for by the woods he means dens of darkness, in which rage and lust hold sway.

It is never quite clear — and was probably never meant by Virgil to be clear — where woods end and underworld begins. The actual jaws of the entrance way form little division; they merely introduce the added metaphor of the house whose thresholds Aeneas must cross one by one. Nor, more important, does the poet articulate the difference between unavoidable external setting and the purely spiritual realm of death and life in death. The same distinction could well be applied to the tale of Nisus and Euryalus. When all is said, the *amor menti* of VI, 133 — the desire of Aeneas to brave entrance into the world of death to meet his father finally in Elysium — nearly parallels Nisus and Euryalus' *ardorem mentibus* (IX, 184), the yearning for heroism, which takes explicit form in the necessity of passing through the Rutulian camp before reaching Aeneas at Pallanteum. Nisus and Euryalus are so overwhelmed by temptation that subsequent events, both literal and symbolic — the turn to the left and involvement in the labyrinthine woods of death — are inevitable. Their goal is not to be reached. When the choice of complete submission to *furor* and *cupido* is offered Aeneas in Books II and IV (in VI he can view Tartarus with the utter detachment of one watching life change to death but not literally participating himself in the change), he respects the warnings of divinity and retreats. Nisus and Euryalus, in their minor epic, exemplify those who are tempted and yield. Their description follows one of the patterns of which Virgil's imagination was especially fond.

The adventures of Nisus and Euryalus, however, stand apart from the main event of Book IX — the onslaught of Turnus upon the Trojan camp, his entrance thereto and forced withdrawal. But since this development likewise follows a pattern we have been tracing in our analysis of II, it is appropriate to discuss it here.

Virgil's fascination with the potentiality of violence, usually depicted through imagery of enclosure and release, takes a double form in IX. It begins with the Trojan retreat behind the doors of their camp (IX, 38–39):

> . . . per omnis
> condunt se Teucri portas et moenia complent.

The Trojans seek shelter for themselves through all the gates and man the ramparts.

The verbs in this line are both used of the wooden horse, as the men first hide themselves in its belly or retreat into it again when hard-pressed. The Trojans bar the gates (*obiciunt portas*, line 45), this time deliberately penning themselves within as Volcens and his men trapped Nisus and Euryalus in the woods (lines 379–80):

> obiciunt equites sese ad divortia nota
> hinc atque hinc, omnemque abitum custode coronant.

On this side and that horsemen bar the well-known junctions and surround every exit with guards.

Turnus yearns to play the role of Nisus and Euryalus in the Rutulian camp and seeks a way to enter (lines 57–58):

> . . . huc turbidus atque huc
> lustrat equo muros aditumque per avia quaerit.

Raging hither and thither he rides up and down the walls and seeks an entrance where there is none.

He has not yet accomplished his goal, but Virgil hints through his imagery that he soon may, for he is compared to a hungry wolf, with jaws dry with blood, who roars in anger about a full sheepfold. Euryalus, depicted, we remember, in the guise of a ravenous lion, succeeds where Turnus is still thwarted, since Virgil places him within the pens, mangling the helpless flock. One night only, however, separates Turnus from his objective, the very night that sees the challenge and downfall of Nisus and Euryalus.

When the fighting resumes, Pandarus and Bitias, the Trojan gatekeepers, in a moment of unjustified confidence, swing wide the doors (*portam recludunt*). The Rutulians not unnaturally seize the opportunity (line 683):

> inrumpunt aditus Rutuli ut videre patentis.

The Rutulians break into the entrance-ways when they see them wide open.

Turnus, too, is apprised of the news. Bitias is soon killed in the struggle and Pandarus, fearful now, closes the gate, leaving some of his comrades shut out and at the same time enclosing some of the enemy within the walls. He does not see that Turnus is among them, and Virgil vivifies the occasion with a brief but all the more effective recapitulation of the same motif of animal and flock (lines 728–30):

> demens, qui Rutulum in medio non agmine regem
> viderit inrumpentem ultroque incluserit urbi,
> immanem veluti pecora inter inertia tigrim.

Madman, because he did not see that he had shut in the army's midst the Rutulian king, who had broken in, and of his own accord had penned him in the city, like a huge tiger among helpless flocks.

From here to the end of the book we watch a gradual change in Turnus from beast of violence, having his will of his victims, like Nisus and Euryalus within the Rutulian camp, to Turnus, still an animal but now hemmed in and forced to give ground (lines 791–93):

> acrius hoc Teucri clamore incumbere magno
> et glomerare manum, ceu saevum turba leonem
> cum telis premit infensis . . .

At this the Trojans more boldly press upon him with great shouting and mass their forces, as a crowd presses with hostile weapons upon a fierce lion.

The parallel with Nisus and Euryalus, now trapped in the woods, continues (one need not point out clear verbal parallels) save that Turnus finds it possible to escape by plunging into the waters of the Tiber.

Abluta caede, cleansed from blood, is the phrase Virgil uses (line 818). The slaughter is to be washed from him in the same ritualistic fashion it must be purged from Aeneas before he sets forth on the journey from Troy (II, 718–20). For Turnus such a rite of purification has a second, but equally impressive, significance. The actual turning-point of the previous battle scene begins at lines 756–59 where, once again using an image of crashing through a barrier, Virgil states that Turnus could have finished the war then and there had he thought to let in his companions (lines 760–61):

> sed furor ardentem caedisque insana cupido
> egit in adversos.

But rage and a mad lust for slaughter drove him fiercely against the enemy.

Once more, as we have seen in the case of Nisus and Euryalus, it is rage and mad desire to destroy which alters the action and changes the animal-like Turnus from pursuer to pursued. The reaction in the narrative is the result of moral collapse when the necessity of fighting gives way before an overwhelming greed for slaughter. The symbolic character of Turnus, as wolf, lion, and tiger, lurking ravenous and then devouring greedily, is established here with a fixity unchanged for the remainder of the epic. Here, above all, he remains *impius Furor*, wandering loose to deal destruction at will, then confined though not yet to the point of the total imprisonment of death. The crucial moment finds him only half-surrounded by hostility, for the Tiber offers, on the other side, both escape and refreshment. The action of Book XII begins with Turnus as a wounded lion, and draws to its conclusion with the hero compared to a stag completely surrounded and brought to bay at the will of a fierce hound. He remains an animal to the last, but a new element of helplessness is present at the end as all solace and refuge yield before the triumphant ferocity of the founder of Rome.

2 ' GAME AND REALITY

For the most part, Book V is not one of the more powerful or dramatic sections of the *Aeneid*. As we turn from the ruin of Troy and from Dido's flaming pyre to the celebrations of games which do honor only to the past, we feel a certain anticlimax. And save for the burning of the ships and the journey to Cumae, little happens which forms a necessary link in the chain of epic story. The book's two most prominent events, the funeral games and the death of Palinurus, seem to stand apart from the main narrative. The one appears as a bow to tradition; the other, a beautiful, but mysteriously elusive and special creation of the poet's imagination. Since, in a superficial sense, neither episode furthers the tale, Book V is often taken to be merely an interlude which Virgil was forced to add to bridge the gap from Aeneas' passionate encounter with Dido (the theme of Book IV) to the living death through which the Sibyl guides him, and to which he must succumb in compensation for knowledge of the future. It is therefore frequently treated in cursory fashion.

As the clear parallels show, the model which Virgil had before him in the first part of *Aeneid* V is the twenty-third book of the *Iliad*. Any such reference to the Hellenic tradition inherited by him is often conceived of as a veiled insult to Virgil, servile imitator of Homer, forced, in the case of Book V at least, by one of the established customs of the epic genre to add the equivalent of Achilles' funeral games in honor of Patroclus. As Servius[1] phrases the objection, in anticipation of some modern critics, it is a book "whose major part is taken from Homer, for all the things which he describes here take place around the tomb of Patroclus." Here was Virgil's last chance to make such a break before the steady pace of the war in Latium began.

Book XXIII of the *Iliad*, therefore, offered Virgil a pattern to follow, and the commentaries are liberally scattered with references to its influence, generally to the point of leaving little room for any originality on the part of the Roman poet. Yet there has never been much doubt that the description of the games has touches which are thoroughly Roman in coloring, and even the most ardent Homerist would admit that Virgil has individualized the portraits of his athletes. They need characterization, after all, for they are mostly minor figures who appear only rarely in later events. On the other hand, the special personal traits of Homer's participants, such as Ajax and Odysseus, must be divined from elsewhere in the *Iliad* and then applied to the incidents of the games, not vice versa. In sum, though Virgil's debt to Homer has been so often noted, little attention has been paid to what is particularly Virgilian about the games of *Aeneid* V. The same must be said of the remainder of the book, even of the moving death of Palinurus, a description which adheres closely to one of the poet's special patterns of symbolism.

Another criticism leveled against Book V is that, since it supposedly lacks a unifying theme or focal idea, it misses the emotional drive and vitality which enliven Books IV and VI, both of which develop around one central event. The two occurrences elaborated at any length during the course of Book V, the games, which dominate its opening section, and the divinely contrived death of Palinurus, with which it draws to a conclusion, are indeed disparate, at least from the narrative point of view. Yet they are united by one theme, which lies just beneath the surface throughout the book — the necessity of sacrifice through suffering, sometimes even self-sacrifice, to reach for, and on occasion to achieve, the goals of heroism. The fact that during the course

65

of the games the sacrifice is never actually forced to the point of the destruction of human life is what separates the games from the main narrative of the *Aeneid*, where death is the constant tragic condition of the hero's progress toward self-knowledge. The games offer a momentary relaxation from this particular tension. But, as Huizinga has brilliantly elucidated in his discussion of the meaning of play, the border-line which separates game from seriousness often appears narrow indeed.[2] Even within the movement of ritual, with which ancient athletic events are usually connected, the contest may take either turn.

The connection with ritual is important. Dedicated to the honor of Anchises and celebrated near his tomb, the games of Book V are a religious rite, bounded on the one hand by the sinuous motion of the genial snake, as it coils and re-coils around the tomb; on the other by the ordered regularity of the boys parading in formation before their elders' admiring eyes. The latter display is also a game, to be sure — and Virgil is at pains to demonstrate its etiology — but its significance depends on the fact that it is no longer a contest but, enhanced by the irony which the youthfulness and discipline of the participants convey, a parody of the actualities of war which are to come. Thus the reader is prepared for the sudden return to reality which soon occurs in the form of the burning of the ships.

In this sense, then, the games form a world apart. They are enclosed within the world of ritual which takes the story out of the violence of life and then, once more, leads back to it. This violence of the outside world, from which the games offer momentary escape, is associated primarily with Palinurus the pilot. He is the central figure of the book's initial episode, and it is with his death that the book concludes. The sea-storm which opens the book, and which, in its unusual strength, forces even Palinurus to cower in fear, is, as we shall see, closely related to the severity and suddenness of his death, and therefore serves to balance the beginning of the book with the end. And when at last the men gain land at Drepanum and prepare for the contests, it seems clearly to be only a momentary respite from powers that are uncontrollable. Death almost claimed the pilot, whose uselessness becomes briefly but sharply clear. The snake of Anchises, which appears from his tomb shortly after Aeneas reaches it, does little to dispel the notion of impending doom. A benign snake in classical literature is unusual. In Virgil, who constantly associates snakes with hidden, unwonted death, as we have seen from Book II, it is all but unique. Its importance here should not be underestimated, for it suggests, through association with ritual, the theme of religious awe which postulates escape out of ordinary life into the sphere of game. It also hints at lurking violence — violence which comes suddenly to life again, even while the games are yet in progress, with the mission of Iris and the firing of the ships. Even in this forceful return to reality Virgil uses some of the imagery associated with the snake of Anchises to portray madness at last revivified.[3] From then on, as the book progresses, the tension reaches a higher and still higher pitch until its climax in the death of Palinurus.

Within this world apart, the world of game, the outside tragic sphere never imposes itself to the point that game becomes a matter of life and death. Elsewhere in the epic, the suffering and sacrifice which typify the particular heroism of the *Aeneid* lead in a series of tragedies to a culmination in Book XII, where death is the only possible outcome. In the games, life always seems to triumph after a brush with death, and the hero, as is the fashion in comedy, is absorbed back into the ranks of the society whence he was singled out to perform. Through the games Virgil takes the reader aside and merely by so doing — by describing events which seem to have little or nothing to do with the epic story — offers a kind of relaxation from the tensions which form the real world of Aeneas. Their subject matter is seemingly remote and special, and the result of each event is always in some sense comic, by however narrow a margin. Yet, happily as they generally evolve, the games are a microcosm of the world at large. It is thus that they are interpreted here, first in terms of themselves, then in relation to the book as a whole, with particular emphasis on the figure of Palinurus, whose role rises beyond importance only in Book V to a symbolic significance related to the total epic.

> Interea medium Aeneas iam classe tenebat
> certus iter fluctusque atros Aquilone secabat
> moenia respiciens, quae iam infelicis Elissae
> conlucent flammis. quae tantum accenderit ignem
> causa latet.

Meanwhile Aeneas, firm in his resolve, held with his fleet a course well out to sea and cut through the waves darkened by the north wind, looking back at the walls which now gleam with the flames of unfortunate Dido. The reason why so great a fire was kindled remains hidden.

These opening lines of Book V pick up the narrative of Aeneas' adventures where it was dropped in order that the final moments of Dido's agony might be described in detail — *interea*, "meanwhile," as if to emphasize that Aeneas' departure and her death are dissociable events in the mind of the hero. The flames, through whose gleam he sets his sails, consume her body and end her love for Aeneas at the same time. The metaphorical wound of love he inflicted, the fire he ignited, become a reality as destructive of the past as it is ominous for the future. Aeneas even looks back (*respiciens*) as he did finally for Creusa, dying in the inferno of the sinking Troy.[4] But here, as there, it is the glance of one ignorant of the necessary human suffering left scattered in the wake of his ideal journey.

Thus Dido's corpse is overwhelmed by fire; thus Priam's ancestral Troy is consumed in flames which destroy the past and, at the same time, seem only to spur Aeneas on his destined way. Fire is always quenched with water in these opening books of the *Aeneid*. Just as the sea voyage of Book III contrasts in this respect with the conflagration of Troy, so now the resumption of the ocean journey serves not so much to counteract the flames of ill-fated love as to equalize them in the scale of the total epic.

Book III concluded with the death of Anchises, that symbol of purposeless, wandering Troy in transition, and in Book V we are not deprived of a similar situation, in which death is the required condition of progress. For Book V, though most of its action takes place on land, is one in which the imagination of the reader is always directed to the sea and hence to the character of the pilot, Palinurus, whom we find guiding the fleet as we plunge into the action, and with whose mysterious death the book concludes in lines of special brilliance.[5]

The opening verses thus serve the same purpose as the two with which Book VI begins; they join the action of the previous book to the one which follows. Yet lines 1–7 have their own intrinsic interest. Though Aeneas may realize that Dido's death is the cause of the flames, the poet never makes this explicit, and hence he carries over into words like *flammis* and *ignem* the ambiguous metaphor of fire become real, central to Book IV. The fire imagery is also important in another way, because it recalls Mercury's threat to Aeneas (IV, 566–67):

> "iam mare turbari trabibus saevasque videbis
> conlucere faces, iam fervere litora flammis . . ."

"Soon you will see the ocean swirling with beams and fierce brands blazing, and the shore glowing with flames."

Such a dread event Mercury promises to bring about unless Aeneas leaves Carthage forthwith. Though the actual result is that Dido herself burns in their stead, she would be quite capable of burning the ships to detain Aeneas and wreak her revenge.

Yet the sight offers a feeling of foreboding as the men ponder what a woman is capable of in madness (*furens quid femina possit*, line 6). The curse which Dido utters against her deserting lover in IV, 661–62, finds its fulfillment here:

> "hauriat hunc oculis ignem crudelis ab alto
> Dardanus, et nostrae secum ferat omina mortis."

"Let the cruel Trojan from the deep drink in this fire with his eyes, and let him take with him the omen of our death."

69

But there is a more far-reaching consequence, one which does indeed accomplish the ominous presage of these initial lines. For it is in Book V that the Trojan women, who are similarly aroused with maddened rage (*actae furore*, line 659), finally do burn Aeneas' ships as Dido herself might have done. The grief and suffering of Dido, Juno's emotional pawn, can in part be traced back ultimately to the suffering of the goddess herself. For, still in Book V, we find Juno (line 608)

> multa movens necdum antiquum saturata dolorem.

up to many tricks, with her ancient resentment still unsated.

Through various wiles, Juno is a prime cause of both events.

It is only with line 8 of Book V that the past is left entirely behind, as the ships confront the violence of a new storm (lines 8–11):

> Ut pelagus tenuere rates nec iam amplius ulla
> occurrit tellus, maria undique et undique caelum,
> olli caeruleus supra caput astitit imber
> noctem hiememque ferens et inhorruit unda tenebris.

When the ships had gained the deep, and no land was any longer in sight, with ocean on all sides and sky everywhere about, then a dark tempest loomed over his head, bringing night and storm, and the wave bristled with darkness.

These lines parallel very closely III, 192–95, where the much-tried band of Trojans, setting sail for points known and yet unknown, runs headlong into a tempest. Then even Palinurus fails to distinguish day from night and loses his way amidst the raging tempest. Once more in V, as the ships battle on their way, Palinurus is at the helm. This time, however, the course is clearer. The pilot knows the direction but the gods, or fortune, are against the journey. Palinurus seems to sense the irony of his own words when he says "I could not hope to gain Italy under a sky like this" (*non . . . hoc sperem Italiam contingere caelo,* lines 17–18). Though he undoubtedly means to speak for his comrades as a whole, his words bear directly on himself. The atmosphere of uncertainty and impending doom which surrounds the ships in Book III here comes to a climax and centers on Palinurus, as he asks, "What are you preparing, Father Neptune?" (*quidve, pater Neptune, paras?* line 14). As he ponders the violence of the present storm in fear for his comrades, he cannot realize that before many days are spent the god of the sea will deliberately contrive death for him alone.

As similar as these lines are to those of Book III, there is one variation which leaves in the poetry an effect of studied ambiguity, the change from *tum mihi* in III, 194, which refers to Aeneas, the narrator, to *olli* in V, 10: [6]

> olli caeruleus supra caput astitit imber . . .

Over his head there loomed a dark tempest.

Were Virgil literally transposing lines, the alteration from first person narrative to third might in itself postulate such a variation. Nevertheless, the word *olli* remains equivocal in the context of Book V. Does it refer to Aeneas or to Palinurus? The distinction is important chiefly because the conclusion of the book seems to offer a close parallelism between the two characters. Suffice it to observe here that the imagery of line 10, ignored in Book III, is elaborated most carefully toward the end of Book V, relative to the figure of Palinurus. Neptune demands one life (*unum caput*) before Aeneas can continue safely on his journey, and as Somnus, the Sleep of death, stands over Palinurus (*supra* of line 10 is altered to *super* in lines 855 and 858), it is his head which he urges the pilot to lay down.[7] Finally, in words which recall Palinurus' own utterance to Somnus that he would not let down his guard against the face and quiet flood of the peaceful sea or "put trust in this monster" (*huic confidere monstro*, line 849), Aeneas calls him too trustful in the sky and calm sea (*nimium caelo et pelago confise sereno*, line 870). The cause of Palinurus' death appears to Aeneas as nothing more than a sudden storm, such as that at the beginning of the book, which swept him overboard. Death outside of nature is a consequence with which Aeneas is not prepared to bargain. But there is much more to Palinurus' death than this. What is important to observe here is the careful and deliberate balance between these opening lines and those that conclude the book, for the imagery of the storm, through which Palinurus himself cannot pass, certainly reappears in the end as Sleep claims him for his own.[8] And Aeneas, perhaps because he is so much a part of the event without knowing it, misinterprets the happening entirely.

With the winds against them, and facing a driving storm through which even the pilot dares not pass, they steer once more to Sicily and the home of Acestes, and prepare to offer the homage of sacrifice and funeral games on the tomb of Anchises, dead now one year. Aeneas proclaims the order of the celebrations and, having poured the requisite libations and addressed his father's spirit with reverence, is greeted by an omen in the form of a huge snake which proceeds from the inmost shrine, licks harmlessly at the offerings, and disappears whence it came, into the bottom of the tomb. The sign seems propitious, and Aeneas, though uncertain whether it is really his father or just a local divinity, commands further offerings to Anchises.

But the description of the snake's appearance offers as much cause for uneasiness as for encouragement. In fact, the whole episode bears a marked likeness to the manner in which the two monstrous sea-serpents devour Laocoön in Book II, with the important difference that, whereas here the reptile appears innocent, there the two beasts showed, from the start, a particularly destructive purpose.[9] The distinction is not quite so simple, however. In their external features the parallels are extensive. Like the serpents in Book II, the huge snake, enormous in its breadth, pulls its folds after it in circles. It glides around the altars (*lapsus per aras*, line 86; and we recall the use of the word *lapsus* in II, 225, as the snakes glide up to the citadel). The serpents from Tenedos had surrounded Laocoön and his sons while the priest performed his sacred duties. In this lies the ambiguity of the picture. Anchises' snake embraces the tomb (*amplexus*, line 86), and the twin creatures had, likewise, "embraced" Laocoön and his children with intent not to cherish but devour (*amplexus*, II, 214; *amplexi*, 218). They lick their tongues (*lambebant*, II, 211) in anticipation, and the snake from the tomb laps at the viands (*libavit*, V, 92). Then, as we read that the one leaves the altar upon which he had fed (*depasta altaria liquit*, V, 93), we are reminded that each of the sea-serpents, in order to make short work of Laocoön's two sons (II, 215),

> implicat et miseros morsu depascitur artus.

enfolds them and with its jaws feeds on their pitiful limbs.

From one sight the Trojans flee in terror (II, 212–13):

> diffugimus visu exsangues. illi agmine certo
> Laocoonta petunt . . .

We flee in terror from the spectacle. They with fixed course seek Laocoön.

Before the present happening the onlookers merely stand watching in amazement (V, 90–93):

> obstipuit visu Aeneas. ille agmine longo
> tandem inter pateras et levia pocula serpens
> libavitque dapes rursusque innoxius imo
> successit tumulo . . .

Aeneas stood aghast at the sight. At last the snake, gliding with long coils among the bowls and polished cups, tasted of the dishes and harmlesly withdrew again to the bottom of the tomb.

Hence the great and obvious difference between the two episodes is not what the snakes do in each case but the manner and degree in which their goal is accomplished.[10] The snakes of Laocoön feed on people and seem to symbolize in their deed the total destruction of Troy by the twin sons of Atreus. The other makes its meal from offerings, and embraces only what is already dead. In a sense, then, Aeneas offers sacrifice to Anchises as a propitiatory gift to the spirit of the years of wandering, which are now almost concluded. In this his deed also prefigures the essential sequence of events in Book V, which consists in the main of one kind of sacrifice after another and culminates — to anticipate for a moment — in the offering of Palinurus both to Neptune and for the future underworld journey. In fact, the action of the priestess in VI, as she sacrifices to the gods of Hades before setting out (lines 243–44, 247) —

> quattuor hic primum nigrantis terga iuvencos
> constituit frontique invergit vina sacerdos . . .
> voce vocans Hecaten caeloque Ereboque potentem.

Here first the priestess set in line four bullocks with dark backs and poured wine over their foreheads . . . calling aloud on Hecate, powerful in heaven and in hell . . . —

is akin to the rites which Aeneas now fulfills (V, 96–99):

> . . . caedit binas de more bidentis
> totque sues, totidem nigrantis terga iuvencos;
> vinaque fundebat pateris animamque vocabat
> Anchisae magni Manisque Acheronte remissos.

According to custom he slaughters two sheep and as many pigs, and the same number of dark-backed bullocks. He poured wine from bowls and called on the spirit of great Anchises and the ghost released from Acheron.

In brief, this offering to Anchises and his ominous snake is the first of a series which culminates only in the arrival of Aeneas himself in the underworld, like the bough which he carries, dead and yet very much alive.[11]

In no way disturbed by the omen, Aeneas immediately lists the order of the games and prepares the prizes. The first competition is the boat race, whose story lasts 171 lines and is the most elaborately detailed of all the events; in fact, it is a little tale all to itself.[12] Four ships, chosen from the entire fleet as part standing for the whole, start the race, but at its conclusion only two arrive unscathed. After Aeneas has set a rock well out to sea as the turning point (*meta*) of the course, the boats rush headlong over the waters like chariots breaking forth from newly opened gates.

The first incident of the race centers upon the boat of Gyas. With all four competitors apparently pulling neck and neck, Gyas shouts to his helmsman, Menoetes, to cleave a path closer to the rocks of the goal (lines 162–65):

> "quo tantum mihi dexter abis? huc dirige gressum;
> litus ama et laeva stringat sine palmula cautes;
> altum alii teneant." dixit; sed caeca Menoetes
> saxa timens proram pelagi detorquet ad undas.

"Where are you going so far off to the right? Steer this way. Stick to the shore and let the left oar graze the rocks. Let others keep to the deep water." He spoke, but Menoetes, fearing the hidden rocks, twists the prow toward the open sea.

The result is that the ship of Cloanthus, choosing the way which the timorous Menoetes had feared, surpasses that of Gyas, who, in his wrath, hurls Menoetes overboard (lines 175–77):

> in mare praecipitem puppi deturbat ab alta;
> ipse gubernaculo rector subit, ipse magister
> hortaturque viros clavumque ad litora torquet.

He hurls him down from the high poop headlong into the sea. He himself takes over the guidance of the tiller and, now captain, urges on his men and twists the rudder shoreward.

This episode seems to anticipate the death of Palinurus, in the mock heroic, even comic, fashion whereby much connected with the games contrasts with the highly serious events which follow. The episode of Menoetes takes place in the midst of the flood (*medio in gurgite*, line 160), a phrase that would become clearer to Virgil's commentators were they to turn to the mention of *gurges* in line 814 to denote the place where Neptune promises that the dead Palinurus will be found.[13] The several prominent verbal repetitions point up the similarity of the two situations. Menoetes falls headlong into the sea (*in mare praecipitem*) and Palinurus, too, topples headlong into the waves (*in undas praecipitem*, lines 859–60). Menoetes is hurled by Gyas from the lofty stern, the same place held by Palinurus in line 12 and later taken by Somnus for his violent dealings with Aeneas' helmsman. Gyas then undertakes the direction of the ship as does Aeneas, who himself guided the ship through the waves of night (*ipse ratem nocturnis rexit in undis*, line 868). In the end Gyas fails through lack of a helmsman. Nor can Aeneas very well plot the course of a ship bereft of its helm. He is sublimely, though unknowingly, in the hands of the gods.[14]

Thus Gyas commands Menoetes and Somnus, Palinurus, although only Palinurus actually dies. Since Gyas, by taking over the direction of the ship after the helmsman's loss, also plays the role Aeneas assumes at the book's conclusion, he combines in himself the roles held by two people in the story of Palinurus. Aeneas, for his part, knows nothing of Sleep, though in a sense it claims a share of him. The major difference in the two episodes, however, is the fact that Menoetes does not die. Instead (lines 178–80):

> . . . gravis, ut fundo vix tandem redditus imo est,
> iam senior madidaque fluens in veste Menoetes
> summa petit scopuli siccaque in rupe resedit.

. . . Menoetes, barely yielded up at last from the sea bottom, a man already old, weighed down with his dripping garments, grasps the top of the rocks and sinks down on the dry crag.

The humor of the situation, clearly apparent to those watching the byplay, stands in marked contrast to Palinurus' own description of his death in VI (lines 358–59, 361) where he tells how

> ". . . iam tuta tenebam
> ni gens crudelis madida cum veste gravatum . . .
> ferro invasisset praedamque ignara putasset."

76

". . . now, weighted down with dripping garments, I would have reached the shore in safety had not the cruel folk, thinking me booty in their ignorance, assailed me with the sword."

The peril and escape of Menoetes anticipates just this tragic situation.[15]

As the first part of the race centered on a special clash between Cloanthus and Gyas, so now the remaining two boats, captained by Sergestus and Mnestheus, vie in overtaking the lagging, pilot-less Gyas. This time the action centers on the *scopulus* itself, the sounding rock which all are striving to round. Here Mnes-theus appears a type of minor Aeneas (he uses words spoken by Aeneas elsewhere in the book), urging on his men to overcome Sergestus. He attains his wish (lines 202–4),

> namque furens animi dum proram ad saxa suburget
> interior spatioque subit Sergestus iniquo,
> infelix saxis in procurrentibus haesit.

for while Sergestus in madness presses his prow closer toward the rocks and enters into the region of danger, unhappily he sticks upon the jutting rocks.

If the previous episode suggests a parallel with the death of Palinurus, this one could be said to anticipate the final events of the book, which follow immediately upon the helmsman's loss. The danger caused by Aeneas' lack of a pilot is emphasized as the fleet approaches the treacherous rocks of the Sirens (lines 864–66):

> iamque adeo scopulos Sirenum advecta subibat,
> difficilis quondam multorumque ossibus albos
> (tum rauca adsiduo longe sale saxa sonabant) . . .

And thus now in its course it approached the rocks of the Sirens, once perilous and white with the bones of many (then the crags sounded hoarsely afar from the unceasing surf).

The final threat posed to Aeneas, the seafarer, of dying ship-wrecked on the rocks of the Sirens before attaining his goal of Italy and Cumae, Sergestus confronts here, in a much simpler fashion, and fails. Virgil speaks of the adventure of his ill-fated boat (*spatioque subit Sergestus iniquo*) in a manner similar to the way he describes Aeneas' fleet passing by the Sirens' rocks (*scopulos Sirenum advecta subibat*). And, though Aeneas escapes, Virgil seems also to be anticipating here, in comic vein, the book's conclusion. Sergestus was maddened at heart, the passion of the moment leading him to forget the mean course which would win the day in the end. Thus, in striking too near the rocks, he fell victim to the opposite fallacy from that which proved the undoing of Menoetes (and with him Gyas), a desire to steer at too great a distance from the dangerous reef.[16] Gyas is like Sleep, counseling that which Palinurus is unwilling to believe or to follow. Yet Palinurus must die, just as Sergestus, in following the opposite extreme, must suffer shipwreck. Palinurus would avoid the Sirens' crags. Aeneas must of necessity skirt them and come out unscathed through the workings of divine will.

And thus Mnestheus, surpassing Sergestus, comes into the final stretch, like a dove frightened from her rocky nest (lines 213–17):

> qualis spelunca subito commota columba,
> cui domus et dulces latebroso in pumice nidi,
> fertur in arva volans plausumque exterrita pennis
> dat tecto ingentem, mox aëre lapsa quieto
> radit iter liquidum celeris neque commovet alas . . .

Even as a dove, whose home and sweet nestlings are in a rocky hiding-place, is suddenly startled from her cave, she takes flight from her home toward the fields and in her terror makes a great flapping with her wings. Soon, gliding through the quiet air, she cleaves a liquid path, not moving her swift pinions.

Though the dove imagery is important for the archery contest which soon follows and for the descent of Somnus, it is the sequence of the simile itself which is of most interest here. The narrowness of the cave, the confinement of the rocky haunt wherein the dove has her nest, alludes to the closeness of Mnestheus' recent conflict with Sergestus. The whole setting, particularly the rocky den, offers a figure for the reef on which Sergestus grounds and the crags of the Sirens from which Aeneas' fleet is steered. Having escaped from its cave, the dove gradually loses its fear. Though roused (*commota*) and frightened at the outset, in the end it does not even move its wings (*commovet alas*). It is this new peace, itself reflected in the quiet air and liquid path, which leads back into the description of Mnestheus (lines 218–19):

> sic Mnestheus, sic ipsa fuga secat ultima Pristis
> aequora, sic illam fert impetus ipse volantem.

Thus Mnestheus, thus the Dragon of herself cleaves in flight the water's final stretch. Her own momentum bears her along as she flies.

After the reef comes the calm freedom of the open air and sea, through which Mnestheus now glides without rowing as the boat cleaves its own way. It is likewise in the calm of night, with the ocean still as marble, that Sleep soon comes down to claim Palinurus, plunging him into the watery waves, while the very seas (*ipsa aequora*, Sleep says) bear the boat along. Here it is Mnestheus who suggests Aeneas, whose final hazard is the Sirens' crags. And Sergestus, whom Mnestheus now passes by, wrecked on the rocks and calling in vain for help (*frustra vocantem auxilia*, lines 221–22), is but a small, comic shadow of Palinurus as he dies in the calm sea of the final journey, calling upon his comrades in vain (*socios nequiquam vocantem*, line 860).[17]

The last part of the race, in the smooth waters near the end, remains between Mnestheus and Cloanthus, and the latter wins the day by vowing sacrifice to the gods of the sea. At this, Neptune intervenes on Cloanthus' behalf and, swift as an arrow, the boat shelters itself in the deep harbor (*portu se condidit alto*, line 243). So also, by the good offices of the god of the sea, Aeneas arrives safely at Cumae, at the very beginning of Book VI:

> Sic fatur lacrimans, classique immittit habenas
> et tandem Euboicis Cumarum adlabitur oris.

He spoke thus in tears and, giving rein to his fleet, glides at last to Euboean Cumae's shores.

Near the end of Book V, Venus prays to Neptune (lines 796–97):

> "quod superest, oro, liceat dare tuta per undas
> vela tibi, liceat Laurentem attingere Thybrim . . ."

"As for the rest, grant them, I pray you, to sail safely over the waves, grant them to gain Laurentine Tiber."

Neptune, aware of what is nearer to hand, answers her request by a promise (line 813):

> "tutus, quos optas, portus accedet Averni."

"According to your wish, he will gain in safety the harbor of Avernus."

Rome itself is less important to him than the last leg of the journey, to the land of the dead to learn of Rome. For Aeneas in actuality, as for Mnestheus within the context of game, the final stretches of his sea journey (*ultima aequora*) are at hand.

Sergestus too escapes, though, like a snake crushed by a wheel or beaten by a passing wayfarer and left to languish on a rock, he seems at first half dead, pulling his coils after himself in vain (lines 276–79):

> nequiquam longos fugiens dat corpore tortus
> parte ferox ardensque oculis et sibila colla
> arduus attollens; pars vulnere clauda retentat
> nexantem nodis seque in sua membra plicantem . . .

Fleeing in vain, he twists his body in long coils, still fierce in part, flashing fiery eyes and raising his hissing neck aloft. Part of him, lamed by the wound, holds him back, writhing in knots and twisting in upon his own limbs.

In the end, however, gaining motion like the dove, Sergestus enters the harbor under full sail. As in the case of the dove simile, ideas previously latent come to the fore through the imagery. The snake has been wounded by a wayfarer and left on a rock [18] in the same way that Sergestus went aground on the cruel reef.

Yet he manages to pull himself off (*revulsus*, line 270), like the snake gradually moving forward, coiling in on itself. But the snake is half dead, and the ship, too, appears (line 271)

> amissis remis atque ordine debilis uno . . .

with oars lost, and crippled in one tier.

Part lives on, part dies — the very fate of Aeneas' fleet with Palinurus lost (*amisso*, line 867). And he also dies tearing part of the helm with him in his fall (*puppis parte revulsa*, line 858).

Thus, in brief, the various episodes of the first race suggest a comic microcosm of the final stretches of Aeneas' journey which embrace the loss of pilot, narrow escape from shipwreck, and final safe arrival at a destination. The race thus serves further to unify the book and, in part at least, to polarize it around the figure of the doomed pilot.

The theme of victory by sacrifice, of achievement gained only through death, which in the games always ends in the comic relief of narrow personal escape, is the focal idea of the rest of the contests. Second comes the foot race, which is very briefly described. Its main interest lies in the misfortune of Nisus, who had at first led the field. It was near the end, however (lines 328–30),

> . . . levi cum sanguine Nisus
> labitur infelix, caesis ut forte iuvencis
> fusus humum viridisque super madefecerat herbas.

when unfortunate Nisus slid on some slippery blood, which had poured out where bullocks had by chance been slain and had dampened the ground and green grass.

The motif of offering, which occurs frequently during the book's course, is here centered on the figure of Nisus, who could be said to sacrifice himself for the sake of Euryalus, who wins the race. Aeneas finds him innocent (*insons*) in the face of fortune's wiles, the same adjective that is ascribed to Palinurus in line 841. But once again, in mock contrast to the stirring drama at the book's end, the hero rises to gain one of the prizes of victory.[19]

Aeneas prepares to bestow upon the victor in the boxing contest that follows a bullock bedecked with gold and fillets, like the bull which Ascanius in Book IX promises to immolate should he subjugate Numanus. In this instance the theme of sacrifice, once established, is dropped during the course of the fight. We have only a hint of what might come in line 413 when Entellus displays his gloves which, he adds,

> "sanguine cernis adhuc sparsoque infecta cerebro."

"you see still dyed with blood and spattered with brain." [20]

At the beginning of the fight Dares seems first to be winning the day by a dexterity which the massive, less agile Entellus does not possess, but soon the tide turns. Finally Aeneas, anticipating thoughts Somnus is soon to utter over Palinurus, warns Dares, *ex post facto*, to yield to a higher power, especially when it seems to have the backing of the gods (lines 465–67):

> "infelix, quae tanta animum dementia cepit?
> non viris alias conversaque numina sentis?
> cede deo."

"Unfortunate man, what great madness has seized your mind? Do you not see that the strength belongs to someone else and that the divine will is adverse? Give in to the god." [21]

Death was again almost successful, but not quite. Dares is, as Entellus puts it, narrowly recalled from death (*revocatum a morte*, l. 476). His place is taken by the prize bullock against which Entellus swings his gauntlet (lines 480–81):

> . . . effractoque inlisit in ossa cerebro:
> sternitur exanimisque tremens procumbit humi bos.

He broke into the skull and shattered the brain. The bull shuddered, collapsed, and lay lifeless on the ground.

Dares is spared through the sacrifice of the bull. But this comes closest of all events in the games to human sacrifice, and thereby forms another link in the chain which soon leads to Palinurus.[22]

The next and final event of the games is archery, and the target, borrowed from Homer's description, is a dove hanging by a cord from the ship's mast. Here, at last, contest and fulfillment, sacrifice and purpose, have the same result, the death of the dove which becomes both goal and victim. The picture of the terrified bird itself is taken partially from the comparison examined earlier of Mnestheus to a dove soaring forth from her hidden nest. At first, like the bird in the simile, it trembles on frightened wing and everything round about echoes with noise. Is it the terror of the dove the poet is depicting, as would be only natural, or the joy of the onlookers? The ambiguity seems deliberate, for the two emotions are closely tied together now that death is the actual purpose, as it is in none of the other contests. Death in earnest, threatened against a living creature, has replaced mere vying for athletic honors. The dove is tied, and freedom, when it briefly comes, is soon cut off in death. When Mnestheus severs the cord which binds the bird to the mast, it has a momentary free flight toward the dark heavens (*atra volans in nubila*, line 512), like the dove in the simile flying toward the fields (*in arva volans*, line 215).

But even the first arrow shot from the twanging bow (*nervo stridente sagitta*) aimed at death. In a similar manner Virgil describes the actions of the Dira who brings death to Turnus, screeching through the sky (*stridens*) like a poison dart sped from a string (*nervo per nubem impulsa sagitta*: XII, 856), against whose wound there is no remedy. It is not long until Eurytion accomplishes the fated deed, and the dove (lines 517–18)

> decidit exanimis vitamque reliquit in astris
> aetheriis fixamque refert delapsa sagittam.

falling dead, left its life among the stars of heaven and in downward course brought back the arrow which had pierced it.

She flutters dead, paralleling the trembling bull sacrificed shortly before by Entellus (*exanimis*, line 481). Yet in the collapse of her lifeless body and the ascent of her spirit upward, she anticipates both the moment of Palinurus' death (lines 838–39) —

> cum levis aetheriis delapsus Somnus ab astris
> aëra dimovit tenebrosum et dispulit umbras . . .

when light Sleep, gliding down from the stars of heaven, parted the darkening air and dispelled the shadows . . . —

and the departure of Sleep back toward heaven (line 861):

> ipse volans tenuis se sustulit ales ad auras.

He soared toward the air above, flying on light wings.

In its very fall, the dove suggests Palinurus, helpless against a fate which is both incomprehensible and inescapable.[23]

As if to alter the mood of doom present and to come, the poet seems to turn the arrow of Acestes, which now shoots heavenward and in its course catches fire, into an omen of good, just as he changes the fire in Book II from destructive to beneficent through the omen of Iulus' hair. Thus on a more hopeful note Virgil prepares for the end of the games, but here, as in the appearance of Anchises' snake, it is a total impression of violence and destruction that seems to remain, not any final attempt to palliate it. Even though it appears of great value as presage of the future, the omen is described in highly ambiguous language. Aeneas accepts it as propitious, but its significance in relation to the imagery of Book V could scarcely be so conceived. Acestes twists his shaft toward the heavenly breezes, and (lines 525–28)

> . . . volans liquidis in nubibus arsit harundo
> signavitque viam flammis tenuisque recessit
> consumpta in ventos, caelo ceu saepe refixa
> transcurrunt crinemque volantia sidera ducunt.

flying amid the liquid clouds, the arrow caught fire, showed its path from the flames and, burning away, vanished into thin air, as often shooting stars, detached from the sky, run their course, trailing their tresses across the heavens.

Henry, in his *Aeneidea*, refers the sign to a future deification of Acestes.[24] One doubts, however, that Virgil's intention here was to convey, without further elucidation, a meaning which has nothing to do with the remainder of the *Aeneid* or even with the future course of Rome. Without broadening the search, a perfectly satisfactory explanation of the omen can be found in the events that follow in Book V, in which case it falls into the series of supernatural manifestations which make the book turn now to the past, now to the future, through the disclosures of divinity. Henry is correct that death is involved. The dove, we remember from the lines shortly before, though her body plunged to earth, left her life among the stars of heaven. In a very similar manner, and at a time not long distant, Somnus departs after fulfilling his baleful mission against Palinurus:

> ipse volans tenuis se sustulit ales ad auras.

He soared toward the air above, flying on light wings.

Manifestly the line refers to the god betaking himself back to his starry realms, but Death has somehow taken possession of Palinurus and, although he tells us in Book VI of his struggle to gain the shore through the violent swell, his life, too, now makes its company among the winds, *tenuis*, almost unseen, like the ominous arrow of Acestes.

It is not only death which the symbolic arrow seems to predict but also destruction by fire, an anticipation, it could be said, of the burning of the ships. But before this occurs, there is one final piece of entertainment, once more a mock exposition of the truth to come, in the parade of Iulus and his companions. The previous conflicts, only because they were supposedly entered upon in the spirit of a game, all ended short of death — often, as we have seen, by the narrowest of margins. Now little Iulus sets up his forces in mimic battle array (lines 583–87):

> inde alios ineunt cursus aliosque recursus
> adversi spatiis, alternosque orbibus orbis

impediunt pugnaeque cient simulacra sub armis;
et nunc terga fuga nudant, nunc spicula vertunt
infensi, facta pariter nunc pace feruntur.

Next they enter on other marches and counter-marches, their positions facing each other. They intertwine circle with opposing circle and initiate in arms pretended warfare. And now in flight they bare their backs and turn their spears in hostile fashion; now making peace they ride off side by side.

They put on their show before the faces of their parents and the eyes of their dear ones. Indeed, Virgil emphatically repeats, the boys mirror in their young faces their parents' looks (*ora parentum*, line 553). Yet the phrase, in relation to the total epic scheme, recalls more sorrow than joy for the present episode. We cannot help but recall, for instance, that at one of the more striking moments of Book II it was before the very eyes of his parents (*ante oculos . . . et ora parentum*) that Polites dies, pursued by Pyrrhus to the feet of his father.[25]

Irony surely lurks in the two similes used to enhance the description of the maneuvers of the warrior boys. The first, a comparison between their weaving course and the famous Labyrinth of Daedalus, occurs in lines 588–93:

ut quondam Creta fertur Labyrinthus in alta
parietibus textum caecis iter ancipitemque
mille viis habuisse dolum, qua signa sequendi
frangeret indeprensus et inremeabilis error:
haud alio Teucrum nati vestigia cursu
impediunt . . .

As of old in mountainous Crete it is said that the Labyrinth contained a path woven of dark walls presenting treacherous deceit in its thousand ways, whereby the undetected and irretraceable maze confounds the signs marking return: in similar fashion the Trojan youths interweave their steps as they go.

This strange scene of the house of the Minotaur and others like it, products of the genius of Daedalus, are, of course, part of the scheme which decorates the temple of Apollo at Cumae described at the beginning of Book VI, of whose imagery it forms a brief but important part.[26] Hence this simile may look to the future, to the last and greatest of the *errores* of Aeneas.[27] The next picture certainly appears to glance at what lies ahead. The boys also seem (lines 594–95)

> delphinum similes, qui per maria umida nando
> Carpathium Libycumque secant luduntque per undas.

like dolphins who, as they swim through the liquid flood, cut a path in the Carpathian or Libyan seas and play amid the waves.

On the shield of Aeneas, in the final calm before the storm at Actium, Virgil, in the place where Homer forges the eternal ocean of life which surrounds the world of Achilles and Hector, puts dolphins playing (VIII, 671–74):

> haec inter tumidi late maris ibat imago
> aurea, sed fluctu spumabat caerula cano,
> et circum argento clari delphines in orbem
> aequora verrebant caudis aestumque secabant.

Among these things the picture of the swollen sea spread far and wide, all of gold, but the dark flood foamed with hoary crest, and in a circle bright dolphins of silver swept the waves round about with their tails and cut through the surge.

The quiet sea of Book V is transformed into the picture of Actium's swollen flood, but the sea creatures still cavort and cut the waves as before. Yet a violent change occurs, for in the midst of this brief idyllic scene we suddenly come upon brazen fleets and a battle scene with Mars arrayed (*instructo Marte*).[28] Iulus also arranged his battle lines (*instruxit*, line 549) but only in mock imitation of war.[29] Here again, as in all the other episodes of the games, the seriousness of the future looms large in the happy present. And, as for Iulus himself, it must not be forgotten that it is his careless deed in Book VII which helps to start all the bloodshed.

This *lusus Troiae*, performed by Iulus, is an example of the order and perfection of game as seen in the grace and exactitude of a set piece which cannot be broken without spoiling the mood entirely. This very perfection, however, focuses our attention once more on one of the tensions developed within the sphere of game, namely, that it is beyond what is regularly human because death is avoided. The meaning of the *lusus Troiae* hovers between the two poles of complete escape and complete involvement with real life. It is like most games because it admits of no destruction or violence to its participants. And, after all, only children are performing it under the watchful eyes of their teachers and within limitations which demand precise order for their fulfillment. But even here there remains in the background the potentiality of war as fought by men whose goal is death, not stage play. The images never get beyond the labyrinth and the dolphins, but each looks potentially further ahead to future hazard; and one, as pointed out above, probably recurred to Virgil when he was describing the clash at Actium over which Apollo presided like the teachers over their charges in Book V, but with a purpose far less benign. Orderly as the exhibition is, it anticipates disorder of the most bloody sort.[30]

The setting of the games is stylized and, in general, deliberately unreal. At line 604 we return, with sudden violence, to the world of the present.

The spirit of emotion which appears somewhere in every book of the *Aeneid* comes now in the person of Juno's minion Iris. Here she is scarcely more than a personification of Juno's suffering, as is Allecto in Book VII, whom she resembles in detail. The unhappy Troades offer the perfect prey for her wiles (V, 618–19):

> ergo inter medias sese haud ignara nocendi
> conicit et faciemque deae vestemque reponit.

Therefore, knowing well how to work harm, she hurled herself into their midst, putting aside the features and dress of a goddess.

Ready to harm, as is Allecto, she thrusts herself among them. The verb *conicit* is important, and forms, with the elaboration which accompanies its various appearances, the main metaphorical strand of the episode. Her suggestion is to burn the ships, and, claiming that Cassandra has appeared to her in a dream offering burning torches and that Neptune also abets her suggestion by furnishing torches on his altars nearby, she seizes one (lines 642–43),

> sublataque procul dextra conixa coruscat
> et iacit . . .

and raising it aloft with her right hand, she brandishes it mightily and throws.

The women in their turn, led by an aged dame not unjustly named Pyrgo, recognize the goddess (lines 659–62):

> tum vero attonitae monstris actaeque furore
> conclamant rapiuntque focis penetralibus ignem;
> pars spoliant aras, frondem ac virgulta facesque
> coniciunt . . .

Then indeed, awestruck at the marvels and driven by madness, they cry out and snatch fire from the inner hearths. Some despoil the altars and hurl leaves, twigs, and brands.

The original metaphor of "hurling," inherent in *conicit* of line 619, here becomes a reality, for, just as Iris threw herself into the crowd of women and hurled the first brand, so now, driven by the contagion of her madness, they all join in tossing the torches upon the ships.

The parallels between this turn of events in Book V and the Allecto episode in VII are worthy of further mention. As her first weapon to arouse madness (and one of Virgil's two favorite instruments of destruction), Allecto had used a snake, which she threw at Amata (*conicit*: VII, 347). The manner in which she assaults Turnus, her second victim, is yet more akin to the way Iris acts against both women and ships (VII, 456–57):

> sic effata facem iuveni coniecit et atro
> lumine fumantis fixit sub pectore taedas.

89

Having spoken thus she [Allecto] hurled a torch at the youth and stuck in his breast brands smoking with dark light.

And of course the same rage seizes Turnus as seized Amata, a *furor* pictured by the poet as a fire which causes water to seethe in a cauldron and sends up billows of smoke toward heaven, much like the black ash which Aeneas now sees floating up in a cloud from the flaming ships. Indeed the madness of the women is transferred to the roaring fire which with loosened reins (*immissis habenis*), like a horse run wild, rages through the burning fleet.

The torch is to be taken both literally and symbolically at the same time. It is the actual instrument whereby the fire starts, and yet it also symbolizes the madness which Juno imparts through her servant. And when the women have finished their baleful deed and, losing their rage, revert to their former selves, the poet adds that Juno was shaken from their hearts (*excussaque pectore Iuno est*, line 679). Though the image may refer to the throwing off of a bit, it seems even more apposite, when taken in conjunction with the passage dealing with the madness of Turnus quoted above, to find in it a final reminder of the torch of Juno's madness, implanted in women and ships alike and then quenched.[31]

The ships now take on human characteristics for a moment, as the poet's metaphors lend another special touch to the imagery of fire. Like the flame of love which consumes Dido, imparting a silent wound which lives beneath her breast (*vivit sub pectore*: IV, 67), the fire lives deep in the sodden wood (*udo sub robore vivit*). Furthermore, the flame, in the form of a *pestis*, creeps into the whole body (*toto corpore*, line 683) of the ship as if it were a person, again like Dido, also the victim of a disease (I, 712), or Turnus, pierced by the maddening torch of Allecto, likewise personified as a *pestis* in VII, 505.

The destruction of the ships, however, forms little more than an interlude in the total design of Book V. The sentiments which the women utter — that they have too long borne the trials of seafaring and would prefer to settle down on land with a city of their own — are those which must have been foremost in the mind of Aeneas and certainly bulk large in the subsequent episodes with Acestes and Anchises. The women burn the ships because they symbolize, for them at least, the years of seemingly fruitless wandering to which all have been subjected. When, not long after, Anchises appears in a dream to Aeneas, he urges his son to accept the suggestion of Nautes to found a city and people it with those (lines 713–14), as Nautes puts it,

> ". . . amissis superant qui navibus et quos
> pertaesum magni incepti rerumque tuarum est . . ."

"who survive, though their ships were lost, and who dislike the grand design of your enterprise."

Nautes looks, in general, to the conclusion of another segment of Aeneas' history and specifically to those who wish to remain in a world which is neither Troy nor Rome. Anchises' speech, as we shall see below, looks to the future. He urges Aeneas (lines 729–31):

> ". . . lectos iuvenes, fortissima corda,
> defer in Italiam. gens dura atque aspera cultu
> debellanda tibi Latio est."

"Bring to Italy chosen youths, bravest of hearts. For you must fight in Latium a hard race whose ways are rough."

Those who make the final journey are to form a group few in number, but nevertheless possessing strength and courage for war. In other words, as the emphasis shifts from former events toward those which are to come, there is a consequent and parallel shift from sea to land, from the dangers of an ocean voyage to the risks of war. The action of the women in burning the ships marks the transition. The ships are no longer necessary and hence ought to be destroyed, as symbols of the past years of frustrated wandering. Aeneas, in setting sail on the final voyage to Cumae, sacrifices animals to Eryx and the storms. At this point the ships themselves are duly offered to Neptune. It was from the four altars of Neptune that the women snatched their destructive brands; in the end, four ships were lost, victims of the fire-plague. A token bestowed on the god of the sea for the whole lot, they form one in the series of such offerings. The last and greatest is soon to come.

There are two episodes, brief in outline but important for what follows, between the burning of the ships and the death of Palinurus: the nocturnal visitation of Anchises, which results in the decision to leave the colony behind in Sicily, and the conversation Venus holds with Neptune, who promises safe arrival in Latium.

Anchises, as noted, urges rest for the weary, but primarily he holds forth the prospect of war. Even before this comes about, however, Aeneas must visit the depths of Avernus and, seeking out his father, learn the subsequent history of his race and of the city his descendants will found (lines 735–37):

> "huc casta Sibylla
> nigrarum multo pecudum te sanguine ducet.
> tum genus omne tuum et quae dentur moenia disces."

"Hither the holy Sibyl will lead you, after you have offered much blood of black sheep. Then you will learn of your whole race and of the walls to be yours."

The conversation with Anchises thus fulfills an important function in turning the mind of Aeneas (and of the reader) from a fruitless past toward the view ahead with fixity of purpose. In particular, Anchises shows clearly that what follows between this point in Book V and the opening lines of Book VI is specifically the start of the voyage to the underworld. Aeneas is now to enter the world of the dead in order to gain a knowledge of future events which begin to take place only at the end of Book VIII.

But first he must make the journey. He offers a new sacrifice, three bullocks to Eryx and a lamb to the tempests (lines 774–76):

ipse caput tonsae foliis evinctus olivae,
stans procul in prora pateram tenet extaque salsos
proicit in fluctus ac vina liquentia fundit.

He himself, his head bound with leaves cut from an olive, stands far out on the prow and, holding a cup, throws the entrails into the salt sea and pours flowing wine.

By making a vow to sacrifice a white bull on the shore and to perform this same propitiatory act (lines 237–38) —

". . . extaque salsos
proiciam in fluctus et vina liquentia fundam."

"I shall throw entrails into the salt sea and shall pour flowing wine." —

Cloanthus had won his sea race. The course is only happily completed by a sacrifice to Neptune. And this, in so many words, is exactly what the god of the sea stipulates to Venus when he states (lines 813–15):

"tutus, quos optas, portus accedet Averni.
unus erit tantum amissum quem gurgite quaeres;
unum pro multis dabitur caput."

"According to your wish, he will gain in safety the harbor of Avernus. One alone will be lost whom you will seek in the ocean. One life will be offered for many."

Palinurus is this offering.[32] The promised sacrifice of Cloanthus is a slight and comic version of the highly serious ending of the book. Nevertheless, it does serve as further evidence of the unity between the earlier games and the remainder of the book. Father Neptune himself, *pater ipse* (the *genitor* of line 817), pushed Cloanthus' boat into port and promises now to do the same for Aeneas. It is perhaps no coincidence that the bevy of sea nymphs which accompanies him as he stills the waves for Aeneas' safe journey (lines 822–26) contains at least one member, *Panopea virgo*, from the chorus of Phorcus which joined him in aiding Cloanthus (lines 239–40). Once the idea of the sacrifice of Palinurus has been decided, the swelling sea must of necessity grow calm.[33]

At this happy turn of events — a divine manifestation that his course is correct — Aeneas is pleased and orders the yardarms to be stretched with sails (*intendi bracchia velis*, line 829). Before the boat race the men stood in anticipation, with arms straining at the oars (*intenta bracchia remis*, line 136). But the race for Palinurus and Aeneas, unlike that of Gyas and Menoetes, is now in deadly earnest as the coming of night sets the stage for the book's final adventure.

As throughout Book III, Palinurus, the pilot, leads forth the fleet at the journey's start (line 833–36): [34]

> princeps ante omnis densum Palinurus agebat
> agmen; ad hunc alii cursum contendere iussi.
> iamque fere mediam caeli Nox umida metam
> contigerat . . .

First, in front of all, Palinurus led out the close convoy. Toward him the rest were ordered to set their course. And now dewy Night had nearly touched the midway mark in the heavens.

The reader's thoughts immediately return to the games. Palinurus is the leader, *princeps*, as Gyas had been before the loss of Menoetes. The imagery further hints at the idea of a race, now in earnest, especially the phrase *cursum contendere*, an echo of line 291 where Aeneas made ready the prizes for those

> hic qui forte velint rapido contendere cursu.

who here might wish by chance to compete in the swift race.

In line 834 the words would be translated as "set their course," but there remains, in the phrase *ad hunc*, the idea that Palinurus not only sets the pace for the fleet but also, like the rocks of the boat race, is the goal toward which all must strive. Ironically, he is not only the cynosure of all the ships behind him but about to be the special victim of Somnus and Neptune.

It is Virgil's habit to make the description of natural events, which grace the epic story, fit the special happenings at hand.

The ambiguity of journey as race is also transferred to the image of Night, which now touches the midway mark in the sky (*mediam caeli metam*, line 835).[35] This is the only occasion where Virgil uses the image of the *meta*, borrowed from the race course, to describe the passing of night. But its appearance here could scarcely be more fitting, since Aeneas is indeed approaching the turning-point, the crucial juncture of the journey to Cumae. After Palinurus' death, the rocks of the Sirens, anticipated in the rocks which formed the *meta* of the boat race, must immediately be skirted and only then is all smooth sailing into the Sibyl's harbor.

Yet, as the previous lines have made clear, it is on Palinurus that all eyes are now focused, as he becomes the special target of Somnus. The particular aspect of the *mise en scène* described in lines 836–37 —

> . . . placida laxabant membra quiete
> sub remis fusi per dura sedilia nautae.

The sailors, stretched upon hard benches under their oars, relaxed their limbs in quiet sleep . . . —

is a favorite of Virgil's especially when something of a violent nature is in the offing.[36] On a previous occasion involving Palinurus, we were told of his liveliness while sleep overspread the tired limbs of the other men (*fessos sopor irrigat artus*: III, 511). It is the metaphor inherent in the word *irrigat* which is elaborated now in lines 854–56, as Sleep exercises control over his victim:

> ecce deus ramum Lethaeo rore madentem
> vique soporatum Stygia super utraque quassat
> tempora, cunctantique natantia lumina solvit.

Behold the god shakes over each temple a branch steeped in the dew of Lethe and dripping with the might of Stygian sleep. Though he struggles, Sleep loosens his swimming eyes.

Out of the many passages in the *Aeneid* that present a similar situation, lines 250–53 of Book II seem most appropriate to mention:

> Vertitur interea caelum et ruit Oceano nox
> involvens umbra magna terramque polumque
> Myrmidonumque dolos; fusi per moenia Teucri
> conticuere; sopor fessos complectitur artus.

Meanwhile the sky revolves and night rushes from the ocean, surrounding with deep shade the earth, the heavens, and the wiles of the Greeks. Throughout the fortress the Trojans lie stretched in sleep as slumber embraces their tired limbs.

Sleep is the central image of each passage. In one case it embraces, as the snakes had just "embraced" Laocoön and his sons; in the other it is poured, to fit the water imagery of the book. The snakes sought Laocoön specifically, but we also find the army of the Atridae seeking the well-known shore (*litora nota petens*), with a purpose as quietly destructive as that of Somnus while he is seeking Palinurus (*te, Palinure, petens*: line 840). The soldiers are met by their confreres, gliding (*lapsi*) out of the horse. Here it is Sleep who appears slipping down from the stars (*delapsus ab astris*). The enmity against Troy which is divided among the snakes, Atridae, and the wooden horse, is centered in Book V not on a city but on the lone figure of Palinurus.

Laocoön was doomed to fail before the fatal *monstrum* of the horse which, seemingly lifeless, teemed with a deadly burden. Palinurus confronts his *monstrum* (line 849) in the form of the calm but treacherous sea. The snakes of death creep over the sea and enfold in their fatal embrace, fittingly enough, the priest of Neptune, who screams in vain for help. In the same manner we find Palinurus calling often and in vain upon his comrades (*socios nequiquam saepe vocantem*). Sleep has already long held them in its grip as it held the Trojans and now holds Palinurus. The *monstrum* is always opposed by someone who sees through it, yet nevertheless in the end dies in its power. Palinurus successfully opposed the sea in Book III, gave way before it at the opening of Book V, and now becomes its victim.

Palinurus has no will of his own as the sleep of death descends with birdlike motion and then, paradoxically, assumes human shape, urging him to take his rest. *Pone caput,* lay down your head, Somnus commands, a phrase which ostensibly looks to sleep but in effect ironically reflects Neptune's decision that *unum caput,* one life, would be sacrificed for all the others. Likewise the duties (*munera,* line 846), which Somnus now claims he will enter upon for Palinurus, are not only his tasks as helmsman but also the rites of death, demanding as they do a gift or prize for Neptune. When Palinurus resists, the god shakes over him his magic bough "steeped in the dew of Lethe."

The sprinkling with dew, as it appears again in VI, 230, is usually part of the lustration of those present at a funeral or the laying-out of the corpse. Here the shaking of the bough seems to symbolize preparation for death, like the binding of the victim's temples in preparation for a sacrifice.[37] Certainly the associations of words such as *Lethaeo* and *Stygia* suggest the underworld as well as Neptune's realm. Palinurus is clearly a sacrifice to the past. He may also be a propitiatory offering leading to life in the future.

Then Sleep flings him into the sea, Palinurus tearing with him a part of the ship and dragging the helm as well. Sleep wings its way back into the heavens, and the fleet, putting trust in Neptune's words, glides safely onward (*promissisque patris Neptuni interrita,* line 863). In his headlong plunge Palinurus not only leaves the fleet without a guide; he renders the ship useless by pulling the helm along with him. So when Aeneas assumes Palinurus' role, it is over a ship which is incapable of control. In his death and in his disfigurement of the ship, Palinurus demonstrates that there is no need either for helmsman or for the helm by which he navigates.

Since the direction of destiny had thus far remained unsure, Aeneas had set his sights on the world of the navigator, on the heavens and its pattern of stars, on the external, in a word, which must serve when inner conviction is lacking. The sea is henceforth to mean nothing more in the life of Aeneas, and Palinurus symbolizes in his person the death of that part of Aeneas which pertains to voyaging, to wandering, and to a meaningless search for a goal which has, almost until this very moment, remained unstipulated. The pilot is one thoroughly versed in the reality of the sea, as opposed to those charmed by its superficial beauties. Aeneas is not fated, like Captain Ahab or Mark Twain's river pilot, to penetrate into the deeper meanings of the ocean and its symbols. Palinurus, who is, must die by virtue of the knowledge and loyalty he symbolizes.[38]

His death is, then, a figure for the death of a total concept or, better, of a sphere of existence. Fighting for what in his own terms he thought was right, he must yield to a higher fate and a different world.[39] The reason that the women burn the boats earlier in the book is that the ships denote change of place, search, and the restless sea rather than stable life on land. Not that the future holds peace, but only that Aeneas' purpose becomes fixed.

In his sorrow, Aeneas prophesies (line 871):

> "nudus in ignota, Palinure, iacebis harena."

"Palinurus, you will lie naked on an unknown shore."

This particular description of manner and place of death is one which recurred to Virgil at crucial and imaginative junctures. From the preceding books of the epic, two examples seem especially important. Aeneas, in his tale to Dido of the death of Priam, once monarch of all Asia, grieves that now (II, 557–58)

> . . . iacet ingens litore truncus,
> avulsumque umeris caput et sine nomine corpus.

He lies upon the shore, a huge trunk with head torn from shoulders, a corpse without a name.

The head torn from the shoulders is replaced, in the case of Palinurus, by the rending of the boat, *parte revulsa*, but in other respects the descriptions are remarkably parallel.[40] These strange lines are in each instance partially divorced from their context and hence stand out in the narrative. As the death of Priam seems to symbolize for Aeneas himself the end of any connection with Troy, so with Palinurus dies the need for seafaring. And in each case the aftermath is the necessity of search for a higher goal.[41]

The burning of Troy, the first in a series of ordeals by fire for Aeneas, soon yields place to the second trial, the attempt by Dido to seduce Aeneas from his fated way. She also dies, cursing her deserting lover (IV, 620):

> "sed cadat ante diem mediaque inhumatus harena."
> "But let him fall before his time, unburied on the open sand."

The imprecation seems to point not so much to the future Aeneas, founder of the Roman race, as to Dido herself, who does indeed die before her time (*ante diem*: IV, 697), and to Palinurus, naked on an unknown shore (*nudus in ignota harena*), to Aeneas, the seafarer of Book V, who must continue further on his journey. Both Dido and Palinurus are parts of him which he must put behind as he plunges into the underworld for the clarification of his destiny. The last trial is the burning of the ships, intimately and symbolically connected with the death of the pilot who guides them. The loss of Priam and Anchises releases Aeneas from the historical past, from Troy and from the years of wandering, while the deaths of Creusa and Dido fulfill the same purpose on an emotional level. With the chief exception of Iulus, who is the future, Aeneas is to a great extent released from any human attachment as he prepares to meet his father in the land of the dead.[42]

Though the figure of Palinurus looks to the past, as sacrifice to Neptune, it also seems, in part, to anticipate the future in the capacity of propitiatory offering to the underworld. To understand this, and several of the niceties of Virgilian expression, we must turn to the Homeric model for Palinurus, the ill-fated Elpenor who, like Palinurus, dies an untimely death and reappears shortly thereafter to his leader in the underworld.[43]

The events take place in *Odyssey* X and XI, where Odysseus leaves Circe and sets out to visit the land of the dead. Meanwhile, Elpenor has fallen off a roof, unnoticed by his companions. It is therefore in an unburied state that, like Palinurus, he comes before his leader begging for the rites of burial. Virgil has taken note of more than the superficial aspects of the description. Circe allows Odysseus to depart, but makes a condition that he visit the underworld and talk to Tiresias, the seer. But the hero, worried about the safety, or even the possibility of such a voyage, asks (*Od.* X, 501–2)

"O Circe, who will be the pilot for this journey? Never before has anyone reached Hades on a black ship."

To calm his not unnatural fears, Circe replies (lines 505–7):

"Let not lack of a pilot for your ship in any way trouble you, but set the mast, spread aloft the white sails, and sit down. The breath of Boreas will bear her along."

Homer explicitly states that, though the ship may need a helmsman to keep it steady, it is the breezes themselves which will direct its course. The ship cannot, indeed must not, reach the land of the dead under human guidance. It is this thought which Virgil has borrowed and then refined in his own imagination from the Homeric portrait of Elpenor. Palinurus is no longer needed.

It is possible that Elpenor may have been the pilot in an earlier version of the *Odyssey*. Like Palinurus for Aeneas, he certainly seems to stand for an aspect of Odysseus, perhaps his youth, which is now lost forever. And Aeneas himself is journeying to the dead in order to gain a renewal of life, but on a different level entirely. We have spoken before of his necessary inability to become deeply involved in the events through which he passes in the first five books of the epic. He is forced to exist only on the most superficial level; hence his failure to comprehend the death of Palinurus, the man whose life involves a complete understanding of the sea. Though fostered by the meeting with Anchises in Book VI, Aeneas' actual rebirth into depth of purpose does not occur until he has made his way, in Book VIII, to the source of the river of life which is the primitive but beautiful village of Evander. Only then, braced by the tension between Evander's pastoral life and the heroism of Hercules, the tension which should be his own, is he fully prepared to assume the destiny which is his mother's gift.

And all this begins now, in Book V, in the magical journey on which Aeneas is about to embark. *"Ferunt ipsa aequora classem"* — "The very waters bear the fleet along" — Somnus says to Palinurus as his first inducement to relinquish his position. But the phrase rings true, in spite of the pilot's disbelief and innate mistrust, for the poet has just stated a few lines earlier that the winds carry the fleet along (*ferunt sua flamina classem*, line 832). The breezes of the air and the very waves carry the ship along, a point the poet repeats at the end of the book in proof of the fulfillment of Neptune's promise (line 862):

> currit iter tutum non setius aequore classis . . .

And just as before, the fleet runs a safe course through the waves.

The mysterious journey of life into death has begun for Aeneas, as it had for Odysseus, and no human agency is necessary to see it through to completion. Not unlike Odysseus, whom Homer describes as in a state bordering on death during his homeward journey from the land of the Phaeacians, so now Aeneas, figuratively speaking, must die to arrive at the land of the dead as well as to be reborn into vitality of purpose from his experiences there. With this new atmosphere of divine control, Palinurus is out of place and, though he resists, there can be no opposition to his appointed doom.

With the helmsman lost, the fleet and Aeneas undergo a new trial (lines 864–66):

> iamque adeo scopulos Sirenum advecta subibat,
> difficilis quondam multorumque ossibus albos,
> (tum rauca adsiduo longe sale saxa sonabant).

And now in its course it thus approached the rocks of the Sirens, once perilous and white with the bones of many (then the crags sounded hoarsely afar from the unceasing surf).

Into these three lines Virgil compresses an episode which takes up a considerable portion of the twelfth book of the *Odyssey*.[44] Since the basic counterpart of *Aeneid* VI lies in the journey which Odysseus has just completed before he must sail past the islands of the Sirens, Virgil has reversed the order of events with startling symbolic effect. There is a deliberate and necessary contrast between the knowledge (and hence kind of temptation) which the Sirens purvey and that provided by the visit with the dead in *Odyssey* XI. The Sirens know all things and are parallel in this sense to the Muses. But they are Muses of the sea; their wisdom is barren and empty when compared to that which the goddesses of Helicon offer from their clear springs and Olympian heights.[45] Superficially they personify the hidden dangers of a calm sea, the *placidi pellacia ponti*, the lure of calm water, to borrow Lucretius' phrase, and it is against this that Palinurus is on his guard as he is drawn into their orbit. To Odysseus they do not so much present the attractions of false knowledge as seek to seduce him into everlasting involvement with the world of the sea. While he wanders, the hero, falling under the spell of Circe, Calypso, and an immense variety of other temptations, loses his existence in terms of Troy and Ithaca. He exists in a no-man's-land where his life remains unknown to those outside this sphere. The Sirens, and the heap of bones which surround them, typify the life and death of the individual within this strange context of nonexistence. Hence their real temptation consists in offering knowledge without experience — experience which can be gained only in the real world from which they offer perpetual escape.

On the other hand, the appearance of the ghosts in *Odyssey* XI bestows true knowledge, from the dead about the living, from the past yet of the future. Indeed, they tell Odysseus, as the false seduction of the Sirens could not, that he is going to escape from the world of nonexistence and wandering and regain the stabilized human sphere of war and peace, of Achilles' shield.

Why, then, should Virgil add that the boat of Aeneas begins to drift toward the rocks of the Sirens at this particular moment? Aeneas has been, up to a certain point, modeled on the wandering Odysseus. Since his destiny (and it is one much less certain to him than is Odysseus') lies in a future vague both as to time and place, the temptation has been, and could at this one instant remain, to wander. The result would be to absorb a life which is unreal while escaping from that which is fated, and to feed a romantic longing to dabble in all types of experience, leaving destiny to come as it may. Thus far Aeneas' knowledge has resulted only in negation. He has learned what he must not do. Life has been a superficial series of adventures encountered and tests passed, with purpose centered on fulfilling the thoughts and actions of the moment and with only a vague commitment to the future. There has been no deep spiritual understanding of the meaning of life and the involvements of existence.

Hence at the very end of this world the Sirens appear. They are the ultimate trial, and the ships drift inevitably toward them, for they seem to offer, in the form of the white bones, an example of those who, perhaps in spirit alone, were tempted to cling too closely to an existence false to reality. The temptation of the Sirens — the boat drifting without a helmsman on a calm sea — must come to Aeneas before attainment of the spiritual meanings of the future. When understanding is present, there can be no further temptation. This, then, is a crucial moment in Aeneas' journey of life. He now presses on to the knowledge, revealed by his father in the underworld, of a future which is not easy but hard and cruel, fraught with difficulties and yet clear and lending meaning and insight to a life which now turns away at last from the superficial and empty emotions of the moment toward the reality of Rome.

3ᐟHISTORY'S DREAM

As far as the unfolding of the story is concerned, the main purpose of Book VIII[1] is the introduction of Aeneas to Evander and through him to the Etruscans who will supplement his meager Trojan band in the coming war against the Latins. But Virgil has a more important object in view, for, by taking Aeneas actually up the Tiber to the humble abode of Evander, he is able to present a unified picture of the site of Rome as it had been in the past and now is, through the eyes of the exile from Arcadia, and as it will be until the golden age returns after the battle of Actium, a tale we learn from the shield which the god of fire creates for the hero as he prepares for the final conflict with Turnus.

There was nothing in Homer quite like this; no need ever for the hero to be introduced to the reality of a destiny which was not to be his, but which nevertheless takes its start from him. The *Aeneid* is oriented toward history in a way which the Greek epics are not, and in the journey up the Tiber Virgil adds something new and special to established tradition. He opens up the vistas of the future to his hero and tells him how he should order his life in relation to what lies ahead. Perhaps, too, he means to fashion a model in early Rome for Augustus to follow, since the occasion is at hand to renew Saturn's golden age. To no other section of the *Aeneid* does an allegorical interpretation seem quite as applicable as to book VIII.[2] Aeneas absorbs the tradition of heroism in Hercules, of pastoral in Evander and transmits them to Augustus, through the poetry of Virgil. Whether or not Augustus accepted the advice is not a matter for discussion here (we will turn to it briefly in the next chapter). In this respect Book VIII ends in a manner very akin to XII. The conflict is over, the victims either killed, as in the case of Turnus, or paraded before the Romans' admiring eyes. The proud have been conquered, but have the suppliants been spared? Whatever the answer, one possible model is put before Augustus in the simplicity of Evander's Rome, and as Virgil takes his readers from monument to monument, introducing Aeneas and the reader to the glory that was primitive Rome, he cannot avoid dropping an occasional hint that the contrast between the two Romes is not the result of historical progress alone but of ideological change as well.[3] It is for Augustus to return to the old.

But there is more to VIII than a grand tour with allegorical overtones. If such were not the case, it would be nothing more than a narrative of events loosely strung together — arrival at Rome, Hercules' encounter with Cacus, site of Rome, Venus and Vulcan, journey to Caere, description of the shield — and the fact that it has been taken as such is proved by the necessity which many critics feel to defend its unity. Some find the unifying factor in the idea of "wonder" which pervades the book, as Aeneas marvels before so much that is new to him and worthy of admiration.[4] Others search for linking motifs which run through the events, such as the fated demand for Aeneas that he meet the challenge of the future.[5] All such approaches contribute something to our understanding of the book, not because they take our attention from the several historical and topographical problems awaiting elucidation, but because they broaden our focus to embrace the artistry of Virgil in creating this picture of Aeneas and the time-scheme of Rome from Saturn to Augustus. With this same goal in view, I propose to examine here certain aspects of the poetic structure of *Aeneid* VIII and to show how they enhance its major theme, which is not so much the presentation of the glory that was and in some ways continues to be Rome, as it is, almost literally, the birth of Aeneas and his descendants into this glory.

The opening seventeen lines, like the initial verses of Book V, form a study in concentrated action. They convey with the strength of brevity a succinct resumé of all the energy let loose throughout the preceding book. Verb follows verb, adjective follows adjective, with a rapidity unusual in Virgil. Turnus himself is both the cause and center of all this violence. He it is who raises the signal of war, urges on his horse (a symbol for war throughout the *Aeneid*) [6] and brandishes arms. *Impulit arma*, he clashed his arms, the poet says, using a metaphor which takes us back to Juno herself dashing open the gates of war in VII, 621. Her action there has a very similar result as all Ausonia, mounted on horseback, burns for the fray and everyone cries for arms. The preparations now take specific point as Turnus, seeking to defend his homeland, asks Diomedes for aid and advice. The general effect, then, is to summarize in brief compass the events of the world at large, the world of energy which has suddenly grown up from the wild but pastoral land of Latium. Above all, it suggests with intensity the human concerns which are now the lot of Aeneas and which must ultimately force him into long hours of trial and conflict.

Talia per Latium, Virgil says. Aeneas the hero, son of Laomedon, sees all these things throughout Latium, not literally so much as in his mind's eye, forced now only to imagine. The transitional quality of these lines is impressive and important, as Aeneas contemplates like a distant spectator events from which he must momentarily separate himself. It is a crucial time and Virgil stresses it by repeating two lines, 20–21, from the very instant in IV (lines 285–86) where Aeneas decides a course of action in his planned departure from Dido. The result here, however, is a further spiritual withdrawal, described by one of

the most suggestive similes in the epic (lines 22–25), where
Aeneas' mind is

> sicut aquae tremulum labris ubi lumen aënis
> sole repercussum aut radiantis imagine lunae
> omnia pervolitat late loca, iamque sub auras
> erigitur summique ferit laquearia tecti.

like a light flickering from water in a brazen bowl, a light which, struck
off its surface by the sun or the reflection of the moon's glittering rays,
flies about everywhere. And now it rises into the air and strikes the high
fretted ceiling.

The starting point of the simile is a comparison of the thoughts
of Aeneas, turning this way and that, to the light reflected off
water, flitting back and forth within a closed space.[7] The light
itself, however, is caused by sun and moon, by outside forces of
nature, but the movement of the simile is conceived as occurring
within a room, shielded, as it were, from external existence, only
mirroring it. The outside world, if viewed in relation to the
book's opening lines, seems to be that of Italy, typified in the
character of Turnus. He symbolically began the war by striking
his steeds (*acris concussit equos*: line 3) and is the indirect cause
of Aeneas' thoughts, of the *lumen repercussum*, as it jumps here
and there, ranging far and wide, *late*, the same word used already
twice before in these very lines, in close conjunction with a play
on the word *Latium*, to describe the extent of the world through
which the future conflict will rage.

But the emphasis lies more on the enclosed space, on the room
itself, being, as it were, the mind of Aeneas upon which reality
plays but which is somehow apart from it. The sudden change
from the politics of upheaval to the quiet of night and the soli-
tude of Aeneas dreaming on the Tiber's bank, which follows
immediately, can be explained particularly well in terms of the
masterstroke of this simile. By showing us Aeneas' mind at work
Virgil prepares the way for exactly what is about to happen
—another retreat from reality on the part of the hero, this

time into a world of magic and idealism from which he learns much and which, as always in the *Aeneid*, equips him still further for the future. Like Alice's bold journey through the looking-glass and into the room on the other side, this brief vision of Aeneas' inner thoughts prepares the way for his momentary submission to the pastoral life beyond the bounds of actual human strife. It offers a deliberate withdrawal into a world nearer to perfection, which gains its very charm by contrast to the world of violence with which it is so aptly juxtaposed here. Book VIII develops the tension between the two worlds of nature and power and suggests their ultimate reconciliation in Aeneas and in the shield he carries. Now at the start Aeneas is, in a figurative sense, to be reborn, certainly initiated into the genesis of Rome, as the appearance of the Tiber prepares him for the journey up the river to meet Evander. It is the simile which makes possible the transition from one world to the other with such facility.[8]

Before turning to the speech of the Tiber, it is worth looking for a moment at the line which precedes his opening words (line 35):

> tum sic adfari et curas his demere dictis . . .

Then he spoke thus to him and took away his cares with these words . . .

This line is repeated twice elsewhere in the *Aeneid*, and the contexts are instructive. The first is at II, 775, where the vision of Creusa, suddenly come to Aeneas from the ruins of Troy, parallels the appearance of Tiber (*visa*, II, 773, is changed to *visus*, VIII, 33). But the careful reference back does more than equate ghost and dream. It returns the mind of the reader to the downfall of Troy, just as Creusa's speech looks to the arrival at the Tiber (II, 781–82):

> "et terram Hesperiam venies, ubi Lydius arva
> inter opima virum leni fluit agmine Thybris."

"And you will come to the land of Hesperia where Lydian Tiber with gentle course flows through fields rich in husbandmen."

Hence it is not strange that the first allusion of Tiber, in his speech of comfort to Aeneas, is back to Troy, as he addresses him (VIII, 36–37):

> "O sate gente deum, Troianam ex hostibus urbem
> qui revehis nobis aeternaque Pergama servas . . ."

"O thou sprung from the race of the gods, who bring back to us the city of Troy from its enemies and preserve Pergamum for eternity . . ."

One context anticipates, one reviews the other. One foresees Aeneas' safe arrival in Italy and renewal of Troy, the other announces that this has at last occurred, that Troy has been transplanted to the more productive soil of Italy.

The other previous use of VIII, 35, is at III, 153. Once more a vision (*visi*: III, 150), here of the Penates to Aeneas as he dreams, and once more there is a close similarity of context. This extends even to atmosphere, for III, 147 —

> nox erat et terris animalia somnus habebat.

It was night and on earth sleep held all creatures —

clearly anticipates VIII, 26–27:

> nox erat et terras animalia fessa per omnis
> alituum pecudumque genus sopor altus habebat . . .

It was night and throughout all the lands deep sleep held the tired races of birds and beasts.

Moreover, the actual setting in III of moonlight journeying in through windows recalls the simile we have just examined which precedes the vision of the Tiber. But it is the similarity the event bears to Creusa's exhortation which demands further inquiry. For the Penates, too, prophesy that Italy is the fated land. No other place of settlement will serve. And when Tiber addresses Aeneas in the lines which begin *O sate gente deum*, he merely refers closely to III, 148–150, where Aeneas dreams of his own household gods,

"effigies sacrae divum Phrygiique Penates,
quos mecum a Troia mediisque ex ignibus urbis
extuleram . . ."

"the holy images of the gods and Phrygian Penates, which I had taken
with me from Troy and from the midst of the city's flames."

It is only by carrying both himself and his familiar gods that he
can truly be said to bring back the city of Troy from its enemies.
And it is these very Penates, saved from the city's downfall, that
Tiber promises are at last assured of a lasting home (*certi*: VIII,
39). Thus Virgil enhances the change from Troy to Rome by
clear and provocative allusion to crucial events in the past that
led gradually to new-found stability. The collapse of Troy (Book
II) gave place to Troy in transition, searching for a new home
(Book III), and this, in turn, yields now to the fixity of purpose
which only the very certitude of Tiber makes a reality in Book
VIII.

The first thing Tiber mentions in his speech is that at last
Aeneas has obtained the promised land. He soon adds an interesting detail (lines 40–41):

"neu belli terrere minis; tumor omnis et irae
concessere deum."

"And do not be terrified by the threats of war. All the swollen wrath of
the gods has subsided."

Proof will be given, he adds, of the truth of his remarks by the
appearance of a portent in the form of a pig with thirty offspring,
symbolizing first that Aeneas has discovered the spot at which the
initial settlement will be founded. And thirty years later, his son
Ascanius will lead hence the expedition to establish Alba Longa.

There seems at first no definite relationship between the sub-
sidence of the wrath of the gods, the sow, and Aeneas' journey
to Pallanteum. The initial clue Virgil gives that there is a connection between such diverse things is also supplied by Tiber
himself, who promises to make smooth the journey up-river
(lines 57–61):

"ipse ego te ripis et recto flumine ducam,
adversum remis superes subvectus ut amnem.
surge age, nate dea, primisque cadentibus astris
Iunoni fer rite preces, iramque minasque
supplicibus supera votis."

"I myself will lead you along the banks, straight up the stream, so that as you go you may overcome the adverse current with your oars. Come now and awake, goddess-born, and when the stars begin to set, offer due prayers to Juno. Overcome her wrath and threats with prayerful vows."

Here we learn that the anger and menace of the gods, mentioned before in general terms, are specifically those of Juno, and that, in order to progress any further on his journey, Aeneas must offer her due sacrifice as an additional appeasement of her wrath. The repetition of the verb *supero* also makes it clear that there is a deliberate connection between the anger of Juno and the river itself. The very rise and fall of the river's flood symbolizes the state of her feeling. The river can never be conquered, Tiber appears to say, until the hatred of Juno subsides. And this is exactly what happens after the required sacrifice of the pig has been performed (lines 84–87):

quam pius Aeneas tibi enim, tibi, maxima Iuno,
mactat sacra ferens et cum grege sistit ad aram.
Thybris ea fluvium, quam longa est, nocte tumentem
leniit, et tacita refluens . . . substitit unda . . .

Good Aeneas sacrifices the pig to you, even to you, mighty Juno, as he performs the holy rites, and places her with her young upon the altar. During that whole night long, the Tiber calmed his swollen flood and, staying his current, stood still with silent wave.

Aeneas may overcome the adverse current with the help of the river god and his own oars (each useless without the other). But Juno, too, must be won by prayers and suppliant vows. The swelling of the river (*tumentem fluvium*) is parallel to the *tumor* of Juno's anger, mentioned in line 40, and as the flood is calmed so her emotion subsides to the point where Aeneas can pray successfully against it.[9] The sacrifice of the pig, then, could be said to have a twofold meaning. It looks to propitiation of Juno. But such a sacrifice in turn is directly connected with Aeneas' preparation for a new adventure symbolized by the prophetic qualities of the pig, namely a further advance in his own knowledge of the future of Rome. And hence the river, too, possesses both a negative and a positive aspect. Tiber seems to separate for a moment from his swell. He must control the violence of his flow (he can do so only after Aeneas has performed the requisite sacrifice) as if it typified an emotion contrary to his own feelings. Here *leniit* is the key word, used regularly by Virgil of attempts to appease the destructive aspects of unreason.[10] But, when the flood subsides, the Tiber becomes, as the god himself had prophesied, the direct link between Aeneas on the river bank and the site of Rome; between the potentiality, at which the omen of the pig hints, and the actuality of Aeneas' realization of the past and future of Rome. The Tiber's calm, therefore, prepares the way not only for Aeneas' journey but for a change inherent even in the opening lines of the book, from irrational force to love and birth, from Juno in fact to Venus, who plays a key role in the remainder of the book.

In order to look more closely at some of the niceties of Virgil's imagery in these early lines of Book VIII it is worth examining briefly the inseparable relationship between Aeneas' continuing progress and the necessity of sacrifice to calm the wrath of Juno and some of the forms this connection takes. The interrelationship is posed, as so much else basic to the epic's structure, in the speech of Juno near the opening of Book I as she pledges force to destroy the Trojans, asking (lines 48–49):

> ". . . et quisquam numen Iunonis adorat
> praeterea aut supplex aris imponet honorem?"

"And does anyone still worship the divinity of Juno or place on her altar a suppliant's offering?"

No special victim is proposed here in appeasement. Juno wishes, by marshaling the power of Aeolus and his winds to her destructive intent, to do away with the Trojans effectively, completely, and with one blow. As Neptune finally stills the swollen waters after the storm (*tumida aequora placat*: I, 142), we think of the Tiber's flow and realize that the goddess' wrath nearly claimed all its sacrificial victims at once. During the remainder of the epic Juno never again in any single episode endangers the lives of all, as she does in the opening sea-storm. But she does demand that Aeneas become the very suppliant for whom she searches in Book I and that the various stages of his fated journey be marked by sacrifice to her.

The important prophecy of Helenus in III, 374–462, is the first crucial revelation to Aeneas of this necessity. After detailing as much of future events as the fates and Saturnian Juno allow — among them the appearance of the sow at the Tiber's mouth — Helenus makes one important warning (lines 435–39):

> "unum illud tibi, nate dea, proque omnibus unum
> praedicam et repetens iterumque iterumque monebo,
> Iunonis magnae primum prece numen adora,
> Iunoni cane vota libens dominamque potentem
> supplicibus supera donis . . ."

"This one thing, more important than all else, I will foretell to you, goddess-born, and repeat my words again and again as a warning: worship first in prayer the divinity of mighty Juno, willingly chant vows to her and overcome the powerful mistress with suppliant gifts."

One need not stress how close this is to Tiber's demand that Aeneas overcome Juno's wrath with suppliant offerings (*supplicibus supera votis*). The initial occasion of the needed sacrifice follows shortly in Book III when the Trojans find themselves first touching Italian soil. The second, much more crucial to the epic story, happens at the end of Book V in the death of Palinurus. At this time Aeneas is still completely unaware of the idea of sacrifice and its link with Juno.

The relationship of this event with the opening of Book VIII — and it is a very close one indeed — might best be realized by asking what Virgil means when he describes the night during

which the Tiber calmed his swollen flood as one which was long
(*quam longa est*). Why the emphasis on the length of the night?
Once more there seems to be a connection with Juno, in this
case the length of time it takes to calm the wrath of the goddess
when the propitiatory offering, here in the guise of the pig, has
taken place. The swelling wrath is transferred to the Tiber,
which in turn typifies, in its slowly decreasing flood, the gradual
faltering of opposition to fate on the part of Juno and to at least
this particular segment of the destiny of Aeneas. The *longa nox*
of VIII defines a specific night and its strange supernatural occurrences. Yet because of the word *longa*, its implications reach
beyond the mere temporal progress of a few hours to the broader
pattern of the *Aeneid*. Virgil himself gives the key in V, 783–84,
where, in reference to her heavy anger and insatiable heart,
Venus describes Juno to Neptune as one

> "quam nec longa dies pietas nec mitigat ulla,
> nec Iovis imperio fatisque infracta quiescit."

"whom neither length of time nor any piety soothes, nor does she grow
quiet, broken by the power of Jupiter and by fate." [11]

And this *longa dies* of Book V, the long passage of time in which
Aeneas had demonstrated his *pietas* to human and divine alike,
is paralleled by the *longa dies* which, according to Anchises (VI,
745), must elapse before every taint is washed from a soul, leaving it newly purified and prepared for return to the world above.
Yet the occasion in V is a good deal more specific. Venus well
knows that this is another crucial moment in her son's career as
he prepares to set sail on the journey to the underworld. He has
performed all the requisite sacrifices, it would seem. Yet Venus
quite rightly suspects that it is exactly at such an instant that the
madness of Juno might flair up — a madness which she cannot
explain but which, given scope in the storm of Book I, almost
caused the death of her son and the collapse of future Rome. It
is not so much that he is about to make another sea journey as

that this particular journey is both transitional and final. Neptune fully realizes the situation (lines 801–2):

> "saepe furores
> compressi et rabiem tantam caelique marisque."

"Often have I suppressed the rage and monstrous madness of sky and sea."

And in his words he scarcely hides a reference to the madness of Juno. Yet he knows that a higher sacrifice is demanded to propitiate Juno (and partially himself), now that this particular phase of the *longa dies* is drawing to a close. This sacrifice is to be that of the pilot Palinurus (lines 814–15):

> "unus erit tantum amissum quem gurgite quaeres;
> unum pro multis dabitur caput."

"One alone will be lost whom you will seek in the ocean. One life will be offered for many." [12]

The result of Neptune's decision is by now not unexpected. Having soothed the heart of the goddess, he yokes his horses and glides lightly over the waters (lines 820–21):

> subsidunt undae tumidumque sub axe tonanti
> sternitur aequor aquis, fugiunt vasto aethere nimbi.

The waves sink down, and the flood, swollen under the thundering axle, subsides with its billows. The storm-clouds flee from the wide heavens.

The strange thing here is that there has never been any previous mention of a storm. In fact, we have heard exactly the opposite description of the condition of the sea shortly before as the Trojans prepare to set sail with a favorable wind astern. Once more we find Virgil working not with literal, so much as with symbolic, description. As in VIII and, at least partially, as in Book I, the poet's mind associates the idea of swollen water's being calmed with due sacrifice to the gods, usually to Juno, but on this occasion to Neptune as well. Hence, to return in summary to Book VIII, the *longa nox* remains both general and particular as it is rounded out in the gradual calming of the Tiber's swell. The sacrifice of expiation has occurred, and it is only a matter of one long night — the long night of propitiation and change — before the wrath of Juno gives way, at least momentarily, before the destined course of Rome, specified in V by the irrevocable voyage to the underworld, in VIII by the magical journey up the Tiber.

A third instance of preparatory offering is to be found in the opening lines of Book VI, centering around the dialogue of Aeneas with the Sibyl and the plucking of the golden bough. Since this episode carries a close and intense parallelism with the initial events of VIII, it is worthy of detailed examination. The Sibyl fulfills at the beginning of Book VI much the same role as Tiber in VIII. When the priestess catches sight of the Trojans looking at the sculptures of Daedalus, she chides them for wasting time and demands the sacrifice of seven bullocks and seven ewes (lines 38–39). How preliminary this is and how minor (it is like Aeneas' sincere but naive offering to the tempests in V when compared to the death of Palinurus) we can see from the first reaction of the Sibyl when possessed by the god. We are told that she grew to more than human size and that her heart swelled with wrath (*et rabie fera corda tument*). The reason for this is not simply that she has become the medium of Apollo, ready to prophesy. She is angry because the gods are angry and hence her violent cry to Aeneas (lines 51–53):

> "cessas in vota precesque,
> Tros" ait "Aenea? cessas? neque enim ante dehiscent
> attonitae magna ora domus."

"Are you slow to vow and pray, Trojan Aeneas?" she says. "Are you slow? for not till then will the great portals of the shrine be shocked into gaping open."

Interpreting her words quite literally, Aeneas replies by vowing a temple to Apollo and a shrine to the Sibyl herself. This seems to appease her sufficiently to allow her to prophesy the coming struggle in Latium. It also gives Aeneas the opportunity to make his real request — to be granted admission to the underworld to visit his father. After noting the difficulties in such a journey, she prescribes two necessities before the actual entrance to Hades can be gained, namely the burial of Misenus and the plucking of the golden bough. These two events, which look to the end of past wandering and to Aeneas' preparation for an interlude during which he is, like the bough, alive and yet dead, are splendidly intertwined and played off against each other in the lines which follow, as Aeneas fulfills the Sibyl's requests.

In spite of the disparity in the number of lines, a close parallel exists between this complex of events and that which precedes Aeneas' voyage up the Tiber in Book VIII. In each case there is a prophecy of the trials that future events hold in store and how best these can be surmounted. In each case we find Aeneas vowing suitable honors in recompense, not only as a thank offering to the prophet, but because both Sibyl and Tiber symbolize in language and gesture the anger of the gods which must be appeased. Above all there is a remarkable similarity in the preparatory *signa* of bough and pig which are put before Aeneas, the one to pluck, the other to sacrifice, before he can begin the respective journeys for which Sibyl and Tiber help him prepare. An examination of the relationship between these symbols will set in relief some of Virgil's varying goals in Books VI and VIII.

We first hear of the pig during Helenus' prophecy in III, 389–93:

> "cum tibi sollicito secreti ad fluminis undam
> litoreis ingens inventa sub ilicibus sus
> triginta capitum fetus enixa iacebit,
> alba, solo recubans, albi circum ubera nati,
> is locus urbis erit, requies ea certa laborum."

"When at a time of trial you will find a sow lying near the waters of a secluded stream, a mother sow which has just given birth to a litter of thirty beneath the oaks by the shore (white, as she lies on the ground, white her litter around her), this will be the location of the city, here a sure respite from your troubles." [13]

The last four lines are in essence repeated by Tiber at VIII, 42–46, and to these he adds a further explanation:

"ex quo ter denis urbem redeuntibus annis
Ascanius clari condet cognominis Albam."

"And, after the passage of thirty years from this time, Ascanius will found the city of Alba, of shining name."

We would be inclined to leave the whole episode as an example of allegory — the whiteness of the pig giving its name to Alba Longa, the thirty piglets merely signifying the passage of thirty years before the city's foundation — were not the details of the sow's actual appearance so vivid (lines 81–83):

ecce autem subitum atque oculis mirabile monstrum,
candida per silvam cum fetu concolor albo
procubuit viridique in litore conspicitur sus.

But behold, a portent sudden and amazing to see. Through the wood a white sow is seen, lying on the green shore, of one color with her white brood.

In tracing through the poet's imagery a connection between the bough and the pig, we are first reminded that the bough is part of an *ilex* tree (VI, 209) and the pig is to be discovered lying under an *ilex*. *Per silvam* seems an unnecessary elaboration unless we have recourse to the setting of the bough within a vast wood (*silvam immensam*: VI, 186; *nemore in tanto*: VI, 188). And there is a common image of greenness, too, for the pig lies on the verdant shore, while the doves of Venus first alight on the greensward (*viridi solo*: VI, 192) as they lead Aeneas toward the bough which, in its comparison to mistletoe, is said to grow green with fresh leaves (*fronde virere nova*: VI, 206). The pig's brood is unmistakably white (*fetu albo*). The bough itself is found on a tree which, as the Sibyl describes it, possesses *auricomos fetus*, golden-haired fruit, and, as one detail in its likeness to a piece of mistletoe, the bough is said to be discovered growing on an alien tree with fruit of bright yellow (*croceo fetu*). Finally, and here the similarity is most direct because Virgil in his entire work uses each word only once, the pig is *concolor*, in harmony with its setting and surrounded by its snowy brood. The bough, on the other hand, sends off a *discolor aura*, a contrasting gleam, because of the many tensions posed by the opposition of light and dark it betokens, tensions which its locale only superficially manifests.[14]

Herein lies symbolically one of the differences between the two journeys that Aeneas is about to undertake. The first looks to the strange combination of life in death to which Aeneas, living amid those who are no longer alive, must submit. The other manifests only the brightness of birth into a new life. It is not without reason that Virgil uses the same verb, *procumbo*, to describe the sow lying on the shore that he had previously utilized to depict Aeneas asleep by the river awaiting the dream of the Tiber (line 30) and that he would again, crucially enough, in the first scene on the shield of the wolf suckling the twins (line 631), a point to be examined later in some detail. For this is a book where birth is an essential concept and to which all the patterns of imagery, whatever their own interrelationships, are subordinated. Both the pig and the bough are passports into a new sphere of existence, each quite distinct, and they manifest their differences accordingly. But it is important not to dismiss their similarities. Each is a necessary offering to Juno. The bough, we learn, is deemed sacred to nether Juno (*Iunoni infernae dictus sacer*: VI, 138), to be plucked and displayed as token. Yet in fact the sacrificing of the sow serves the same poetic purpose as the initial use of the bough in Book VI. For when Aeneas and the Sibyl first approach Charon to enter his boat and gain passage across the Styx, he not unnaturally offers objection. At this the Sibyl displays the bough, whereupon the wrath of his swollen heart subsides (*tumida ex ira tum corda residunt*: VI, 407). This, of course, is almost exactly what happens to the *tumor* of Juno, as manifested in the Tiber's swollen flood. It means that all opposition to change has collapsed. In Book VIII it proclaims the real commencement of a new life. Aeneas lies down on the shore not only to dream about but soon to become part of the begetting of Rome, first through his own thoughts and then as allegorized in the sow and her offspring.[15]

The parallels between Books VI and VIII do not end here. But before returning to them it is best to look first at Virgil's description of this supernatural journey up the Tiber to the future site of Rome. It is accomplished with all brevity. After the sacrifice of the pig, the reaction of the river, as we have seen, is immediate (VIII, 86–90):

> Thybris ea fluvium, quam longa est, nocte tumentem
> leniit, et tacita refluens ita substitit unda,
> mitis ut in morem stagni placidaeque paludis
> sterneret aequor aquis, remo ut luctamen abesset.
> ergo iter inceptum celerant . . .

During that whole night long, Tiber calmed his swollen flood and, staying his current, stood still with silent wave in such a way that he might calm his watery flood into a smooth pool or silent mere and the rowing might be effortless. Therefore they hasten on the journey they had begun.

At this manifestation of divine favor, the men happily begin the journey which takes them, after a day and a night, to the humble settlement of Evander (line 101):

> ocius advertunt proras urbique propinquant.

Quickly they turn the prows shoreward and approach the city.

Here, as so often elsewhere, Virgil has taken the clue for some details from a scene in the *Odyssey* particularly rich in symbolic associations — in this case the landing of Odysseus on the coast of Phaeacia. Driven through the anger of Posidon at the mercy of wind and wave for two full days after his departure from Calypso, the hero, son of Laertes, finally swims within striking distance of land and, after being once more drawn back into the ocean's swell, finds himself in a haven where it is only the adverse current of a river flowing into the sea which forces him from shore. Odysseus prays (V, 450)

"But take pity, lord. I call myself your suppliant."

This thought, at least, is echoed in Aeneas' entreaty to Tiber as one who had already shown pity for his misfortunes (*miserantem incommoda nostra*: line 74). Even more startling is the similarity in the instances of the effect of prayer (V, 451–53):

Thus he spoke, and forthwith the god stayed his current and held back the wave, creating a calm for Odysseus and bringing him safely to the river's mouth.

The river magically makes its waters smooth so that Odysseus can safely land in a manner not unlike the way the Tiber calms its floods so Aeneas can go his journey.

The focal symbol for Odysseus, coming as he does from the violent ocean, lorded over by Posidon, into this haven of peace and security, seems to be the strange olive growing near the stream, which sports from a single stock one half that is wild, the other tame. The wild olive typifies, perhaps, the sphere of high adventure now left behind as Odysseus gradually begins to return to the civilization and stability of homeland and family, which the tame olive seems to denote. Phaeacia is in one sense the subtlest of temptations offered to the hero in his wanderings, because in it he is forced to view a family life of rare beauty. And hence as he draws nearer the point where he must be absorbed back into his own it causes him both to remember and to forget. The stream beside which Odysseus now walks, led by Nausicaa, takes him toward a city too perfect, from which he must ultimately escape in a state which borders on death.

Virgil pondered this pattern closely. But Aeneas' journey up the river to Evander's city is the approach to a paradigm which, in his case, must be embraced and not soon denied. He will change it by adding the fire of heroism which it had but rarely seen. He too must again withdraw into the world of a grim and hard reality, but not before he has absorbed and made his own the virtues which Evander's world has to give him. The special qualities — in fact the peculiarly Virgilian intonation of this whole passage, as Aeneas journeys up the Tiber to be initiated into the new life which the palpability of Rome's past and future presents — can best be discerned by continuing a juxtaposition with Book VI. Virgil himself is, as usual, the finest commentator on his own text.

It should be recalled that the stage for entrance into this new world was set during the initial lines of Book VII, and the mood that that moment created, though constantly violated within VII itself, should be re-established here. Dawn had come (VII, 27–36)

> cum venti posuere omnisque repente resedit
> flatus, et in lento luctantur marmore tonsae.
> atque hic Aeneas ingentem ex aequore lucum
> prospicit. hunc inter fluvio Tiberinus amoeno
> verticibus rapidis et multa flavus harena
> in mare prorumpit. variae circumque supraque
> adsuetae ripis volucres et fluminis alveo
> aethera mulcebant cantu lucoque volabant.
> flectere iter sociis terraeque advertere proras
> imperat et laetus fluvio succedit opaco.

when the winds fell and suddenly every gust subsided, and the oars labored in a slow calm. And then Aeneas spies from the water a large grove. In the middle of this the Tiber broke with his beautiful stream toward the sea in swift rapids, yellow and filled with sand. Around and above, different birds, accustomed to the banks and the river's channel, soothed the air with song and flew about the grove. Aeneas bids his comrades change their course and turn the prows to land. And happily he enters the shady stream.

The sudden calm of the winds and the quiet of the ocean's surface, like the magical harbor in which Aeneas finds shelter after the storm of Book I, help generate an atmosphere in which life itself forms the basic image. The grove, as often in Virgil, is a symbol of initiation and acceptance of the new. The mention of the river's channel (fluminis alveus) likewise adds an important element to the developing picture. Like so many others elaborated in Books VII and VIII, the image was first stated in III not only in the oracle's general command to the Trojans to search for their mother of time past (*antiquam matrem*) but also, more particularly, in the description of the very moment they first touch the Italian shore (III, 509–11):

> sternimur optatae gremio telluris ad undam
> sortiti remos passimque in litore sicco
> corpora curamus: fessos sopor inrigat artus.

Having drawn lots for the oars, we lie down at the wave's edge on the bosom of the kindly earth and all along the dry shore seek rest for ourselves. Sleep refreshes our tired limbs.

Ilioneus adopts the image in his attempt to persuade Latinus that (VII, 233)

> "nec Troiam Ausonios gremio excepisse pigebit."

"Ausonia will not regret that she received Troy to her bosom."

Juno, too, turns the image to her own ends as, shortly after, she cries (302–4)

> "quid Syrtes aut Scylla mihi, quid vasta Charybdis
> profuit? optato conduntur Thybridis alveo
> securi pelagi atque mei."

"How have the Syrtes helped me, how Scylla or gaping Charybdis? They have gained their desire and are hidden in the channel of the Tiber, careless of the ocean and of me."

In thus speaking she adopts (with only a slight change from *alveus* to its cognate *alvus*) a figure we have seen twice applied in scornful fashion to the wooden horse. The first is in II, 401, when Virgil describes how terror drove some of the Greeks back into the horse's belly:

> scandunt rursus equum et nota conduntur in alvo.

They climb again into the horse and are buried in the well-known belly.

Much later, in IX, 150–52, Turnus, comparing himself and his men attacking the beleaguered enemy to the Greeks before Troy, says that this time the Trojans need anticipate no subtle guile:

> "tenebras et inertia furta
> Palladii caesis summae custodibus arcis
> ne timeant, nec equi caeca condemur in alvo . . ."

"Let them not fear darkness or the craven theft of the Palladium, with the guardians of the high citadel slain. We will not lurk in a horse's dark womb."

Here all the potentiality of the occasion is present in the verb *condo* which, as Juno uses it, could look either to hidden deception or to the establishment of something violent, ready to burgeon and burst forth. The sinister ambiguity is also constantly applied to the wooden horse. To Juno's mind, at least, the settlement of the Trojans at Tiber mouth is both creative and evil.[16]

Though the image is in fact realized in the mother sow and her litter, it is anticipated here at the opening of VII. For Aeneas and his men the beautiful stream, with its dark grove re-echoing with the songs of birds, can only mean a form of reception which denotes the possibility of new life, salvation, and happiness. The effect is redoubled by contrasting these lines with the description of the entrance to the underworld through which Aeneas and the Sibyl must pass, a contrast Virgil could well have had in mind. Among the physical details of the rugged cave, which is the access to the world below, the poet places particular stress not only on the dark woods which protect it — the Tiber too is *opacus* as the darkness of the grove overshadows the water — but on the lack of the very birds whose presence lends so much to Aeneas' realization that he has at last reached the Tiber. It is a cave (VI, 239–42)

> quam super haud ullae poterant impune volantes
> tendere iter pennis: talis sese halitus atris
> faucibus effundens supera ad convexa ferebat:
> [unde locum Grai dixerunt nomine Aornon.]

over which no birds at all could safely make their winged way, such was the breath which came pouring out from the dark jaws toward the vault of heaven. For this reason the Greeks named it Avernus, the Bird-less Place.

Once more, as in the case of the bough and the pig, the juxtaposition stresses the difference between the two worlds, typified by Books VI and VIII, of death and birth.

Subsequent events reinforce this contrast, for the next stage of the underground journey leads to the bank of the Styx, to the dialogue with Palinurus who waits patiently at its edge (as does Aeneas, dreaming by the side of the Tiber) and then to the encounter with Charon, the great ferryman himself. We examined above similarities between Tiber and the Sibyl, both preparing Aeneas for the developments ahead to which he must submit. Charon, too, seems to demand, as does the Tiber in flood, the propitiation of divine wrath, but once the bough has been displayed, he can willingly accept Aeneas for his journey across the Styx. So also Tiber himself will reduce his current — will himself become the ferryman — that Aeneas may travel easily to Pallanteum. Though the Styx is specifically associated with the land of the dead and though, in VIII, the Tiber fits splendidly into the book's basic pattern of imagery, stemming from the idea of birth, nevertheless in both instances Virgil stresses the fact that a river must be navigated before Aeneas can be allowed to continue on his way, a river presided over by a god who counsels and then approves.[17] As Aeneas first looks out incredulously over the Styx, the Sibyl explains (VI, 323)

"Cocyti stagna alta vides Stygiamque paludem . . ."

"You are looking at the deep pools of Cocytus and the Stygian marsh."

And it is into just such a state that Tiber calms his waters (VIII, 88–89)

mitis ut in morem stagni placidaeque paludis
sterneret aequor aquis, remo ut luctamen abesset.

that he might calm his watery flood into a smooth pool or quiet mere, that the rowing be effortless.

Further parallels are numerous.

There is one interesting variation, however. Only after the conversation with Palinurus does Aeneas of necessity meet Charon. Virgil introduces his opening questions with the following lines (VI, 384–89):

> Ergo iter inceptum peragunt fluvioque propinquant.
> navita quos iam inde ut Stygia prospexit ab unda
> per tacitum nemus ire pedemque advertere ripae,
> sic prior adgreditur dictis atque increpat ultro:
> "quisquis es, armatus qui nostra ad flumina tendis,
> fare age quid venias iam istinc, et comprime gressum."

Therefore they continue on the way and approach the stream. But when from the waters of the Styx the boatman saw them making their way through the quiet grove and nearing the shore, thus first he speaks and of his own accord reproves: "Whoever you are, who in armor approach our stream, come, tell me even from there why you have come, and check your steps."

The phrase *ergo iter inceptum* Virgil uses again in VIII, 90, as the Trojans begin the journey up the Tiber, but the last part of the sentence, *fluvioque propinquant*, is changed to *urbique propinquant* in VIII, 101, as the Trojans near Evander's city. In Book VIII it is before the city, not the river, that Aeneas must undergo a real challenge in the person of Pallas who, like Charon and Cerberus in the underworld, faithfully guards the entrance to his pastoral paradise and opposes anyone who dares enter without due cause. Here again quotation in full is necessary. The people are celebrating a day sacred to Hercules and performing the stipulated rites (lines 107–113):

> ut celsas videre rates atque inter opacum
> adlabi nemus et tacitis incumbere remis,
> terrentur visu subito cunctique relictis
> consurgunt mensis. audax quos rumpere Pallas
> sacra vetat raptoque volat telo obvius ipse,
> et procul e tumulo: "iuvenes, quae causa subegit
> ignotas temptare vias? quo tenditis?" inquit.

When they see tall ships gliding among the dark woods and men leaning over silent oars, all are terrified by the sudden sight and rise up, leaving

the banquet. Bold Pallas forbids them to break off the sacred rites and,
seizing a spear, rushes himself to meet them, and from a mound afar
cries: "Youths, what reason has driven you to try unknown paths?
Whither do you make your way?"

Aeneas and the Sibyl, too, make their way through the silent
woods. Likewise the Trojan ships are said to glide through the
grove as the men ply silent oars. Aeneas, alive in the world of
the dead, is just as much a prodigy to Charon as the ships of the
Trojans are to Pallas because of their unreal approach, full of
armed men and moving smoothly along even though the way lies
up-river. And when Virgil tells how the people are terrified by
the sudden sight (*terrentur visu subito*), he continues the idea
of Aeneas as a sudden portent since the wording is only a variation upon a similar phrase he applies to Aeneas gazing in
amazement at the tribes of people yet unborn who nevertheless
will constitute Rome's future (*horrescit visu subito*: VI, 710).
The Sibyl answers the challenge of Charon by displaying the
bough, and Aeneas puts the barking Cerberus to sleep with a
drugged cake. Only after this can they leave the bank of the
Styx and commence the next part of Aeneas' journey to his
father. To Pallas Aeneas offers an olive branch, symbol of peace
and friendship. This is the key gesture after which (VIII, 125)

> progressi subeunt luco fluviumque relinquunt.

They walk forward into the grove, leaving the river behind.

With this ends the first segment of both Books VI and VIII.[18]

In the opening lines of VIII the dominant figure is the river
Tiber which remains in part what the contrast with the Styx
suggests, the river of life on which lies Rome, its past and present, and above all its future, imagined in the mind of Aeneas,
but as yet intangible. It is in a sense like the river Lethe from
which Dante must drink before entering the earthly paradise at
the end of *Purgatorio*, a river which contrasts as clearly with the
streams of blood flowing through the *Inferno* as Tiber does with

Styx.[19] It is not impossible that Virgil, too, is thinking back to that section in Book VI where Anchises begins to enumerate his offspring, the future glories of Italy. Symbolically, at least, the Tiber is like Virgil's Lethe of VI; it brings to fruition the process which the draught of Lethe starts, the force of rebirth and regeneration. Anchises looks to the future only in the joy of his thoughts. Aeneas must be reborn, as it were, though he does not need to drink of Lethe's waters because, in escaping still living from the world of the dead, he manifests a revitalization of himself and his purpose which now becomes both clear and constructive. But purpose is not yet enough. Rome itself and its heritage must be discovered. Now, at last, on the banks of the Tiber and in the city itself, it is into a peculiarly rich and evocative ambiance embodying tradition and perspective, which Evander puts before him, that Aeneas is initiated as he leaves the river's edge and, entering the sacred grove, joins in the worship of Hercules.

The next segment of Book VIII begins in the grove and ends after Aeneas has entered the house of Evander at nightfall (line 369). As often in Virgil, a poetically strategic and portentous introduction leads to a developmental passage in which action is stressed more than symbolic interplay. In Book II the dialogue between Laocoön and horse, Sinon and snake, anticipates the actual destruction of Troy which Virgil vivifies by depicting Aeneas walking through the center of the city and finally reaching the palace of Priam. Book VI finds him first conversing with the Sibyl, who knows the future and realizes the tension between personal motivation and historical validity inherent in Aeneas' life, and then afterward plucking the golden bough. Only thus is he prepared to walk through the underworld to the division of the roads and the discovery of his destiny. Book VIII makes this destiny come alive, but, as in the way through VI before the confrontation with Anchises, it is a destiny first realized by reviewing the past. In VI it takes the very personal form of the conversations with Palinurus, Dido, and Deiphobus, who summarize the major events thus far in Aeneas' life, events which roused emotions he must now put behind him as his orientation changes toward realization of future grandeur. Book VIII likewise presents a survey of the past but is retrospection with a much broader, less personal sweep. Above all, if the river journey looked symbolically to the reception of Aeneas into the actuality of present and future Rome, the subsequent narrative expands the idea of birth through the majesty and perspective of genealogies, all of which, though the roads lead from various angles, center directly upon the simple hut whither Evander directs his guest.

The strands of descent and evolution are impressive. First Aeneas traces the common ancestry he has with Evander; then Evander remembers happily his meeting with Anchises. So the bonds joined by heritage are further linked by personal acquaintance. Arcadia and Troy converge by their separate ways on Rome. But of equal importance with those who have come from the outside is the specially rich heritage which the site of future Rome itself offers. Evander will have more to say on this later. At the moment he introduces Aeneas into the ritual of Hercules. In particular he details the reason why Hercules was so revered at Rome. In this, too, the outside world merges with life at Rome because the victorious Hercules on his way back to Greece with the cattle of Geryon stopped at the site of Rome and slew the monster Cacus who had long tyrannized the defenseless people. This is a paradigm which Aeneas must ponder, Evander realizes. Evander's own city may be a reflection of his Arcadian homeland, but even here, into what must nearly approach the pastoral ideal, there crept evil and violence in the person of Cacus, violence which must be suppressed by the hero Hercules. If it was Hercules' mission to rid Rome of this dread creature, how must Aeneas now feel as he ponders, from the momentary serenity proffered by the refuge of Rome, the madness of war which awaits his return to the reality of the outside world?

The description of the Cacus adventure is not without its specifically Virgilian motifs, for, like the winds in Book I and the horse in II, Cacus is a further transformation into epic story of the figure of *impius Furor*.[20] Actually, the ambiguities in the description of *Furor* at I, 294–96, tempt one to see in Cacus a very close approximation indeed:

> Furor impius intus
> saeva sedens super arma et centum vinctus aënis
> post tergum nodis fremet horridus ore cruento.

Unholy wrath, sitting within upon fierce arms, bound with a hundred brazen knots behind his back, will roar dreadfully from his bloody mouth.

Like *Furor*, Cacus seems neither wholly man nor wholly beast. At one point he is called half-man (*semihominis*, VIII, 194) and at another half-beast (*semifer*, line 267), and he partakes of the nature of each both in figure and behavior. He is called a monster, (*monstrum*), and in this parallels both the wooden horse and the giant Polyphemus of Book III, since all three are distinguished for their gigantic size.[21] Whatever resemblance to a human being he possesses seems derived from his father Vulcan whose violence is not tempered here toward greatness, as it is later in the book, but aggravated into beastlike force. This surpassing ugliness is enhanced by Cacus' treatment of those around him (lines 195–97):

> . . . semperque recenti
> caede tepebat humus, foribusque adfixa superbis
> ora virum tristi pendebant pallida tabo.

Always the ground was warm with fresh blood, and faces of men, attached to the defiant doorposts, hung pale in gruesome decay.

Virgil seems to have the same fearsome qualities in mind, still further enhanced if this is possible, in his later description of the tyrant Mezentius who now threatens Rome's peace (lines 483–88):

> quid memorem infandas caedes, quid facta tyranni
> effera? di capiti ipsius generique reservent!
> mortua quin etiam iungebat corpora vivis
> componens manibusque manus atque oribus ora,
> tormenti genus, et sanie taboque fluentis
> complexu in misero longa sic morte necabat.

Why should I tell of his dread murders, the brutal crimes of the tyrant? May the gods save this for himself and his offspring! Nay, he even joined dead bodies to living, fixing hand to hand and face to face (loathsome torment) and as they flowed with blood and gore, he killed them thus by lingering death in a dread embrace.

The Cacus episode offers Aeneas the chance to follow the example of Hercules and rid Italy of unwanted despots. Mezentius will be one of the first to follow in Cacus' footsteps and will suffer accordingly.

But the actual clash between the fire-breathing monster Cacus, whose name proves him to be evil, and Hercules, the heroic demigod, must have appealed to Virgil as well, for here too his description fits into the familiar pattern of events which surrounds any figure partaking of the characteristics of *impius Furor*. This power of darkness lives in a cavern so deep as to be untouched by the rays of the sun. It is into this cave that he drags the cattle stolen from Hercules and it is here that he retreats when pursued by their enraged owner. He imprisons himself, not unlike the winds suppressed in their cave or the Greeks enclosed within the belly of the deep and hollow horse (*sese inclusit*, line 225). But Hercules brooks no delay and spies his means of entry in a huge rock which towers over the cave (lines 236–40):

> hanc, ut prona iugo laevum incumbebat ad amnem,
> dexter in adversum nitens concussit et imis
> avulsam solvit radicibus, inde repente
> impulit; impulsu quo maximus intonat aether,
> dissultant ripae refluitque exterritus amnis.

This, as it sloped from the ridge toward the river on the left, he struck, straining against it from the right, and tore it up, wrenched free from its deep roots. Then suddenly he hurled it. At this thrust, the mighty heaven thunders, the banks leap apart, the river in fear stays its current.

Like the opening lines of the book, with which these have much in common, the description gains power through the sequence of verbs. One is especially important, *impulit*, for it is a word which appears more than once in connection with manifestations of *Furor*. It is utilized in the description of Aeolus' release of the winds. Laocoön throws his spear (*impulerat*) futilely at the wooden horse, not fated yet to be revealed. Juno pushes in the gates of the temple of Janus (*impulit*) and a land formerly at peace becomes the helpless prey of strife.

Here in Book VIII the result is not madness escaped but rather only revealed (lines 241–42):

> at specus et Caci detecta apparuit ingens
> regia, et umbrosae penitus patuere cavernae . . .

But the cave, huge home of Cacus, stands clear and uncovered, and the shadowy caverns deep within lie exposed.

Virgil seems here to be varying one of the more striking details in his description of the loading of the wooden horse (II, 18–20):

> huc delecta virum sortiti corpora furtim
> includunt caeco lateri penitusque cavernas
> ingentis uterumque armato milite complent.

Here into its dark side they covertly lock a select body of men chosen by lot, and fill up its huge caverns and belly deep inside with armed soldiery.

There follows immediately a comparison of Hercules' gesture opening the cave of Cacus to a sudden gaping of the earth which reveals the underworld to view. The spirits of the dead do not rush to escape but only tremble, forced to look upon the light.[22] It is a picture of evil, of a realm hated by the gods, and as such adds still further to the impression of Cacus as a figure both

wicked (κακός in Greek) and a power of darkness (*caecus*).[23]
The subsequent battle within the cave finds Hercules victorious,
defender of light and life, as reasoned heroism triumphs over
irrational, almost subhuman madness. But even Hercules is for
the moment said to blaze with madness (*furiis*, line 219; *furens*,
line 228). His is not to absorb and reapply the pastoral humility
of Evander. To combine the qualities of both Evander and
Hercules is reserved first for Aeneas.

Thus the river bears Aeneas into a realm where, even in the
past, all has not been serene, and the grove, crucial always in
Virgil at moments of change, offers initiation into a pattern
which demands heroism in the face of violent opposition but yet
postulates that this very heroism adapt itself closely to the spirit
of Evander's pastoral realm.[24] The legend of Hercules and the
cattle thief is much more than simply another incident in the
past to help inform Aeneas' conception of his new role. It is a
spiritual inheritance with implications which extend, in terms
which border even on allegory, far beyond Evander and even
Aeneas himself. Before Virgil clarifies this still further, two more
narrative sections intervene which comprise the actual walk from
the river to the center of the city. The first is Evander's description of the ancestry of those who lived on the site of Rome, beginning with the indigenous *fauni* and nymphs and extending
to his own arrival.[25] The tale is rich in implications since there
was once on this very site of Rome a golden age of Saturn which
lasted (lines 326–27)

> deterior donec paulatim ac decolor aetas
> et belli rabies et amor successit habendi.

until little by little a lesser, decadent age took control, and the madness
of war and greed.

But the main narrative purpose of these lines is to interweave
the newer traditions of Arcady and Troy, already united in the
meeting of Aeneas and Evander, with the past of Rome itself.
Spiritual inheritance and genealogical background receive visible

expression in the monuments themselves by which Aeneas and his host now pass, as they make their way through the Carmental gate to what will one day be the Roman Forum but which now resounds with the bellow of cattle (lines 359–61):

> Talibus inter se dictis ad tecta subibant
> pauperis Euandri, passimque armenta videbant
> Romanoque foro et lautis mugire Carinis.

Speaking thus among themselves, they approach the house of poor Evander. They see cattle all about, lowing in the Roman Forum and the brilliant Carinae.

The word *subibant* has special importance. It had appeared, we recall, at an earlier equally critical stage of ritual progress as Aeneas and Pallas first leave the river bank and enter the grove (*subeunt luco*). Evander makes clear the significance of the recurrence (lines 362–63):

> ut ventum ad sedes, "haec," inquit, "limina victor
> Alcides subiit, haec illum regia cepit . . ."

When they came to his dwelling, he says, "This threshold victorious Hercules entered, this house received him . . ."

By imitating this same gesture Aeneas acknowledges acceptance of Rome, and in particular of Hercules' part in its foundation. The moral lesson Evander soon supplies: "Fashion yourself worthy to be a god by despising riches," he tells Aeneas. Once again it is hard to avoid intimations of allegory, all the more because not many lines have passed since Virgil drew a deliberate contrast between the Capitolium in Evander's day and in his own (line 348):

> aurea nunc, olim silvestribus horrida dumis.

golden now, once bristling with woods and thickets.

But this is secondary to the fact that Aeneas' action marks the end of a further progression in the growth of the hero as he makes his way up the river to become part of the Roman tradition. By separating the book into two almost equal parts, the

135

falling of night forms here a particularly expressive division between realization of this past, drawn from so many diverse traditions and united on the site of Rome, and announcement of the future, of events near at hand in which Aeneas prepares to participate and of those still more remote which he can only contemplate on the shield with wonder and dismay.

There is continuity, and yet change as well — continuity, because the embrace of night, enfolding Aeneas and earth with its dusky wings, leads directly to the love scene of Venus and Vulcan; but change, too, since the opening lines of the new episode have little to do with Evander's Rome (lines 370–72):

> At Venus haud animo nequiquam exterrita mater
> Laurentumque minis et duro mota tumultu
> Volcanum adloquitur . . .

But Venus, with her mother's heart not unjustly fearful at the threats of the Laurentes and the harsh tumult set in motion, speaks to Vulcan.

Line 371, in itself almost a brief summary of the initial verses of the book,[26] takes the reader's mind back to the original impulse behind Aeneas' journey and associates Venus not with her son's momentary escape into Evander's pastoral idealism but with the violence of the impending conflict and the necessity for action. In reviewing the past and noting the possibility of danger, we plunge into the future.

Venus is still fulfilling her role as mother of Aeneas — the word *mater* is conspicuous in line 370 — but we are now introduced to a strange new Venus as well, protecting her offspring and shielding him from danger as always, yet now relishing action and fostering the creation of arms for conflict in a way hitherto not her wont. The theme of appeal for arms is as central in her subsequent speech to Vulcan as her position as Aeneas' mother (*arma rogavi*, line 376; *arma rogo*, line 383). The tone of the scene is established even before Venus poses her request (lines 372–73):

> . . . thalamoque haec coniugis aureo
> incipit et dictis divinum aspirat amorem . . .

And in the golden nuptial chamber of her husband she begins thus and breathes divine love into her words.

Once more birth is the outstanding theme, triumphant not only in the mother's relationship to her son but in the subsequent love-scene which introduces, through a symbolic tableau, the basic imagistic pattern to be elaborated in the remainder of the book. We have seen in the case of Cacus what ruinous consequences the misdirected use of fire's violence can have. Here, by the calming influence of rational and creative love, Vulcan, the spirit of fire, is wooed and won. So it is that the weapons which result from the union, even if forged with war's fires, are tempered with much for which Venus is the symbol. And though love yields to necessity in the search for arms, it is the combination of Venus and Vulcan which is all-important.

As he wrote this little episode, Virgil clearly had in mind Lucretius' description of the embrace of Venus and Mars incorporated in the proem to the first book of *De Rerum Natura*. When Virgil speaks of Venus breathing divine love into her words, in the passage quoted above, he is merely centering on a specific occasion the power which Venus exerts over all nature in Lucretius' vivid account (I, 19),

> omnibus incutiens blandum per pectora amorem . . .

as she instills winning love into the hearts of all.

It would seem, too, as if Lucretius' initial address to Venus as mother of the sons of Aeneas (*Aeneadum genetrix*) — the goddess invoked as protector of all her descendants in a resounding opening note — gives way in Virgil before the more specialized needs of the moment as Venus begs arms for her son, *genetrix nato* (line 383). But even here, as Virgil follows his regular procedure, the symbolic introduction of a longer episode, often restricted in scope, yields in due course to the wide sweep of events which it intimates. Venus' specific and present interest in her son takes grander shape in the vision of the whole race of her future offspring (*genus omne futurae stirpis*), depicted on the shield which is forged as a result of her appeal to Vulcan.

Her request is successful only after a time (lines 387–92):

> Dixerat et niveis hinc atque hinc diva lacertis
> cunctantem amplexu molli fovet. ille repente
> accepit solitam flammam, notusque medullas
> intravit calor et labefacta per ossa cucurrit,
> non secus atque olim tonitru cum rupta corusco
> ignea rima micans percurrit lumine nimbos.

The goddess spoke and, as he hesitated, she caresses him with snowy arms and cherishes him in soft embrace. Of a sudden he received the familiar flame. The accustomed fire passed into his marrow and ran through his collapsing limbs, even as a fiery streak, bursting from the thunder's roar, runs through the clouds with gleaming flash.

Herein lies one of the more conspicuous paradoxes of the remainder of the book. To have the god of fire warmed by Venus not only reverses the Lucretian situation but changes our whole conception of Venus as she has thus far appeared in the *Aeneid*. The imagery adds a further ambiguity because it is with snowy arms that she cherishes him, and this conjures up the shining beauty of the goddess of love and with it all the associations of water, pastoral, and motherhood usually linked with her. Yet it is her beauty which imparts the flame to Vulcan. Again Virgil turned to Lucretius for his model. Indeed Mars in the opening lines of *De Rerum Natura*, overcome by the everlasting wound of love (*aeterno devictus vulnere amoris*; I, 34), had once suffered much the same reaction to her charms as Vulcan here, enchained by undying love (*aeterno devinctus amore*: line 394). Again, however, it is the difference in the results which Virgil stresses by drawing attention to the inherent parallels. This is no Venus lulling the powers of war to sleep so that nature can create at peace. Rather, as her lover soon realizes, this is a new Venus, bent on conflict, the flame of whose love becomes metaphorically the very fire which helps forge the shield, through the intermediary of Vulcan himself. The embrace which follows, full of further Lucretian reminiscences and with the same ambiguity between fire and water now translated into even stronger sexual terms, completes the little episode.

The transition from bedchamber to Cyclopes' cavern where Venus' request is carried into fact is another superb example of Virgilian art. It is effected through a comparison of Vulcan to a housewife at her loom deep into the night (lines 407–15):

> Inde ubi prima quies medio iam noctis abactae
> curriculo expulerat somnum, cum femina primum,
> cui tolerare colo vitam tenuique Minerva
> impositum, cinerem et sopitos suscitat ignis
> noctem addens operi, famulasque ad lumina longo
> exercet penso, castum ut servare cubile
> coniugis et possit parvos educere natos:
> haud secus ignipotens nec tempore segnior illo
> mollibus e stratis opera ad fabrilia surgit.

At that time when, in the mid-course of the now waning night, first repose had banished sleep; when a woman, whose trial it is to make life endurable with her distaff and Minerva's humble work, rouses the flame that slumbered in the ashes, adding nighttime to her work, and sets her servants to some long task by lamplight so that she might keep chaste her husband's bed and bring up her small children: in such a way and no less eagerly the god of fire then rose from his soft couch to go about his forge's work.

Time of night is the initial source of the comparison. But there is no mistaking a further relationship between the servants of the woman in the simile and Vulcan's Cyclopes, busy at their forges even during the night's small hours. This relationship is fostered by her first gesture, to rouse up the coals of the sleeping fire.[27] In putting his slaves to the forging of Aeneas' armor, Vulcan, god of fire at his work of creation, is essentially doing the same thing, on a far grander scale, as the good wife weaving her web. At this point, however, the simile might have run its course, but a further reason is added for the woman's nocturnal occupation, namely, that she can live her life chastely and bring up her small children. The mention of her husband's bed refers the reader back forthwith to Vulcan's golden nuptial chamber (*thalamo coniugis aureo*) and to the frequent mention of either Venus or Vulcan as *coniunx* in the subsequent episode. In this case the small children mentioned in the simile become Venus' descendants — Aeneas and his children — whom it is now Vulcan's purpose not only to defend but, almost literally, to create as he molds for Aeneas on the shield the fame and fortune of his heirs (*famam et fata nepotum*).

For further clarification of this episode one might add here a word on the importance of the goddess Minerva. As the opening of *Georgic* I intimates, she is regularly to be considered a pastoral divinity, discoverer of the olive and guardian of the household — the goddess, in fact, of chaste marriage. But she is likewise the patroness of arts and crafts to whom, for example, the wooden horse was dedicated. Both roles are inherent in the simile which, through the affection of Venus for Vulcan as well as for her son, accomplishes for the moment one more reconciliation between the pastoral and heroic worlds, of fire and water, power and love, as it helps translate the reader out of Evander's realm into the underground cavern of the Cyclopes.

One of the chief excellences of *Aeneid* VIII arises from the interplay of contrasting episodes juxtaposed, a rhetorical technique which goes hand in hand with the symbolic tensions forming the book's artistic core. The description of Venus' love as a thunderbolt coursing through darkening clouds may serve as a warning gesture that her wish to make war and Vulcan's desire to put his fire at her disposal will soon merge in a scene in which Virgil makes use of some of his favorite images. Nevertheless, in spite of any such glance at the future, their meeting ends on a note of quiet (lines 404–6):

> . . . ea verba locutus
> optatos dedit amplexus placidumque petivit
> coniugis infusus gremio per membra soporem.

Having spoken these words, he proffered the desired embrace and throughout his limbs sought quiet sleep, relaxing upon the bosom of his spouse.

This situation in part recalls Aeneas asleep on the Tiber's bank (*seramque dedit per membra quietem* — he gave over his limbs at last to sleep — Virgil writes in line 30, as Aeneas prepares for his reception into Evander's peaceable kingdom). The episode of Vulcan in the cave of the Cyclopes breaks the momentary calm in a manner not unlike that of Cacus shattering the spell of early Rome's pastoral serenity. There is much in common here. The association with Vulcan and his fire and the characteristic Virgilian image of the cave as a place of suppressed power combine to create a kindred setting.

But there is also one large difference, which stems from the mood already set through the Venus-Vulcan meeting. The potentiality for which Vulcan stands can be of two kinds, it would seem. The figure of Cacus, we recall, was half beast (*semifer*). His human (or, better, divine) forebear was Vulcan, the rest of him pure beast. His life as a consequence was bent on force that was purely destructive. When, on the other hand, the attributes of Vulcan are combined with those of Venus, the result is the channeling of energy into a pattern of order wherein fire is forced to mold the armor of a heroism strong but reasoned.

The locale changes again at line 454, as the night which began with the meeting of Venus and Vulcan leads to dawn rising over the city of Rome (lines 455–56):

> Euandrum ex humili tecto lux suscitat alma
> et matutini volucrum sub culmine cantus.

The kindly light and the birds of morning, singing beneath his rooftop, roused Evander from his humble abode.

If in the previous brief scenes the book's new orientation toward the future had been sketched in tentative symbolic outline, now it becomes clear in actual fact as Evander, through conversation with Aeneas, describes the dangers to come, but notes that all Etruria is ready to join forces in the coming conflict. In the beginning of Evander's speech Aeneas is simply the great leader of the Trojans (*maxime Teucrorum ductor*); only at the end can he be addressed as bravest leader of Trojan and Italian alike (*o Teucrum atque Italum fortissime ductor*). Italy is now to be his as well as Troy. But this grand portrayal of the strength to be put at Aeneas' disposal narrows suddenly, as Evander concludes his talk, to the figure of Pallas, his only child, whom the aged king promises to send also with Aeneas (lines 515–17):

> "Pallanta adiungam; sub te tolerare magistro
> militiam et grave Martis opus, tua cernere facta
> adsuescat, primis et te miretur ab annis."

"I shall add Pallas. Under your tutelage let him grow accustomed to endure warfare and the heavy work of Mars and to behold your deeds. Let him admire you from his earliest years."

It is this last announcement more than anything else which causes Aeneas' reaction to Evander's speech (lines 520–22):

> Vix ea fatus erat, defixique ora tenebant
> Aeneas Anchisiades et fidus Achates,
> multaque dura suo tristi cum corde putabant . . .

Scarcely had he spoken thus, and Aeneas, son of Anchises, and faithful Achates held their eyes downcast and pondered many a hardship in their sad hearts.

The words of the last line parallel closely those of VI, 185, where Aeneas also ponders many things in his sorrowing heart (*haec ipse suo tristi cum corde volutat*). There his sad thoughts spring not only from grief for the mysterious death of Misenus, but also from doubt concerning the future, particularly heightened as he contemplates the huge forest in front of him which somewhere within it contains the emblematic golden bough. He utters a brief prayer for help and then (VI, 190–93)

> vix ea fatus erat geminae cum forte columbae
> ipsa sub ora viri caelo venere volantes,

et viridi sedere solo. tum maximus heros
maternas agnoscit avis . . .

scarcely had he spoken thus when twin doves by chance came flying
from heaven before his very eyes and settled on the green grass. Then
the mighty hero recognized the birds of his mother.

The situation in Book VIII is in some respects quite similar, the
most important change being that in VIII the words *vix ea fatus
erat* are applied to Evander, not Aeneas. In each case Aeneas,
experiencing a period of doubt, has reached so crucial a moment
that nothing less than a sign from heaven is needed to show him
how he must make his decision and willingly enter upon the
next step in his progress. The sign always fits the moment. In
Book VI the doves of Venus appear and lead her son to the
bough. At the beginning of VIII, where Aeneas is again hesitant
about what the future holds in store, Tiber prophesies the sow
and her litter which Aeneas does indeed come upon when he
awakes, and which serve as omens for the first half of the book.
Here too it is Venus, now in her newly espoused role of warrior-
goddess, who sends the prodigy (lines 524–29):

namque improviso vibratus ab aethere fulgor
cum sonitu venit et ruere omnia visa repente,
Tyrrhenusque tubae mugire per aethera clangor.
suspiciunt, iterum atque iterum fragor increpat ingens.
arma inter nubem caeli in regione serena
per sudum rutilare vident et pulsa tonare.

For suddenly from the sky a thunderbolt came flashing with a roar, and
all things seemed for a moment to collapse. The peal of Tyrrhenian
trumpets screamed across the sky. They look up. Again and yet again
the tremendous noise resounded. Among the clouds in a clear part of
the heavens they see arms grow red through the bright sky and crash
in thunder.

Aeneas recognizes the sound as he had recognized the doves in
VI. Yet he begs not to be asked to explain the meaning of the
token and acknowledges only that he is called to a war that is
near at hand which will cause much slaughter and end in the

punishment of Turnus. Virgil's imagery supplies a hint of the realization which Aeneas suppresses.[28] *Fragor*, a thunder-clap, forms part of a sign twice elsewhere in Virgil. It is with a sudden crash, *subito fragore* (II, 692), that the comet which convinces Anchises of the necessity of departure from Troy first makes its presence known. But there is another instance even closer to that of *Aeneid* VIII. It is a *terque fragor*, a triple peal of thunder, as seems also to be the case here, which announces to Eurydice the necessity of irrevocable return to the underworld (*Georgic* IV, 493). A similar doom is proposed in *Aeneid* VIII, denoting something much more specific than the general slaughter which is all Aeneas divulges of his perception. It appears at least probable that Venus is foretelling to her son the death of Pallas in the conflict ahead. Evander, we recall, had just entrusted him to Aeneas before the sign occurred, and certainly the subsequent lines suggest that the father himself felt something ominous in the proceedings. It is doubtful if Virgil would have observed here that this was their last parting (*digressu supremo*, line 583) did he not wish to clarify the omen to his reader as well as to Evander and Aeneas.

Aeneas and Evander offer up ewes duly chosen as oblation in preparation for departure and in honor of Hercules and the pact upon which they had agreed. But, as we find so often in the *Aeneid*, the rudimentary bestial sacrifice which is demanded at moments of change, and which serves as a sop to the superficies of religion, is accompanied by a much higher and more important human offering claimed as token of progress and the realization that Aeneas has entered a new sphere which must be propitiated. Aeneas on occasion is completely unaware of this double challenge, as at the end of Book V. However, the strange interplay of sacrificial offering, burial of Misenus, and rending of the bough, with which VI opens, must necessarily leave its imprint on the mind of Aeneas. Here, it would seem, the hero fully realizes the demands of fate. The sacrifice of Pallas appears in this sense appropriate to Virgil's purpose and to the pattern characteristic of such offerings. Being the child of Evander, Pallas looks to the future of the race, to the continuity of the pastoral humility so important to Evander, and necessary for the development of Rome. As such, he admirably suits the emphasis which the second half of Book VIII places not only on birth but on the future of Aeneas and Rome. This adds further to the implications of the loss which Aeneas must suffer, because the child of the golden age, which the descendants of Aeneas will re-establish on the banks of the Tiber and toward which the story of the shield triumphantly leads, will die even before the first stage has been achieved. So also will Aeneas.

The omen notwithstanding, Aeneas and his followers depart and make for Caere where Venus appears, bringing her son the armor of Vulcan. With the description of the splendid shield, the book draws to a powerful conclusion. Here, as always, setting is a crucial factor while the poet builds up the meaning of a scene. As at the book's opening we find ourselves suddenly in a grove by which flows a stream, in this case all enclosed by mountains and dark forest (lines 597–99):

> est ingens gelidum lucus prope Caeritis amnem,
> religione patrum late sacer; undique colles
> inclusere cavi et nigra nemus abiete cingunt.

There is a large grove beside Caere's cool stream, held sacred by tradition and revered far and wide. On all sides hollow hills enclose it and a forest of dark fir girds it about.

One has a feeling, from the subsequent lines, that before he retreats down into this holy grove Aeneas first surmounts a high ridge, whence he can see the whole of the Etruscan forces spread out in front of him. Fittingly enough for such a pastoral book, the grove and the day are sacred to Silvanus, god of fields and flocks. It is a place of seclusion, refuge, and momentary escape, qualities which the description of Venus' arrival further stresses. She only begins to speak (lines 609–610)

natumque in valle reducta
ut procul egelido secretum flumine vidit . . .

when from afar she saw her son in a hidden valley, protected from in-
trusion by the cool stream.

Such a magical moment partakes of the ritual quality present
at certain decisive occasions in the *Aeneid*. One might mention,
for example, the conclusion of the epic's opening scene when,
after the storm, Aeneas makes his way into a strange harbor
girded by mountains and overshadowed by thick woods wherein
ships need no anchor. At only one other instant, however, are
the parallels in imagery so close as to convince the reader that
the contexts can offer valuable commentary the one on the other.
I refer to the introduction to the last part of Book VI, as Aeneas
and the Sibyl turn away from gazing at Tartarus and from contemplating the punishment of the damned, to plant the bough
for the last time and enter the fields of the blessed in search of
Anchises. Musaeus directs them. First they must climb a hill
from which all the shining lands below are visible to them. Then,
after they leave the heights for the valley, they come upon Anchises surveying, from deep within a hidden vale (*penitus con-
valle virenti*, line 679), the souls of those fated to return to the
world above. They recognize each other, and Aeneas attempts
in vain to embrace his father, in strong contrast to the ease with
which he clasps his mother as she delivers the arms in Book VIII.

Thus far the parallels are purely factual, but Virgil proceeds
in VI to add a further, more incisive, description of the location
of the souls (lines 703–5):

Interea videt Aeneas in valle reducta
seclusum nemus et virgulta sonantia silvae,
Lethaeumque domos placidas qui praenatat amnem.

Meanwhile Aeneas sees in a hidden valley a secluded grove and the
rustling bushes of a wood, and the river Lethe as it glides past peaceful
dwellings.

Here is a similar setting boasting a secluded valley (*valle re-*

ducta), a remote wood, and, above all, location beside a stream. The one is the water of Lethe from which spirits to be born again must drink; the other is sacred to Silvanus. But each fulfills an excitingly parallel role in its own book and thereby serves to draw the two books still closer together.

The Tiber, we have seen, is the introductory symbol of Aeneas' birth into a new life, a life which first concentrates on a review of the past. It corresponds to the river Styx which, in Book VI, must be crossed before Aeneas can truly be said to arrive in the world of the dead to meet, initially, one by one the individuals who stand for salient events in his past life. The challenge of the future is also present in both books, prefaced in each instance by the secluded grove through which runs a brook. This common initiation into events to come takes the form in VI of Anchises' review of the heroes who are ultimately to build the glories of Rome. In VIII it is realized in the shield whose contents are the future affairs of Italy and the triumphs of Rome or, as redefined by lines 628–29,

> . . . genus omne futurae
> stirpis ab Ascanio pugnataque in ordine bella.

the whole race of future stock, sprung from Ascanius, and its wars fought one by one.

The shield's first scene returns so strikingly to the basic imagistic pattern we have been following throughout Book VIII that it merits detailed analysis (lines 630–34):

> fecerat et viridi fetam Mavortis in antro
> procubuisse lupam, geminos huic ubera circum
> ludere pendentis pueros et lambere matrem
> impavidos, illam tereti cervice reflexa
> mulcere alternos et corpora fingere lingua.

And he had portrayed the mother wolf lying in the green cave of Mars. Around her teats twin boys hung playing and fearlessly licked their mother. Bending back her shapely neck, she fondled them one by one and fashioned their bodies with her tongue.

The inspiration for this passage, as we observed also for the meeting of Venus and Vulcan, is the opening lines of *De Rerum Natura* — and not without design, since the initial union which created the shield and looked to the future only through the imagery of birth is here echoed as the actual future begins to unfold. The setting in a green cave (*viridi in antro*) is typically pastoral.[29] The phrase, for instance, is used in *Eclogue* I, 75, to denote part of the landscape from which Meliboeus thinks he will be torn forever. There is one important detail, however, which implies the opposite of pastoral. It is a cave belonging to Mars. The parallels with Lucretius are instructive in outlining this tension. The wolf lies on the ground (the verb used is *procumbo*) as Mars on the limbs of Venus (Lucretius has the participle *recubantem*). The image of the twins hanging from the breasts of their wild nurse (*pendentis pueros*) is likewise borrowed from Lucretius' picture of the breath of Mars hanging from the goddess' lips (*pendet resupini spiritus*). And the figure of Mars pillowing his shapely neck (*tereti cervice reposta*) leads directly to Virgil's wolf, bending her neck so as to lick the cubs (*tereti cervice reflexa*).

If we were to transfer the general impression conveyed by Lucretius' initial presentation of Venus to the opening scene on the shield of Aeneas, we would be tempted to find just one more example of the spirit of violence being lulled to sleep by creativity personified. But it must not be forgotten that the wolf of Mars is doing the cherishing here.[30] She it is who is "fashioning" the future of Rome. Nature has reversed itself. If we compare the behavior of the Martian wolf elsewhere in the epic, for instance at IX, 565–66, its attitude here seems all the more astonishing. But Virgil is not without a purpose.

The imagery looks in two directions. From one vantage point it summarizes, through stress on the idea of birth and generation, the essential imagistic core of Book VIII. To this the position of the episode with which the story of the shield begins lends force, being part of the foundation of Rome itself and the first in a series of generations which form Rome's greatness. Take the word *procubuisse*, for example. It is used, as we previously noted, twice elsewhere in the book and a review of the contexts is instructive. The first occasion finds Aeneas lying down on the shore, asleep before the Tiber appears (*procubuit*, line 30). The word would seem without any special meaning save for the fact that some fifty lines later (line 83) the same verb describes the condition of the white sow which lies on the green shore (*procubuit viridique in litore*), like the wolf whom Vulcan depicts stretched in the green cave (*viridi in antro procubuisse*). Aeneas' entrance into Rome, past and to come, through the Tiber journey, is reinterpreted symbolically in the prodigy of the pig, which greets him as he awakes and whose sacrifice paves the way for the voyage up the river. Thus the idea of generation is also carried over from the *sus feta*, the mother pig with her white brood (*albo fetu*), to the *fetam lupam*, the wolf suckling the twins in the shield's first episode.

This is only half the story, however. We are never allowed to forget that the design on the shield consists not only of the offspring of Ascanius, but also of wars to be fought in the future. The concept of generation is still present but it is now combined with the necessity of war. As such, the initial scene of the shield fits in equally well with the second half of the book, commencing with the mating of Venus and Vulcan, water and fire, pastoral and power, which produces, if on the shield alone, a burgeoning race whose chief glory will be its triumphs in battle. The poet's use of Lucretius in each instance, introducing first the new world of Aeneas' future and then, with much broader sweep, the vision of Roman history from the twin sons of Mars to Augustus, makes the connection all the clearer. And though the wolf reverses its wonted role, nevertheless the potentiality of the beast of Mars in these surroundings leads the reader to accept the fact that henceforth pastoral peace must give way constantly to the violence of war.

And this is the story of the shield — violence ultimately leading to peace. It reaches a climax first in the juxtaposition of Catiline and Cato, with its reference to the underworld which contains both Tartarus and Elysium, punishment for the wicked and reward for the just. Good and evil confront each other most vividly, however, in Virgil's surpassing realization of the battle of Actium, as the might of Augustus, of Rome and its gods, triumphs in bloody conquest over the forces of Cleopatra and her monstrous divinities. The scene opens with dolphins leaping into the waves, but this pastoral serenity of sporting fish yields to the terrific clash of foe with foe. Nevertheless, from the description of Augustus' return in triple triumph, with all races and nations in abject surrender at his feet, one feels that Virgil too felt himself keenly admiring, at least for the moment, that peace gained through might which was the glory of the regime he felt called upon to eulogize and which forms so important a theme in *Aeneid* VIII.

4' TRAGIC VICTORY

Turnus is the central character of Book XII,[1] and not merely because he is the last and most important in the series of Aeneas' victims. The future of an entire race is now in the balance. Individuality is also at stake, but here individual freedom becomes a matter linked closely with corporate destiny. Turnus and the people of Latium stand in hopeless opposition to Aeneas and the fated triumph of Rome. Turnus, as we shall see, in many ways resembles Dido who, because of the madness which in her case sprang from love, stood as a lone antagonist to Aeneas and, while destroying herself, anticipated the downfall of her whole race. But Turnus stands as well for Italy and consequently absorbs into himself for the final clash all the challenge of Mezentius and Aeneas' other foes, all the pastoral freedom of Camilla, the heroine of Book XI, as he begins the last attempt to oppose destiny against insuperable odds.

As the epic reaches its climax, Aeneas on his part undergoes a change which offers a noteworthy commentary on the course his story has taken. During the first six books and even beyond, Aeneas is the protector of his helpless folk, looking to a future of which he knows nothing and at the same time fending off every hostility in his path. Book II, for instance, presents him as futile defender of his city in the face of inevitable destruction and savior of only a pitiful remnant. There, madness rules triumphant among the Greeks, but Aeneas, though he ponders giving in to his impulse to slaughter Helen, obeys the moderate, creative spirit of his mother who teaches commitment to the future, not reprisal for the past.[2]

By the time Book XII is reached, however, history's inevitable progress has imposed upon Virgil a reversal of this scheme. Aeneas, the cherisher of his Trojan folk against wiles human and divine, should ideally have become by the epic's conclusion not only the founder of the Roman race, but the first of a people which would ultimately re-establish the golden age after the forces of madness have at last been defeated at the battle of Actium. In reality he remains the person who imposes Troy on Italy.

Turnus, on the other hand, as the leader of the opposing forces, exhibits his characteristic rage (*violentia*), which at the climax of Book XII is mitigated only in death. But now he is the last hope of his people and even though wrath governs his acts to some degree, its object is protection of his own in the face of an enemy who appears to be stealing both his kingdom and his bride. The primary change — and it is one which must have forced on Virgil at least a partial revaluation of his epic's purpose and achievement — is in the figure of Aeneas, forced by circumstances to adopt a position not unlike that of Turnus himself in Book XII or the Greeks in II, where violence, even needless violence, is created to attain an end.

Book XII is in many ways the best constructed book of the *Aeneid*, particularly rich in associations with the rest of the poem. Its structure is revealed most clearly by juxtaposing the evolution and interplay of symbol and event to the unfolding of the third *Georgic*, in the same way as the poetic perspective of Book VIII gains greater structural clarity when placed next to VI. This comparison will take its proper place in the pages which follow as we turn once more to an examination of Virgil's mind operating through certain salient patterns of poetic exposition. There is no single, predominant type of imagery coloring the poetic essence of the book as is the case with Book VIII. Rather, many allusions to former events work their imaginative magic in conjuring up before the reader crucial moments of the past which lend added meaning to the present. In no other book of the *Aeneid* does the analysis of imagery shed more light on the work's historical and philosophical significance.

Immediately in the opening lines we learn that Turnus is now the cynosure of all eyes, as the routed Latins place all their hopes for survival in him. Nothing daunted at the thought of meeting Aeneas, he rages all the more. In Virgil's words, he blazes with his own unappeasable anger and rouses his spirit (*ultro implacabilis ardet / attollitque animos*). He is, through the poet's eyes, a lion wounded whose strength is still unimpaired (lines 4-9):

> . . . Poenorum qualis in arvis
> saucius ille gravi venantum vulnere pectus
> tum demum movet arma leo, gaudetque comantis
> excutiens cervice toros fixumque latronis
> impavidus frangit telum et fremit ore cruento:
> haud secus accenso gliscit violentia Turno.

Just as in Punic fields a lion, when he has been gravely wounded in the breast by hunters, then at last moves forward into battle and, joyfully tossing his flowing mane from his neck, breaks without fear the marauder's piercing arrow and roars with bloody mouth: in like manner, once he is set ablaze, Turnus' wrath swells.

Here, too, Virgil follows his usual procedure by introducing at the start of the book images which will prove significant when elaborated and varied in subsequent lines.

Turnus is in character. Earlier in the epic, and especially in Book IX, he had often appeared in the guise of a ravenous animal, as wolf either outside a sheepfold or having caught a helpless lamb; as tiger within a herd, or lion forced to retreat. This time, however, the animal is wounded, and inasmuch as Turnus has by no means literally been stricken, this poses the question of exactly what relationship Virgil wished to be drawn between the simile of the lion and the actual events which the metaphors of the passage reinterpret and project.

The imagery would appear to lead the reader in two directions which, in turn, the action of the book as a whole follows. In the first place, everything points to war. The lion, Turnus, though hurt with a grievous wound, takes to arms as if he were human, prepares weapons against his attackers, and fearlessly breaks the shaft with which he has been hit. But by his careful delineation of the lion's pursuers, the poet stresses another point as well. First, in line 5 they are called hunters (*venantum*), but this vague appellation is made a great deal more specific with the singular *latro* in line 7. The word appears only here in Virgil and, though most commentators usually bestow on it the sense of "brigand" or "common soldier," perhaps we are justified in looking beyond this meaning. Aeneas himself can most readily be taken as the leader of the hunters, for in Turnus' eyes, at least, Aeneas would appear a robber in his quest for empire. And, although the word *latro* is unique in Virgil, the equally derisive *praedo*, which also means "robber," is three times applied to Aeneas in the last six books as the Latins become aware of his motives.[3] Above all, we should take note of lines 483–84 of Book XI where the Latin matrons beseech the help of Minerva against this new Trojan Paris:

> "armipotens, praeses belli, Tritonia virgo,
> frange manu telum Phrygii praedonis . . ."

"Tritonian maid, mighty in arms and presiding over war, break with your hand the spear of the Phrygian robber."

The command *frange telum* is, of course, absorbed into the actual phraseology of the last line of the simile under examination. Turnus has confronted the hunter of his land and the robber of his betrothed and for a while survives the onslaught. Indeed, Aeneas has thus far had only partial success in his fight to conquer Italy.

There is also another, no less crucial, dimension to these lines, for Turnus' relationship with Lavinia, his betrothed, would seem of equal importance to the challenge of Aeneas, if we look once again at the metaphors with which the poet chooses to enliven this initial simile of the book. It is a common occurrence to find in Latin poetry the actual weapons of war and the scars that result from conflict utilized as metaphors to portray the various stages of love. We may choose as illustration an instance which bears particularly on this moment in XII — the description of Dido at the opening of Book IV (lines 1–5):

> At regina gravi iamdudum saucia cura
> vulnus alit venis et caeco carpitur igni.
> multa viri virtus animo multusque recursat
> gentis honos: haerent infixi pectore vultus
> verbaque, nec placidam membris dat cura quietem.

But the queen, long stricken now by grievous pangs, fosters the wound with her blood and is fed on by hidden fire. Often the man's courage, often the renown of his people, rush back to her mind. His features and words pierce and remain fixed to her breast, nor does her yearning grant her limbs the quiet of peace.

The verbal parallels between these lines and the opening simile of Book XII are precise enough to seem hardly fortuitous. Like the lion deeply wounded, Dido is stricken (*saucia*) with a grievous hurt (*gravi cura*), a wound which she feeds with her blood. The face and words of Aeneas, which cause this grief, remain fixed (*infixi*) in her (and we recall the use of *fixum* for the hunter's weapon in XII, 7). In Book IV Virgil develops the imagery until it triumphs first in the simile of lines 69–73, where Aeneas, in the guise of a hunter, unwittingly strikes Dido, depicted as a doe. The metaphors then take a more realistic form in the actual chase that follows at the end of which Aeneas seizes his quarry. That the poet re-establishes this atmosphere at the opening of Book XII suggests an identification between Dido and Turnus of deeper import than is at first apparent.

In this initial simile of Book XII, moreover, we seem to have another instance in the *Aeneid* where the details of geographical setting can scarcely be considered without meaning. If the imagery of lines 5 and following is meant to recall the plight of Dido, as has been proposed, the setting amid the fields of Carthage merely reinforces such a possible equation. The final line of Book XII, by repeating word for word XI, 831, clearly recollects the death of the warrior maid Camilla at the very moment Turnus is slain. Here, as Book XII commences and the stage is prepared for his doom, Turnus could be visualized almost as a heroic reincarnation of Dido.

The difference lies in the two sides of the simile. Turnus, because of his love for Lavinia, is suffering a wound similar to Dido's in the opening lines of IV, and passion inevitably rules his judgment in some of the decisions which follow. But upon Turnus rests the whole well-being and safety of his people in the strife ahead, a motif only secondary and suggestive in the case of the Phoenician queen. Nevertheless, he is also the last exemplar of all the individual, highly emotional heroism which has opposed Aeneas from the start, and the question which confronts the critic of the epic's final book is whether Aeneas, as he comes face to face with this composite of past antagonism, maintains the standards of reason and restraint he has hitherto called his own. That the answer must be negative appears only after careful consideration of the book's events as seen through the poet's imagination.

One further idea of importance is announced in the final phrase of the simile: *fremit ore cruento,* he roars with bloody mouth. By applying these words to Turnus, Virgil seems momentarily to equate his hero with unholy *Furor,* who, we recall from I, 296, also will roar dreadfully from blood-stained jaws (*fremet horridus ore cruento*). Hence Virgil could well appear to be deliberately placing Turnus in the company of all those whose spirit is ruled by emotion and thoughts of violence. The manifestations of *Furor,* as we saw in the case of Cacus, often combine, in whatever degree, qualities of beast as well as of man. But the chief importance of the position of *Furor* in Book I is that it is imprisoned. For, according to the world view of Jupiter, as he looks ahead to the ideal principate which could be Augustan, though it escape on occasion and wreak consequent harm to the designs of Aeneas and the future accomplishments of Rome, *Furor* will ultimately be confined, raging but harmless. On the less symbolic occasions of epic narrative, as corporate destiny meets individual challenge, death can be the only penalty exacted from anyone who opposes fate. What makes Book XII both intriguing and in part an exception is that at last the downfall of resistance does not occur before the hero has absorbed certain characteristics usually found only in his enemies. His death will in some ways be seen as a victory for Turnus.

This is scarcely to be suspected from the opening lines, in which the innate violence of Turnus holds sway. But the fact that the lion is wounded must not be forgotten. It hints at the literal outcome of the book, where Turnus does indeed fall victim to Aeneas' stroke. Similarly, the metaphorical connection between Turnus and animals is never dropped, reaching a pitiful, not to say ironic, conclusion in the simile of line 749 and following, in which Aeneas has at last become explicitly the hunter in the guise of a dog (*venator canis*), and Turnus, far from being a roaring lion, takes the shape of a pathetic deer. The awesome beast, once brought to bay, is in reality the helpless victim of a much more powerful animal.

The other aspect suggested above of the "wound" imagery also figures prominently in the lines which follow immediately, namely, the relationship between Turnus and Lavinia, the lover and his betrothed, who must be won from or lost to a man for whom emotion means little, destiny all.[4] Latinus, father of Lavinia, attempts to suppress the youth's ardor but instead admits that he himself was in a sense the cause of the uproar (lines 29–31):

> "victus amore tui, cognato sanguine victus
> coniugis et maestae lacrimis, vincla omnia rupi;
> promissam eripui genero, arma impia sumpsi."

"Overcome by love of you, overcome by family ties and by the tears of my sorrowing wife, I broke all restraint. I snatched the promised bride from my destined son-in-law and took up unholy arms."

The *arma impia* are all but equated with the resulting war, which, because Latinus did receive Turnus, could almost be considered a civil conflict. The Sibyl uses the same words to define one form of civil strife at VI, 612–13. But the breaking of the bonds and the consequent assumption of unholy arms remind the reader that once again *impius Furor* has escaped and is ready to go on the rampage — this time, we still assume, in the person of Turnus.

Latinus uses one especially strong image to intensify his speech to Turnus, as he attempts to dissuade the hero from the impending conflict. The result of the present turmoil, Latinus says, is that (lines 35–36)

> ". . . recalent nostro Tiberina fluenta
> sanguine adhuc campique ingentes ossibus albent."

"the Tiber's flood is still tepid with our blood and the spacious plains are white with our bones."

This association of red and white is an evocative one which seems to have appealed greatly to the Roman poets.[5] Its importance here lies in the fact that this very contrast recurs a moment later in Lavinia's reaction to her mother's attempt to keep Turnus from his purpose (lines 64–69):

> accepit vocem lacrimis Lavinia matris
> flagrantis perfusa genas, cui plurimus ignem
> subiecit rubor et calefacta per ora cucurrit.
> Indum sanguineo veluti violaverit ostro
> si quis ebur, aut mixta rubent ubi lilia multa
> alba rosa: talis virgo dabat ore colores.

Lavinia heard her mother's voice, her burning cheeks flowing with tears, as a deep blush, which spread across her glowing face, intensified the fire. As when a man dyes Indian ivory with blood-colored purple or as white lilies grow red when blended with many a rose, such were the colors which appeared on the maiden's face.

Lavinia's blush, prompted by Amata's speech, is caused by Turnus' love for her, and this in turn, in the eyes of Turnus, at least, is why war is necessary as he fights for what he rightly considers his own. Thus the "ivory dyed red" and the "lilies mixed with many a rose" are more intimate counterparts of the white bones near the river of blood, symbols of the war love brings.

As usual the metaphors inherent in the simile are of importance to explain the surrounding text. Both the words *sanguineo* and *violaverit*, for instance, enhance the ambiguity discussed above, in which the imagery describing the love between Turnus and Lavinia was seen to be expanded to the larger context of war. In noting, for example, the connection between *recalent* (line 35) and *calefacta* (line 66), we realize that the reason for her blushes and for the Tiber's warmth are not dissimilar. And the image of blood-red purple recalls both the bloody Tiber and Turnus' strange statement in line 51 that blood also flows from his wound (*nostro sequitur de vulnere sanguis*). This could mean that blood flows from a wound inflicted either by Turnus or upon him, as the case may be. The former is the obvious meaning at the moment, but Turnus himself alludes to the necessity of his own death more than once in these same lines. He leaves the same ambiguity open for himself in line 79:

". . . nostro dirimamus sanguine bellum . . ."

"Let us decide the war by our own blood."

Violaverit we would expect to mean literally "stain," but it too has its place in the expanded context of these lines, for it explicitly connects Turnus' well-known *violentia* (in Book XII mentioned only at lines 9 and 45) with his love for Lavinia and hence links it also directly with the ensuing conflict.[6]

But red is the dominant color in these lines, whether of the

Tiber's waters or of Lavinia's blushes. Turnus utilizes it once more as he establishes the setting of the impending clash (lines 76–78):

> ". . . cum primum crastina caelo
> puniceis invecta rotis Aurora rubebit,
> non Teucros agat in Rutulos . . ."

"When first the morrow's dawn, riding in crimson car, reddens the heavens, let not Aeneas lead the Trojans against the Rutuli."

Rubebit echoes the preceding uses of *rubor* (line 66) and *rubent* (line 68). *Puniceis* strikes a less obvious note, although it follows one of Virgil's more familiar patterns of allusion. First we recall the setting the poet gives to the initial mention of Turnus' future wounding in Punic fields, as if he were telling the attentive reader that there was to be a relationship between Turnus and Dido deeper than he might at first suspect.[7] Moreover, we could well look ahead to the only other appearance in the book of the adjective *puniceus*, in line 750, where Turnus is depicted as a stag, pursued by a fierce hound, but terrified as well by a wall of bright red feathers, *puniceae pennae*, which hems him in. This is the last mention of blood-red, which plays such an evocative and predictive role in these opening lines. It is nearly, but not quite, the last hint at any connection between Turnus and Dido, the only two characters to whose ensnarement and death, in each case intimately connected with Aeneas, Virgil devotes a whole book. Here it is worth taking a moment to explore in further detail how the poet makes the presence of Dido deliberately felt in these early lines.[8]

Latinus' words of caution to Turnus, discussed briefly above, resemble in some measure Dido's final cries of remorse before she dies. With both Latinus and Dido the phrase *quae mentem insania mutat?* — "What madness alters my resolve?" (IV, 595; XII, 37) — makes patent not only the suffering previous decisions have brought but predicts impending doom for self or family as well. In Amata's subsequent speech to Turnus, Virgil is even more explicit in his reminiscences. The very appearance of Amata on the scene is introduced with the phrase *at regina* (line 54), which figures at three decisive moments in Book IV (lines 1, 296, 504). And the immediate addition of the emphatic *moritura* (line 55), predicting her death, takes the mind back to Dido's own opening remonstrance to the departing Aeneas wherein her death also appears imminent (IV, 308, 323). One need quote only a few lines to show how close are both the substance and the verbal usage of the pleas which ensue in each case. Amata cries (lines 56–60)

> "Turne, per has ego te lacrimas, per si quis Amatae
> tangit honos animum (spes tu nunc una, senectae
> tu requies miserae, decus imperiumque Latini
> te penes, in te omnis domus inclinata recumbit),
> unum oro: desiste manum committere Teucris . . ."

"Turnus, by these tears, by whatever respect your mind holds for Amata — for you now are my one hope, the comfort of my pitiful age; all the glory and power of Latinus depend on you, on you our whole tottering house rests — one thing I beg: avoid open combat with the Trojans."

In her words she is in large measure echoing thoughts which Dido had uttered to Aeneas not too long before (IV, 314–19):

> ". . . per ego has lacrimas dextramque tuam te
> (quando aliud mihi iam miserae nihil ipsa reliqui),
> per conubia nostra, per inceptos hymenaeos,
> si bene quid de te merui, fuit aut tibi quicquam
> dulce meum, miserere domus labentis et istam,
> oro, si quis adhuc precibus locus, exue mentem."

"By these tears and your right hand, I beseech you (since now nothing else is left to me in my sorrow), by our wedding and wedlock begun: if I have deserved anything well of you, and aught of mine has found favor in your sight, pity my tottering house and, if there is still a place for prayers, give up this resolve."

Amata's final thoughts look to her suicide, an event (to be discussed later) which in itself offers a further parallel to the fate of the Queen of Carthage. What is important to emphasize here is the pervasive quality of the recollections of Book IV in these introductory verses to XII. It is not only Turnus but those around him as well whom the poet chooses to depict in terms akin to those in which he had portrayed Dido. Latinus, and especially Amata, seem now to be swayed by as much unreason as Turnus while they attempt to prevent him from a conflict which means death for one and for the other at least a partial destruction of his city.

It is an introduction pervaded by emotion, and it is by no means the last time in XII when previous scenes of passionate involvement will be called upon to enrich the reader's perception of what becomes the tragedy of Turnus. Were we to interweave the story of Dido into the fabric of Turnus' death, we might hope that once again the titular hero would somehow not be directly responsible for the death which must unavoidably come. But in Book XII, as both Turnus and Aeneas know, a face-to-face challenge is demanded, and by the book's end Dido's revenge could be called complete because Aeneas, by bringing death to Turnus, becomes a victim of that very unreason which hitherto he had done his best to shun. If Book XII depicts the tragedy of Turnus, it also delineates the gradual submission of Aeneas to the particular *furor* of Dido, inherited by Turnus and also absorbed in part by Latinus and Amata.

But the introduction predicts only part of the end, and that with little certainty, for as we plunge into the action of the book we find Turnus rejoicing in his armor and steeds, which neigh in anticipation of the coming warfare. Yet, even as all are making preparations for the decisive, peace-bringing duel between the heroes, Juno, the goddess whose suffering regularly brings disorder when emotion is least wanted, once more appears upon the scene. She urges Turnus' sister Juturna (lines 157–58)

> "accelera et fratrem, si quis modus, eripe morti;
> aut tu bella cie conceptumque excute foedus . . ."

"Hurry and snatch your brother away from death, if there is any way.
Or waken up war and shatter the treaty they have framed."

Though the battle is now to be a losing one, Juno seems bent
on stirring up as much confusion, on creating as much disorder,
as she had in Books I and VII. In fact, her words of exhortation
to Juturna are not unlike her appeal to the Fury Allecto to help
start the war in Latium (VII, 338–40).[9] This moment in XII
is of necessity the last deliberate manifestation of Juno's wrath.
But something of her present anger is communicated also to
Jupiter at the book's climax. Indeed, it is worthy of mention in
passing that Jupiter himself calls upon one of the Furies as the
epic draws to a close, to show his wrath against Turnus and be
a sign to the hero of his impending death. By then Turnus easily
perceives the fatal meaning of her appearance, and the doomed
hero shouts to his foe (lines 894–95):

> . . . "non me tua fervida terrent
> dicta, ferox; di me terrent et Iuppiter hostis."

"Your heated words do not frighten me, fierce as you are. I fear only
heaven and Jove's enmity."

Juturna sadly returns to her own domain as the passion of Juno
flares for the last time and then subsides. It is Jupiter's turn, with
sudden irony, in hatred of Turnus and in defense of Aeneas, to
appeal to the very creature who had been Juno's tool.

The initial working of this disorder is briefly postponed, however, as Latinus and Aeneas offer oaths stressing that the impending conflict looks only to a long-lasting future peace. Hand-
to-hand combat by the two leaders alone will decide their peoples'
fate. Turnus' *violentia* is willingly subordinated to the necesssity
of fighting Aeneas according to stipulated rules of fair combat
and within sight of those whose destiny depends on its outcome.
The complete lack of discipline and the savagery with which
both sides return to the combat after the breaking of the truce
only contrast the more with the elaborate protestations of peace

which Aeneas and his future father-in-law utter here. They will be made still more meaningless.

Virgil creates another interesting effect as he contrasts the quiet action of Turnus (he speaks not a word) with the previous grandiloquent oaths of Aeneas and Latinus (lines 219–21):

> adiuvat incessu tacito progressus et aram
> suppliciter venerans demisso lumine Turnus
> tabentesque genae et iuvenali in corpore pallor.

Turnus' approach with silent tread increases their apprehension, as he humbly worships the altar with downcast eye, his cheeks wasted and his youthful countenance pale.

The word *suppliciter* is especially important. It leads the reader directly to the final lines of the book where Turnus is the actual suppliant (*supplex*) before Aeneas — indeed to the moment when Aeneas' final action does in fact give the lie to his proud words here preaching peace. Virgil has deliberately drawn the present contrast between the two heroes. Moreover, it remains quite clear that the actions of Turnus at this moment are not those of a hero preparing for a duel in which a glorious outcome could be as readily his as not, but of an already doomed man who is no match for his mighty adversary in actual conflict. The imagery helps paint a picture of a certain innate humility in Turnus. While hinting at disease as a corollary of the "love" motif already established, it above all announces, in terms however veiled, the ineluctability of Turnus' approaching death.

It is not only the figure of Turnus but the whole scene which serves this purpose, for Virgil is following for the last time one of the familiar symbolic patterns in which his imagination operated, here made unusually explicit. Latinus, Aeneas, and Turnus all draw near the altars to offer oaths and perform due sacrifice. So we have seen Aeneas act before on certain crucial occasions, but usually the external sacrifice is accompanied by some higher offering to the gods in token of his progress, be it symbolic as in the case of the golden bough (so closely linked to the burial of Misenus), or human, to take the example of Palinurus. The sudden change of tone as Turnus venerates the altars could well mean that Turnus is himself to be a victim, the last person standing in the way of Aeneas, the last figure of violence set up by Juno to oppose the hero's fated progress. Like Laocoön, Turnus is at once the sacrificer and the sacrificed.

Virgil clarifies this still further with the first words he puts into the mouth of the disguised Juturna as she seeks to break the truce and save her doomed brother (lines 229–30):

> "non pudet, o Rutuli, pro cunctis talibus unam
> obiectare animam? . . ."

"Are you not ashamed, Rutulians, to sacrifice one life for all such as we are?"

She fully realizes the special necessity of Turnus' death in this Virgilian pattern of progress through sacrifice. He is the climactic victim, however, and as Juno too knows, his presence alone prohibits peaceful acceptance of the Trojans by the Italians. It means also the end of her wrath of which Juturna is the last, waning figure. As such Turnus is, in his own setting, akin to Palinurus concerning whom, we recall, Neptune stipulates to Venus (V, 814–15):

> "unus erit tantum amissum quem gurgite quaeres;
> unum pro multis dabitur caput."

"One alone will be lost whom you will seek in the ocean. One life will be offered for many."

At this moment, in Books II and V, the monster of progress would ordinarily assume physical form to revenge itself on its opposers, through sea or serpent. Turnus has some time yet to wait before his death, foreshadowed in the opening simile, and his countrymen before their surrender. But to the Latins' undecided and unknowing hearts Juturna sends a prodigy, in appearance like the snakes of II because it seems to be a divine manifestation of one thing, whereas its true meaning is exactly the opposite. An eagle, Jupiter's minion, pursuing some shore birds, pounces on a swan, but as it bears its booty away, the swan's companions form ranks, give chase to their enemy, and force it to drop its prize and take wing. The Latins are meant by Juturna to see in this bird of Jupiter (*Iovis ales*) a figure for Aeneas, who seizes their princess Lavinia but is overwhelmed and made to leave.

The true significance is somewhat different, and its correct interpretation depends upon the recollection of a similar omen Venus shows her son in Book I in which twelve swans, who had also been the prey of an eagle (*Iovis ales*: I, 394) under the open sky, now seem to gain land in safety, in the same way as Aeneas' ships, harassed by Juno and her followers, have come through their trial safely to the harbor of Carthage. The eagle is in each case the feeling of hostility and violence roused by Juno against Aeneas and the Trojans (this time specified as *litoreas aves*, birds who have actually reached the shore). In the description in XII there is one important change, however. The emphasis now lies not so much on the joy the victorious forces have upon escape, as it does in Book I, but upon the downfall and defeat of their enemy who flees deep into the clouds (*penitus in nubila fugit*).

The Trojans will clearly win the day, but the poet now gives particular attention to the withdrawal of the eagle which can and should stand for much that is to come before the book's conclusion, especially the gradual departure of all those who could in some way be of assistance to Turnus. First, Latinus hides as soon as the truce is broken (lines 285–86):

> . . . fugit ipse Latinus
> pulsatos referens infecto foedere divos.

After the treaty has been violated, Latinus himself flees, taking with him his defeated gods.

In the death scene of Amata as described to Turnus by Saces, Virgil uses the same image (lines 659–60):

"praeterea regina, tui fidissima, dextra
occidit ipsa sua lucemque exterrita fugit."

"Moreover the queen, your most faithful friend, has fallen by her own
hand and in terror fled the light."

It anticipates as well the final departure of Juturna who,
seeing the hopelessness of further defending her brother, buries
herself in the deep river whence she had come (*se fluvio . . .
condidit alto*: line 886). Finally, it predicts the death of Turnus
himself, as described in the last line of the epic, when his life
flees indignant to the shades below (*fugit indignata sub umbras*).
And in so doing, by announcing the death of the last stumbling
block set up in the path of Aeneas and the elimination of the
ultimate personification of Juno's *dolor*, the departure of the
eagle looks to the position of the goddess herself at the epic's
close, aloof because participation in action from now on is fruitless. With the death of Turnus, the suffering and wrath of
Juno cannot have further meaning. Since there is no possibility
of opposition in the future, fate is no longer subject to the buffets
of irrationality. Emotion takes a different, far more subtle course.

But the time is not yet ripe for the destruction of Turnus —
Virgil has much still to tell the reader — and the first important,
direct result of the renewal of hostilities, the wounding of Aeneas,
seems rather a step backward in what would appear to be Virgil's
grand design. Aeneas had begged for peace (*"o cohibete iras,"*
suppress your anger, he beseeches in line 314) and added, not
without a touch of bravado (line 317),

". . . Turnum debent haec iam mihi sacra."

"These rites now owe Turnus to me."

Apparently to fulfill such a boast Aeneas must come near to
death himself. But the dramatic result of the unheralded, un-
claimed arrow which immediately hurtles through the air and
strikes him, is also necessary. While Aeneas languishes away
from the fighting, apparently dying, it is Turnus' chance to rage

victoriously. From this moment on, as the balance gradually swings back into Aeneas' favor, an inexorable progress begins which leads finally to an exact reversal of these roles, to Turnus dying and Aeneas a victim of the very anger he now urges others to suppress.

At the moment, however, Turnus has the upper hand. He once more demands his horses, symbols of war and of his own *violentia*, and Virgil compares him to bloody Mars, whose horses fly faster than the winds and around whom swarm fear, anger, and treachery. The comparison is reinforced shortly later as the enemy scattered by Turnus' onslaught are likened by the poet to clouds which give place as the north wind roars (lines 365–67):

> ac velut Edoni Boreae cum spiritus alto
> insonat Aegaeo sequiturque ad litora fluctus;
> qua venti incubuere, fugam dant nubila caelo . . .

Just as when the blast of the north wind from Edonia roars over the deep Aegean and drives the billows shoreward wherever the winds press on, the clouds flee across the sky.

The combination of winds and horses as fitting companions to *Furor* on the rampage is familiar from the opening scene of Book I. We might well compare this whole simile with I, 84–86, for instance:

> incubuere mari totumque a sedibus imis
> una Eurusque Notusque ruunt creberque procellis
> Africus et vastos volvunt ad litora fluctus . . .

Swooping down upon the sea, they overwhelm it from its lowest depths, East wind and South together, and Southwest, thick with blasts. They roll vast billows toward the shore.

As noted above, this whole series of lines devoted to the prowess of Turnus — lines strengthened by some particularly striking turns of phrase associated with his gruesome actions — contrasts the momentarily victorious hero and the wounded Aeneas, helpless in his tent (XII, 387–90):

saevit et infracta luctatur harundine telum
eripere auxilioque viam, quae proxima, poscit:
ense secent lato vulnus telique latebram
rescindant penitus, seseque in bella remittant.

He rages and strives to pull out the head of the broken arrow and demands
the nearest road to relief: let them cut the wound with blade of sword
and open up the lurking-place of the shaft from deep within. Let them
send him back to war.

In reflecting on the fact of Aeneas' wounding and its dramatic
necessity, we are reminded of Turnus as the lion who fearlessly
breaks the shaft that pierced him (*fixum . . . / impavidus
frangit telum*). This particular image is dropped, to be called
upon again during the death scene of Turnus, not only in the
actual wound inflicted by Aeneas but in the way Virgil describes
the *Dira*, the personification of Jupiter's terror, rushing to the
place of battle (lines 856–59)

> non secus ac nervo per nubem impulsa sagitta
> armatam saevi Parthus quam felle veneni,
> Parthus sive Cydon, telum immedicabile, torsit,
> stridens et celeris incognita transilit umbras . . .

like an arrow, driven by the cord through the clouds, an arrow armed
with the venom of cruel poison, which a Parthian, a Parthian or a Cretan,
perhaps, has shot. Whistling and unseen, it leaps through the swift
shadows.

This is the fatal arrow, sign of the anger of the head of the gods,
the final irrevocable announcement of fate. If for the moment
Turnus can play the part of Mars surrounded by the figures of
fear, wrath, and treachery, it is not too long before he will confront a much more powerful wrath whose instrument is the
sword of Aeneas.

At the moment, however, Aeneas suffers, but help is soon
forthcoming, for as the human hand of Iapyx falters and fails
to provide due relief, his divine mother comes bringing the
needed herbs. It was at a similar moment in VIII that Venus
had made her appeal to Vulcan to provide the arms demanded

by the threatening war. Now she intervenes to help him press the war to a finish. The initial result of his sudden recovery is worth observing. He pronounces a few cautionary remarks to his son; then (lines 441–45):

> Haec ubi dicta dedit, portis sese extulit ingens
> telum immane manu quatiens; simul agmine denso
> Antheusque Mnestheusque ruunt, omnisque relictis
> turba fluit castris. tum caeco pulvere campus
> miscetur pulsuque pedum tremit excita tellus.

When he had uttered these words, the mighty hero betook himself out of the gates, brandishing in his hand his enormous spear. Together with him in close array rush Antheus and Mnestheus, and the whole crowd pours from the abandoned camp. Then the plain swirls with blinding dust and the trembling earth quakes from the tread of their feet.

Once more we note a series of significant parallels with Virgil's depiction, in Book I, 81–86, of the escape of the winds from their cavernous home with the help of Aeolus:

> Haec ubi dicta, cavum conversa cuspide montem
> impulit in latus: ac venti velut agmine facto,
> qua data porta, ruunt et terras turbine perflant.
> incubuere mari totumque a sedibus imis
> una Eurusque Notusque ruunt creberque procellis
> Africus et vastos volvunt ad litora fluctus: . . .

With these words, he turned his spear-point toward the hollow mountain and thrust it into its side. The winds, as in armed array, rush out where the way is opened, and blow with gusts over the lands. Swooping down upon the sea, they overwhelm it all from its lowest depths, East wind and South together, and Southwest, thick with blasts. They roll vast billows toward the shore.

It is now the moment for Turnus and his allies to grow cold with fear, as does Aeneas in Book I when facing the fury of Juno's wrath. Juturna recognizes the sound and treats it as a sign rightly to be feared (XII, 448–49):

> . . . prima ante omnis Iuturna Latinos
> audiit agnovitque sonum et tremefacta refugit.

First, before all the Latins, Juturna heard and recognized the sound and fled in terror.

The reaction by brother and sister is also much the same to the prodigy which Jupiter sends as the introduction to the final moments of Turnus' life.

This description of Aeneas returning to the fray does nothing so much as remind the reader of Turnus' deeds while Aeneas was out of action. When Virgil writes (lines 444–45)

> . . . tum caeco pulvere campus
> miscetur pulsuque pedum tremit excita tellus . . . ,

then the plain swirls with blinding dust and the trembling earth quakes from the tread of their feet . . . ,

we think of the recent comparison of Turnus to Mars under the tread of whose horses faraway Thrace groans (*gemit ultima pulsu / Thraca pedum*). And the splendid accompanying simile, in which the newly recovered Aeneas is compared to a violent storm at sea which portends ruin to the farmers who observe its imminence, seems for a moment to recall to the attention those very winds of Mars and blasts of Boreas which accompanied Turnus' unimpeded slaughter.[10] Moreover, there is one strong hint in this simile that Aeneas is now beginning to reveal the tendency toward violence which had hitherto so often characterized Turnus. For when we learn that Aeneas' storm will bring ruin to the pastoral world, we know that a further touch of insanity will compound Aeneas' wrath. At the moment he has eyes for Turnus alone (lines 464–67):

> ipse neque aversos dignatur sternere morti
> nec pede congressos aequo nec tela ferentis
> insequitur: solum densa in caligine Turnum
> vestigat lustrans, solum in certamina poscit.

He himself neither deigns to lay low in death those who turn from him, nor does he attack those meeting him fairly foot to foot or carrying weapons: Turnus alone he tracks in his search through the thick gloom; Turnus alone he summons to do battle.

The search is now on in earnest; one might almost say the "tracking" begins. Indeed the word *vestigo*, which appears four times in these and subsequent lines (467, 482, 557, 588), suggests a hunt as well as a war. Juturna senses the dread in the situation, and as she herself takes over the reins of Turnus' chariot the poet provides another evocative simile (lines 473–78):

> nigra velut magnas domini cum divitis aedes
> pervolat et pennis alta atria lustrat hirundo
> pabula parva legens nidisque loquacibus escas,
> et nunc porticibus vacuis, nunc umida circum
> stagna sonat: similis medios Iuturna per hostis
> fertur equis rapidoque volans obit omnia curru . . .

Just as a black swallow wings her way through the spacious villa of a rich lord and traverses in flight the lofty rooms, gathering tiny morsels and crumbs for her chirping brood; now she is heard in the empty porticoes, now around the water-tanks: in such fashion Juturna drives her horses through the midst of the enemy and flying on her swift chariot ranges everywhere about.

The tone of these lines seems to acknowledge the inherently helpless situation of Turnus, the fledgling whose hunger, and hence death, is staved off only by a mother searching for scraps in the house of some great lord. The actual details of the simile do more than merely establish atmosphere, however, for they turn our attention back to one of the most arresting moments in Aeneas' past, the death of Polites at the hands of Pyrrhus, and with it to the total downfall of Priam and his city (II, 526–30):

> Ecce autem elapsus Pyrrhi de caede Polites,
> unus natorum Priami, per tela, per hostis
> porticibus longis fugit et vacua atria lustrat
> saucius. illum ardens infesto vulnere Pyrrhus
> insequitur, iam iamque manu tenet et premit hasta.

Behold, however, Polites, one of Priam's sons, slipping out through the weapons of the enemy from the carnage inflicted by Pyrrhus, takes flight in the long porticoes and, wounded, traverses the empty chambers. Pyrrhus follows him in hot pursuit to inflict a dread hurt, and now, even now, grasps him with his hand and presses upon him with his spear.

To call attention to some of the more salient verbal parallels between these two moments, *vacua atria lustrat* seems to anticipate *alta atria lustrat*, and it is not far from *porticibus longis* to *porticibus vacuis*. The mansion of the rich lord could indeed be taken as nothing else than a reminder of the house of the aged Priam, and the thick darkness (*densa caligo*), in which Aeneas presses toward Turnus, seems to re-establish for a moment the atmosphere of the sinking Troy.[11] We will have this whole mood of impending disaster conjured up again with even greater vigor, by means of allusion to Book II, before long. For the present it is especially important to note that Aeneas is no longer the suffering Trojan but, as he follows the windings of Turnus' chariot, becomes akin to the most maddened of all the Greeks who took part in Priam's overthrow. Turnus is more than ever the pitiful victim as Aeneas begins to give evidence of succumbing to the rage which he had up to now denied.

But Turnus retreats as his sister directs the chariot in a twisting course, and while Aeneas debates what way is best to take in further pursuit of his enemy, Messapus attempts to inflict a second wound upon him. At this moment Aeneas's wrath breaks forth without restraint (*adsurgunt irae*, line 494), and he who shortly before had urged calm ("*o cohibete iras*") now reacts with a display of violence rarely paralleled elsewhere in the epic because it is utterly purposeless (lines 498–99):

> terribilis saevam nullo discrimine caedem
> suscitat, irarumque omnis effundit habenas.

In terrible fashion he awakes fierce slaughter indiscriminately and lets loose all the reins of his wrath.

Little does Turnus matter now as Aeneas' rage simply to kill predominates over any other goal. It first takes the form of indiscriminate slaughter on the battlefield. To accompany the grim work in which both heroes are for the moment engaged, Virgil adds a highly ironic aside on future peace and a simile in which fire destroys nature and nature mankind. And each victim is given a more distinctive personal touch than is usually Virgil's wont, to put into relief the callousness of the massacre.

The next stage in Aeneas' madness is even more enlightening. It begins at line 554:

> Hic mentem Aeneae genetrix pulcherrima misit
> iret ut ad muros urbique adverteret agmen
> ocius et subita turbaret clade Latinos.

At this point his beautiful mother put into Aeneas' mind to attack the walls and turn his columns with speed toward the city that he might overwhelm the Latins with a sudden blow.

The first thing that strikes the reader here is the origin of Aeneas' new scheme; that Venus, the *genetrix pulcherrima*, put such thoughts of misery into her son's mind. The whole subsequent episode may be said to fit into the pattern of the destruction by madness which has been a continuing motif of the book and now centers directly on Aeneas. It is all the more strange that Venus is the cause — she who shortly before was the procurer of drugs to heal her son's wound only to send him out forthwith to the ruin of many. It could well be that the poet wished to parallel from elsewhere this developing change in Aeneas from thoughts of reasoned action to irrational violence by putting part of the blame for it on his mother.

The downfall of Aeneas is thus subtly abetted by Venus, whose role has changed as the poem progresses from one who counsels against violence in Book II, to the purveyor — one might with justice say begetter — of arms in VIII; to the fighting goddess who now impels her son not toward purposes of heroic accomplishment such as the shield had depicted for him to emulate, but against a city essentially defenseless, guarded by an old man and citizens unfit for more strenuous action, a city (line 559)

> immunem tanti belli atque impune quietam.
> free from so great a war, unharmed and at peace.

Quiet, it appears, must be broken; needless destruction pursued at any cost.

It is important to notice that in line 564, as an introduction to Aeneas' speech urging on his men to their ruinous work, Virgil uses a variation of one of his favorite phrases: *celso medius stans aggere*, standing in the middle of a lofty mound. Similar words anticipated other moments of great tension — as Anchises sights Italy for the first time, as Aeneas and his small company appear before Pallanteum, as Augustus watches the battle of Actium — but they were never applied to such a negative event as this. It is all the more unusual that the founder of Rome and unifier of Italy, the supposed bringer of peace, should announce concerning Latinus' helpless city that, unless complete capitulation is granted,

"eruam et aequa solo fumantia culmina ponam."

"I shall overwhelm it and I shall place its smoking rooftops on a level with the ground" (line 569).

The attack upon the city looks once more to Book II, to the destruction of Troy and the very moment when the Greeks, led by the son of Achilles, invade the central palace of the aged Priam. The verbal parallels are impressive. Each episode is introduced, for example, with the words *primosque trucidant* (II, 494; XII, 577). Not least in importance is one noteworthy phrase, *ipse inter primos*, applied in Book II to Pyrrhus (line 479) as he leads the way into Priam's sanctuary, and in XII attributed to Aeneas (line 579), pitting his forces against another aged king, scarcely responsible for the rage called forth against him.

Virgil emphasizes his horror of such an action by a simile and by placing particular stress on an event which results from it. The simile compares Aeneas' burning of the city to such a moment (lines 587–92)

inclusas ut cum latebroso in pumice pastor
vestigavit apes fumoque implevit amaro:
illae intus trepidae rerum per cerea castra
discurrunt magnisque acuunt stridoribus iras;
volvitur ater odor tectis, tum murmure caeco
intus saxa sonant, vacuas it fumus ad auras.

as when a shepherd has tracked down bees hidden in a rocky lair and filled it with bitter smoke. Inside, anxious for their community, they rush through their waxen fortress and amidst great buzzing angrily sharpen their stings. Murky vapors swirl through their homes and the rock hums inside with a muffled murmur as the smoke issues forth to the empty air.

Aeneas first appears as a shepherd, but almost as soon as he has written the image Virgil negates its inherently peaceful implications by turning his hero into a destroyer of the pastoral world in what the fourth *Georgic* describes as one of its most orderly forms, the life of the bees. And in the word *vestigavit*, moreover, Virgil repeats one of the strongest images he had used to describe the commencement of Aeneas' search for Turnus, this time turning it against the doomed Latins.[12]

The event that occurs as a result of Aeneas' rash enterprise is the death of Amata, which takes on a symbolic significance far beyond the brief passage in which it is described. The queen, as she sees the enemy approaching without opposition, thinks that Turnus must therefore be dead, and as a result in despair takes her own life, bringing grief to Lavinia and the city. With her suicide and the renunciation of Juno's wrath, which follows shortly thereafter, ends all opposition to Aeneas, save in the figure of Turnus. Amata had to die, as did all those who in the past posed obstacles to Aeneas or whose removal eased the progress toward achievement of his goals.

To clarify his purpose in mentioning Amata's suicide, Virgil recalls again, with the force of brevity, two of the events upon which we have already seen his mind dwelling during the course of Book XII, the doom of Troy and the death of Dido. After first taking note of the scene itself and the setting of the misfortune (line 594)

> quae totam luctu concussit funditus urbem . . . ,

which struck the whole city to its core with grief,

we should carefully observe the effect this news has on Lavinia, Latinus, and the rest of the city (lines 604–10):

quam cladem miserae postquam accepere Latinae,
filia prima manu floros Lavinia crinis
et roseas laniata genas, tum cetera circum
turba furit, resonant late plangoribus aedes.
hinc totam infelix vulgatur fama per urbem.
demittunt mentes, it scissa veste Latinus
coniugis attonitus fatis urbisque ruina . . .

After the saddened women of Latium had received news of this tragedy,
first Lavinia, her daughter, tore at her flowery locks and rosy cheeks
with her hand, then the rest of the crowd round about became maddened
with grief. The halls resound far and wide with wailing. Thence the
woeful rumor spreads throughout the whole city. Hearts lose their courage, and Latinus goes about, his garments torn, dazed by his wife's death
and the city's fall.

What the artistry of Virgil's first accomplishes in this description
is to turn the mind of the reader back to the interior of the palace
of Priam, to the very moment when Pyrrhus, gleaming like a
snake, stands poised on the threshold (II, 486–91):

At domus interior gemitu miseroque tumultu
miscetur, penitusque cavae plangoribus aedes
femineis ululant; ferit aurea sidera clamor.
tum pavidae tectis matres ingentibus errant
amplexaeque tenent postis atque oscula figunt.
instat vi patria Pyrrhus . . .

But inside, the house is a mixture of groans and pitiable turmoil, and
deep within the hollow halls resound with the cries of women. The
shouts strike the golden stars. Then frightened mothers wander through
the vast houses, holding the doorposts in their embrace and planting
kisses upon them. Pyrrhus presses on with his father's strength.

Through his potent use of repeated imagery, Virgil once more
and now for the last time and perhaps most forcefully, depicts
Aeneas playing the part of Pyrrhus, reincarnation of his father's
anger as he annihilates city and king. Virgil has hinted before
that Turnus would soon be in the position of Polites. He now
adds further point to this previous suggestion by posing Aeneas
as the needless destroyer of Latinus' city and, secondarily, of its
queen.

We have known from the start of the book, however, that Amata would die and that her death would be intimately connected with that of Turnus (lines 61–63):

> "qui te cumque manent isto certamine casus
> et me, Turne, manent; simul haec invisa relinquam
> lumina nec generum Aenean captiva videbo."

"Whatsoever trials remain for you in this struggle, Turnus, are mine also. Together with you I will leave this hateful light, nor shall I live as a captive to see Aeneas become my son-in-law."

We had suspected, too, that as a suicide her death might to a certain degree mirror that of Dido. It does more than that. For suddenly, here in Book XII, the fall of Dido, one of the most equivocal and emotional moments in Aeneas' past, is reviewed with particular force. As the Queen of Carthage sank down, her sword dripping blood and her hands spattered (IV, 665–71),

> . . . it clamor ad alta
> atria; concussam bacchatur Fama per urbem.
> lamentis gemituque et femineo ululatu
> tecta fremunt, resonat magnis plangoribus aether,
> non aliter quam si immissis ruat hostibus omnis
> Karthago aut antiqua Tyros, flammaeque furentes
> culmina perque hominum volvantur perque deorum.

a cry rises to the palace roof. Rumor runs riot through the stricken city. The palace resounds with wailing and the groans of women crying, and the heavens re-echo with the loud mourning. It was almost as if all Carthage or old Tyre were collapsing under the enemy's assault, and raging flames were swirling through the dwellings of men and of gods.

The connection of this passage with XII, 604–10, reviewed above, is thorough and close. Amata had vowed that she would never live as a prisoner to see Aeneas become her son-in-law (*nec generum Aenean captiva videbo*), and she holds to her word. As Dido herself states, when assured that Aeneas' departure was settled, if she at least had a little Aeneas to recall his father (IV, 330)

> "non equidem omnino capta ac deserta viderer."

"I would not seem completely vanquished and deserted."

The only real escape from present suffering is the way of death, and this both Amata and Dido choose.

The cry of woe which arises from Dido's city might make one think, the poet observes, that the whole of Carthage was being overwhelmed by some enemy, as flames raged through the dwellings of gods and men alike. The metaphorical exaggeration contains a touch of irony because, in spite of Dido's curse and prediction of war between her country and the city soon to be established by the followers of Aeneas, it is the Romans who would ultimately gain victory and raze Carthage to the ground. If such destruction in IV remains purely symbolic (Dido is metaphorically the only foe captured and put to death), it forms the literal core of the action in II, as Aeneas is forced to endure Troy's fall. But in the destruction of Troy Aeneas had no part, and Dido's suicide can be imputed to him only secondarily, as can the death of Amata. But this crucial moment in XII, upon which Virgil places so much stress, finds pious Aeneas deliberately reveling in the havoc he creates. He appears now to be the person who could destroy not only Dido but her city and people as well. One cannot fully escape the conclusion that Virgil looks to former events to stress the change which now gradually seems to come over Aeneas as the poem draws to a close. Instead of the hounded creature of destiny he becomes himself the creator of a wrath as strong as any posed against him in the past. What should be left at peace is overwhelmed; what should be left for a productive future is ravaged to satisfy passing vengeance.

In the meantime Turnus has not been forgotten, and his reaction to this catastrophe is worth observing. As he pursues a few laggards at a distant spot on the plain, less confident or joyful than before, it is his turn to find himself, like Aeneas in II, standing suddenly still in fright as the sounds from the grief-stricken city reach his ears.[13] His, too, is the opportunity to follow Juturna's advice and continue the needless slaughter, easy in the absence of Aeneas. Death alone is the alternative, when the time of the final clash arrives. The advent of Saces forces Turnus to the realization that he must defend himself and his people. As he cries out (lines 694–95)

"quaecumque est fortuna, mea est; me verius unum
pro vobis foedus luere et decernere ferro . . ."

"whatever fortune brings is mine. It is more honorable for me alone to atone for the truce instead of you and to decide the issue with the sword . . ."

we think back to the moment when the book's action began and to Aeneas' proud boast that the sacred rites owed Turnus to him. In the intervening lines Virgil concentrated on putting before the reader certain attributes of the two heroes, prior to the final conflict. Many of these now culminate in a series of four similes with which the poet interprets these crucial moments.

The initial two are intimately joined. First, the challenge of Turnus is depicted thus (lines 684–90):

ac veluti montis saxum de vertice praeceps
cum ruit avulsum vento, seu turbidus imber
proluit aut annis solvit sublapsa vetustas;
fertur in abruptum magno mons improbus actu
exsultatque solo, silvas armenta virosque
involvens secum: disiecta per agmina Turnus
sic urbis ruit ad muros . . .

As when a rock from a mountain's crest rushes down headlong, torn off by the wind — whether a swirling rainstorm has washed it off or the old age of years creeping past has loosened it — the reckless mass with a mighty bound is borne down the slope and leaps over the earth, sweeping up with it trees, herds, and men: thus Turnus rushes through the scattered ranks to the walls of the city.

Turnus has not been without his destructive moments in the past; he is like the gigantic rock fallen from high above which can gather up and crush flocks, trees, and men in its path. But the boulder has itself been dislodged, the simile emphasizes, by wind, rain or simply old age (*vetustas*). This last detail, in itself a strange reason to give as the cause of a landslide, fascinates for what it tells us of Turnus. A few lines before he had appeared *iam segnior*, now slower than before, like the old horse in the third *Georgic* (line 95). Turnus is now, in the poet's eyes, akin to the aged ash in Book II, which likewise trembles upon a mountain top, assailed by farmers and collapsing in ruin as it is torn from its slopes. Though literally applied to the downfall of Troy, the metaphors of that simile, as we have seen, look to the death of the aged king Priam as well. Here, in the case of Turnus, the rock outworn with years is only momentarily destructive. What is old will soon die. The youth of Turnus means little as his doom reflects the disintegration, in one last pitiful show of force, of all antagonism to Aeneas.

Aeneas, before the clash begins is by contrast the very mountain itself. He is (lines 701–3)

> quantus Athos aut quantus Eryx aut ipse coruscis
> cum fremit ilicibus quantus gaudetque nivali
> vertice se attollens pater Appenninus ad auras.

large as Athos or Eryx or Father Apennine himself, when he roars with his glistening oaks and joyously raises his snow-capped head to the sky.

Remarkably parallel language introduces each of these two similes. Turnus leaves behind (*deserit*, line 683) his sad sister, and Aeneas likewise withdraws from the walls and citadel of the beleaguered city (line 698). Aeneas breaks away from all his tasks (*rumpit*, line 699) as Turnus, too, tears through the midst of the forces to reach his enemy (*rumpit*, line 683).

Yet it is in the contents of the similes that the contrast lies, for while Turnus is compared to a cliff falling in ruin, Aeneas remains the mountain itself, with the grandeur of Father Appenninus. Once again the reader's thoughts are referred to Book IV, to a simile wherein Aeneas, remaining unmoved by the anger of Dido and the entreaties of her sister, was likened by the poet to a mighty oak facing the blasts of Boreas (IV, 441–46). If Turnus here assumes to himself once again all opposition while defining its collapse, Aeneas, for an instant, appears the un-moved creator of destruction, whose fate it is to stand firm while others destroy themselves around him.[14] In XII, however, the actual deed is demanded of him, and no escape from responsibility is possible.

The time draws nearer and, as the final battle commences, Virgil adds yet another simile which, though lengthy, demands from its importance quotation in full (lines 715–24):

> ac velut ingenti Sila summove Taburno
> cum duo conversis inimica in proelia tauri
> frontibus incurrunt, pavidi cessere magistri,
> stat pecus omne metu mutum, mussantque iuvencae
> quis nemori imperitet, quem tota armenta sequantur;
> illi inter sese multa vi vulnera miscent
> cornuaque obnixi infigunt et sanguine largo
> colla armosque lavant, gemitu nemus omne remugit:
> non aliter Tros Aeneas et Daunius heros
> concurrunt clipeis, ingens fragor aethera complet.

As on massive Sila or the height of Taburnus, when two bulls charge brow to brow in fierce battle, the fearful herdsmen give place and the whole flock stands dumb with fear. The heifers await with lowing who will rule the woodland, whom all the herds shall follow. The bulls with great force exchange blows with each other and pierce one another with thrusting horns. They wash their necks and shoulders in a bath of blood as the whole woodland echoes with their bellowing. Thus also Trojan Aeneas and the Daunian hero clash with their shields, and a mighty crash fills the heavens.

Virgil's imagination has turned back to *Georgic* III for the source of this simile. This is not the first occasion of such borrowing in *Aeneid* XII. Lines 103–6, when Turnus is first preparing to enter the fray with his adversary, are taken with only a few changes from lines 232–34 of the third *Georgic*. Since the setting is virtually the same in both instances and throws light on one of the patterns of imagery Virgil was following in the last book of his epic, it is worth dwelling on for a moment.

The pertinent section of *Georgic* III begins at line 209, as Virgil announces that nothing keeps up the strength of animals,

of whatever kind, more than to ward off from them the goads of
love. But it is not so much the wasting of energy that captures
the poet's imagination as the fact that if the two sexes are not
segregated, with barriers of mountain or broad stream interposed,
one male will be forced to do battle with another for an attractive
heifer (lines 215–18):

> carpit enim viris paulatim uritque videndo
> femina, nec nemorum patitur meminisse nec herbae
> dulcibus illa quidem inlecebris, et saepe superbos
> cornibus inter se subigit decernere amantis.

For the sight of a female gradually saps and consumes his strength; nor
indeed do her sweet allurements allow him any thoughts of wood and
pasture. And often she compels proud lovers to decide their claims through
clash of horns.

Were we to look no further, we would discern in these lines one
of the basic themes of *Aeneid* XII — the clash of Aeneas and
Turnus over Lavinia, brought about by the necessity of Aeneas
to come into his fated realm and of Turnus to defend his people
and preserve what he justly considers his own.

The verb *decernere* is focal here and elsewhere in the *Aeneid*.
At XI, 217–19, for instance, as the people murmur against the
cause of the needless deaths which they mourn,

> dirum exsecrantur bellum Turnique hymenaeos;
> ipsum armis ipsumque iubent decernere ferro,
> qui regnum Italiae et primos sibi poscat honores.

They curse the abominable war and the marriage of Turnus. Him they
bid to decide the issue with arms, him they bid decide it with the sword,
since he claims for himself the kingdom of Italy and sovereign honors.

The war is intimately linked with the marriage of Turnus; its
outcome will decide the fate of Lavinia and the course of empire.
After the breaking of the treaty in XII, both sides bring indiscriminate slaughter upon each other (line 282):

> sic omnis amor unus habet decernere ferro.

Thus all are ruled by one passion, to reach a decision with the sword.

But this desire is focused specifically once again on the two heroes, as Turnus cries before the final meeting (line 694–95):

"quaecumque est fortuna, mea est; me verius unum
pro vobis foedus luere et decernere ferro."

"Whatever fortune brings is mine. It is more honorable for me alone to atone for the truce instead of you and to decide the issue with the sword."

And this thought the poet reiterates a few lines later.

The lines quoted from *Georgic* III, however, establish only the reason why a conflict should arise. Those which follow give the reader an example and place it in a setting which clearly anticipates the simile of *Aeneid* XII examined above (*Georgic* III, 219–23):

pascitur in magna Sila formosa iuvenca:
illi alternantes multa vi proelia miscent
vulneribus crebris, lavit ater corpora sanguis,
versaque in obnixos urgentur cornua vasto
cum gemitu, reboant silvaeque et longus Olympus.

A beautiful heifer feeds on vast Sila. The bulls, attacking alternately, exchange frequent blows with great force, and dark blood washes their bodies. With a huge roar horns are turned to assail the charging foe. The woods and broad firmament re-echo.

In the simile Virgil seems to be pondering not only the battle itself but its effect on the world at large, as seen in the fear of the herdsmen and the terror struck into the hearts of the herd. The outcome will decide their future leader, the ruler of the wood. The point is slightly different in *Georgic* III, for there the poet turns his attention to the defeated bull, forced to leave his ancestral lands (lines 224–28):

nec mos bellantis una stabulare, sed alter
victus abit longeque ignotis exsulat oris.
multa gemens ignominiam plagasque superbi
victoris, tum quos amisit inultus amores,
et stabula aspectans regnis excessit avitis . . .

Nor is it customary for the antagonists to stable together, but the defeated bull goes off into the distant exile of unknown parts. Then, bewailing his disgrace, the blows inflicted by his proud conqueror, and the love which he has lost unavenged, he looks back at his stall as he withdraws from his ancestral realm.

As the poet pondered the dramatic development of his epic's final book, his thoughts turned back to this very moment in the third *Georgic*. The defeated bull returns and then with renewed vigor gives battle again to his rival (232–36):

> et temptat sese atque irasci in cornua discit
> arboris obnixus trunco, ventosque lacessit
> ictibus, et sparsa ad pugnam proludit harena.
> post ubi collectum robur viresque refectae,
> signa movet praecepsque oblitum fertur in hostem: . . .

He puts himself to the test and learns to throw anger into his horns, as he thrusts against the trunk of a tree. He provokes the winds with blows and paws the sand in preparation for battle. Then after his strength has been gathered and powers renewed, he advances his colors and charges headlong against his forgetful foe.

We do not learn the outcome. The lines which follow in the third *Georgic* amount to a virtual homily on the trials and terrors of love. But it is interesting to observe Virgil's order as he borrows from these lines in *Aeneid* XII. First Turnus appears as the defeated bull, expelled from his ancestral land but ready to offer challenge again (*G.* III, 232–34 and *A.* XII, 103–6). Yet *signa movet* is not far from *movet arma* in the first simile of XII. Turnus can still fight, but the wound which will ultimately prove fatal has, in a sense, already been inflicted. The pattern suggested by *Georgic* III is reversed. The final decision comes first, as Turnus prepares to lose not only kingdom and betrothed but life as well.[15]

The ironical implications which the simile — one of the longest in the poem — puts before the reader should not be treated lightly. To place at the crucial moment of the epic, when the destiny of nations is about to be weighed in the same balance as the lives of two fated men, lines partially drawn from a context where two maddened bulls clash for the love of an attractive heifer is to raise once again grave doubts about Aeneas, or, more precisely, about how the poet wishes his audience to view his hero's final actions. Much is said about Turnus' love for Lavinia in the opening lines, and even as he prepares for the ultimate meeting with Aeneas he is still the victim of what the poet calls love tormented by madness (line 668). Of any affection on Aeneas' part for the princess we are never told; nor is it ever implied that it existed at all. He can and will be as deliberately ruthless in the case of Lavinia's betrothed as he was himself un-wittingly cruel toward Dido. He is to marry Lavinia following the dictates of fate, not passion. But though love is absent, vio-lence remains, as the two bulls charge each other and the world watches in wonder. The animal nature of Turnus, powerful with the strength of personal involvement, has often been conveyed through metaphor and simile. This is the first time any such im-plication has been suggested concerning the character and achievement of Aeneas. It is not the last.

At this moment, however, the battle begins, and Turnus is immediately put on the defensive as his sword breaks. He flees swifter than the wind Eurus, the poet says, the very phrase he had used to describe the instant in which Hercules first put Cacus to flight (VIII, 223). The difference is that the inhuman monster of Book VIII has the cave in which he can take refuge. Turnus has no such recourse (lines 742–45):

> ergo amens diversa fuga petit aequora Turnus
> et nunc huc, inde huc incertos implicat orbis;
> undique enim densa Teucri inclusere corona
> atque hinc vasta palus, hinc ardua moenia cingunt.

Therefore Turnus madly takes flight, seeking different parts of the plain, and now here, now there, weaves an uncertain circular course. For on all sides the Trojans have hemmed him in with a crowd, and here a broad swamp, there lofty bastions, block his way.

The motif of the *incertos orbis* has been first established at line 481, when Juturna feels the need of avoiding a direct meeting between the two foes and sweeps her brother away from the fatal clash. The lion has been wounded and at first has fearlessly broken the spear and prepared to wage war against his pursuers. But escape is no longer possible. Madness is to be imprisoned (Virgil uses twice the verb *includere*, a favorite in connection with the wooden horse and Cacus alike),[16] and battle is as inevitable as it was between Hercules and the monster son of Vulcan (lines 763–65):

> quinque orbis explent cursu totidemque retexunt
> huc illuc; neque enim levia aut ludicra petuntur
> praemia, sed Turni de vita et sanguine certant.

Five circles they complete in their course and unweave as many, now here, now there. Nor are the prizes they seek light or sportive, but they vie for the life blood of Turnus.

One would expect that *Furor*, in the figure of Turnus, was pinned down for the last time and that from now on a spirit of rationality would prevail, as Juno gives up her hatred and all opposition falters. Such a happy outcome is apparently not Virgil's intent for, as Aeneas presses his chase, the poet adds another provocative simile whose intent is scarcely less veiled than the previous one (lines 748–57):

> insequitur trepidique pedem pede fervidus urget:
> inclusum veluti si quando flumine nactus
> cervum aut puniceae saeptum formidine pennae
> venator cursu canis et latratibus instat;
> ille autem insidiis et ripa territus alta
> mille fugit refugitque vias, at vividus Umber
> haeret hians, iam iamque tenet similisque tenenti
> increpuit malis morsuque elusus inani est:
> tum vero exoritur clamor ripaeque lacusque
> responsant circa et caelum tonat omne tumultu.

He pursues and hotly presses foot to foot against his trembling foe: as when a hunter hound has caught a stag penned in by a stream or hedged about through fear of crimson feathers, and runs upon him with a rush, barking. The stag, frightened by the snares and the high bank, runs a thousand ways to and fro in flight, but the eager Umbrian grabs at him with gaping jaws, and now, even now, holds him or, as if he were holding him, snaps his teeth, deceived with an empty mouthful. Then indeed a din arises. The banks and pools re-echo roundabout and all heaven thunders with the noise.

Here, too, Aeneas is the implacable foe, and, as at line 466 and following, the words call vividly to mind the triumphant manifestation of madness amidst the horror of Troy's collapse, Pyrrhus' vengeful massacre of Polites and Priam (II, 529–30):

> . . . illum ardens infesto vulnere Pyrrhus
> insequitur, iam iamque manu tenet et premit hasta.

Pyrrhus follows him in hot pursuit to inflict a dread wound and now, even now, grasps him with his hand and presses upon him with his spear.

But here it is no lion or fire-breathing giant Aeneas is following, raging and fearless, who can roam at will or shut himself into a deep den, but a simple stag, hemmed in and frightened by a stream and a cord of crimson feathers. And Aeneas, it turns out, is the raging hound who snaps at it and all but holds it in his jaws.[17]

We have observed before the importance of the adjective *puniceus* applied to the red feathers and have dwelt on the association Turnus has with blood. We have also seen how the setting of the first simile, in Punic fields, may possibly be meant to present a deliberate identification between Turnus and Dido as special victims of Aeneas. But there are only two similes in the epic specifically devoted to the hunting of a stag or doe, and Aeneas is involved in both. One has been quoted above. The other, of crucial importance for the metaphors it suggests which are elaborated as the book progresses, occurs at IV, 69–73, where Aeneas is compared to a shepherd and Dido to a deer, struck unintentionally by his shaft. The differences between the two similes could well be said to illustrate the change which seems to come over Aeneas as he prepares to do battle with his last foe. In Book IV he is a shepherd who has hit a doe, she unwary and he ignorant of his actions and of the extent of the harm he has wrought. Moreover, hunter though he is, he remains a human being. Book XII, on the contrary, finds Aeneas nothing but a savage dog, preparing to devour his hapless victim.

Turnus begins the book as the personification of violence, a lion whose vanity has been wounded, willing to rage against a destiny prepared to take from him his bride and homeland. Then for a moment the two foes become bulls challenging one another for the love of a female, Aeneas equated with an animal for the first time. Finally, as the end nears, Turnus has become only the frightened stag, Aeneas its vicious hunter — a hound who has taken to himself all the violence he has felt from others. The suppression of opposition leads Aeneas to a new level of force and violence, in a sense higher than that ever displayed by his antagonists because of the higher ideals shattered.

One brief episode separates this moment from a change of scene to the heavenly council between Jupiter and his consort. Aeneas' spear gets caught in the stump of a tree, but his mother loosens it after Juturna brings her brother the sword he had left behind. A seemingly unimportant incident, it is sufficient to defend its inclusion by noting how it furthers the action. Turnus is delivered fresh armor (his sword had just shattered against Aeneas' divine shield) and Aeneas' spear as a consequence is released from the clutches of the tree. But, since there has never been any mention previously of Aeneas' use of a spear, one seeks another reason for the significance of the episode and finds it in the figure of Faunus, the native Italian god of field and flock and the grandfather of Turnus. To him the tree has been sacred, but the Trojans had ruthlessly chopped it down to clear the field, *nullo discrimine* (line 770) — making no distinction — the same phrase Virgil had applied to Aeneas' mad slaughter not long before (line 498). If the poet means that the Trojans cared nothing for the land and deities of Italy, he also takes note of the fact that now even Faunus is forced to give up protecting his own. For a moment Turnus' prayer to Faunus for help and pity is answered and the tree holds Aeneas' spear with tight grip. But Venus, angered that Juturna can bring Turnus his sword, enters the action for the last time to release the spear.

It is a small triumph, but symbolically a disastrous one, not only for Turnus specifically but also, in spite of the promise Juno is about to extract from her husband, for what is truly Italian. If the death of Pallas dashes any hope for a renewal of the golden age which the pastoral beauty of Evander's kingdom had shown Aeneas as within the realm of possibility, the killing of Turnus is the death of another part of this very kingdom, a part as essentially and deeply Italian, as Evander knows (VIII, 314–15):

> "haec nemora indigenae Fauni Nymphaeque tenebant
> gensque virum truncis et duro robore nata . . ."

"In these groves dwelt native fauns and nymphs and a race of men sprung from tree trunks and hardy oak."

Aeneas acknowledges in VIII the need for one event to occur; the other he perpetrates himself. The help of Faunus is no longer available to Turnus, the aid of Juturna negated, as the scene shifts to the divine realms above.

This last meeting of Jupiter and Juno is another bow to tradition which offers the poet a further chance to digress from the chaos of the present world his imagination is creating and to dwell instead on the miraculous order into which that world will somehow be forged. Juno will give over her wrath. Trojan and Italian will be joined in happy union destined to produce empire on the grandest scale, as the peace for which Aeneas has longed comes into being. We have faced such a prediction at isolated moments before — Jupiter's glorious prophecy in Book I, and the triumphant prefiguring of future power which flashes and thunders across the stage at the ends of Books VI and VIII, where heroism is joined to the pastoral humility of Evander's achievement to form a perfect vision of future Rome. But the ideal view of Aeneas' fated progress through history, ever-present as it is in Virgil's mind, is constantly shattered by the need to clash with the fallible and the emotional, with individuality and with human nature, which of itself gives little thought to the grander, more brilliant schemes of national achievement when life and freedom are at stake.

Before his role is clarified, Aeneas can remain aloof from the responsibility of directly opposing or accepting those who form this antagonistic world; who are touched and even wounded by this unusually emotionless, spiritually guided tool of destiny as he brushes by. For a while there is no defense needed for such an attitude, even to the time in Book VI when he meets former acquaintances and reviews his former life, as he and the Sibyl grope their way along the murky paths of the underworld. Deiphobus and his homeland of Troy, Dido, Palinurus — all were milestones in a journey toward a promised land still shrouded in mystery. There was no necessity for Aeneas to accept the world in which they lived or to give in to the particular emotional crises provoked by the events of which they were the symbols. Destiny and Aeneas, its vehicle, need not yet meet the challenge of the individual.

The end of VI, however, opened up broader vistas, made more apparent by the exploration of the site of future Rome. By committing himself to Italy and to the foundation of the race whence such a splendid future would spring, Aeneas makes a pledge to history which demands that the idealism of his cause be at last pitted against the realities which its achievement necessitates. Aeneas must now fight and accept the challenge he had hitherto disregarded, face Lausus and Mezentius on the field of battle, and feel direct responsibility for the death of Pallas. Above all he must meet Turnus who embodies so much, not only of the strength of Italy against which Aeneas had already stood his ground, but also, much more subtly, of the power of opposition and forced suffering in the past — Troy's doom and Dido's suicide.

The outcome is the copestone of Virgilian pessimism; the ultimate example as well of the suffering and sacrifice demanded in compensation for Aeneas' accomplishments. Through the potent uses of poetic imagery, Virgil has concentrated in and focused upon Turnus key moments of past trial, beginning with Dido and the downfall of Troy, and ending only in the very last line of the poem, which takes the attentive reader suddenly back to the death of Camilla (XI, 831).

Turnus stands for the world of Italy, that strange combination of wildness and pastoral order. In spite of Juno's plea to Jupiter, it is this world which Aeneas destroys, and with a lack of mercy singularly pronounced because it gives the lie both to Anchises' utterances about the future nobility of Roman conduct and to Jupiter's scarcely finished declaration about the happy union to be attained. The tragedy of the destruction of Turnus and his world does much to negate any romantic notion of the *Aeneid* as an ideal vision of the greatness of Augustan Rome, and it negates, too, the image of Virgil as its poet-laureate, preaching moderation, mercy, and a certain humility which such a far-reaching accomplishment as that of Augustus could well bear. The Augustan Age, by creating some order after decades of chaos, in a sense merits the epithet "classical" so often bestowed upon it. But only the most superficial reading of the *Aeneid* as a whole can find in its hero a model for Augustus or, more unfortunate still, a glorification of the accomplishments of Rome through his character and life. The forces of violence and irrationality which swirl around Aeneas, through person and event and their accompanying symbols, lead ultimately not to his triumph over them (even before the conclusion of Book XII his readiness to succumb to their power at almost every turn was offset more by divine interference than by innate strength), but rather to complete submission, whose suddenness in the poem's concluding lines adds a note of emphasis so strong as to be undeniable in any realistic accounting of the total epic.

It is Aeneas who loses at the end of Book XII, leaving Turnus victorious in his tragedy. Aeneas fails to incorporate the ideal standards, proper for the achievement and maintenance of empire, in his struggle with the individual who embodies the emotionality of all opposition, of fallible man against infallible fate. He loses sight of what his father defined as Rome's grand mission (VI, 851–53):

> "tu regere imperio populos, Romane, memento
> (hae tibi erunt artes), pacisque imponere morem,
> parcere subiectis et debellare superbos."

"You, o Roman, remember to rule nations with your sway — these will be your arts — and to impose the tradition of peace, to spare the humbled and crush the proud."

The creation of empire demands the humbling of opposition by a deed of heroism which both equates itself with, and then transcends, human nature. For, paradoxically, it is by an act which both rejects and receives mankind that true heroism can humble itself in order to spare the humbled, and thus can reorder life by accepting the defeated back into society without the imposition of the finality of death. A larger world-view does not stipulate death as the price of empire or falsely equate private hatred with heroic achievement.

This is the one moment in which the two spheres could be reconciled, and individual man subordinated to, and yet united with, the larger universals of history and the development of empire. Aeneas fails, initially, because he kills the suppliant craving pardon at his feet at the very instant when reconciliation would not only be possible, but would prove that the triumph of empire was not at the cost of personal rights and liberty. Instead, the end of the *Aeneid* presents a tragic victory of the very violence and irrationality which Aeneas had up to this point withstood. By giving himself over with such suddenness to the private wrath which the sight of the belt of Pallas arouses, Aeneas becomes himself *impius Furor*, as rage wins the day over moderation, disintegration defeats order, and the achievements of history through heroism fall victim to the human frailty of one man.

Thus it is that as the death-scene commences we find that all the majesty of Jupiter is not so much expressly on the side of Aeneas as it is against Turnus, and that the means he uses to accomplish his purpose is one of the *Dirae*, upon whom Juno had called in Book VII. The instrument formerly used to stir up wrath against Aeneas is now his ally in bringing not only madness but death to his enemy. We learn something of these twin plagues from line 849 and following:

> hae Iovis ad solium saevique in limine regis
> apparent acuuntque metum mortalibus aegris,
> si quando letum horrificum morbosque deum rex
> molitur, meritas aut bello territat urbes.

They dwell by the throne of Jupiter, on the threshold of the fierce king, and sharpen the fears of feeble mortals, whenever the king of the gods plans dread death or diseases, or terrifies guilty cities with war.

This is not the first hint we have had of Turnus' illness. As early as line 46, it will be remembered, the words of Latinus, however well-intentioned, do little to calm his violence. Rather Turnus, the poet says, grows sicker at the attempted cure (*aegrescit medendo*). The *Dira*, the disease personified, who now flaps her wings in front of Turnus to announce impending doom, brings this sickness to the point of death.[18]

Once more it is the programme of *Georgic* III that helps us to observe a part, at least, of Virgil's intent in this final scene. He summarizes his message succinctly at lines 64–68 of that poem:

> solve mares; mitte in Venerem pecuaria primus
> atque aliam ex alia generando suffice prolem.
> optima quaeque dies miseris mortalibus aevi
> prima fugit: subeunt morbi tristisque senectus
> et labor, et durae rapit inclementia mortis.

Let loose the males; send first your flocks to mate and supply one generation after another by breeding. It is the happiest days in the life of pitiful mortals that are the first to flee. Disease and sad old age and toil creep in, and the ruthlessness of harsh death snatches away its booty.

Feed your flocks and breed them while the time is ripe. Live happily while you can, because soon disease or old age will be upon you and, close upon its heels, death. This outline could not be given more cogent expression than in the third *Georgic* itself which adheres quite strictly to such a pattern, beginning with the care and fostering of animals and ending with their utter annihilation, as the plague rages freely through the world of nature, touching even those humans who minister to the victims. It is part of Virgil's plan that the very person who brings this destruction is Tisiphone, one of the *Dirae*. The poet's words in *Georgic* III, 551–53, are intriguingly close to the reasons Jupiter gives for sending the Fury in *Aeneid* XII:

> saevit et in lucem Stygiis emissa tenebris
> pallida Tisiphone Morbos agit ante Metumque,
> inque dies avidum surgens caput altius effert.

Pale Tisiphone rages, let loose into the light from the Stygian shades, and drives ahead of her Diseases and Fear. Growing with every day, she carries her greedy head ever higher.

The two themes which dominate *Georgic* III, then, are exactly these: the fostering of animals (a topic which allows the poet to comment so strongly on the *furor* of love) and their death. One leads directly and inevitably to the other. We have seen the love motif of *Aeneid* XII established with the help of *Georgic* III. Aeneas and Turnus are seen imagistically as bulls quarreling over a female with such madness as to seem themselves to be indeed part of the animal world. But the cloud of death, too, hangs over the epic's final book from the start, as we have observed. Even as we plunge into the action, the breaking of the truce and the various events which are its result, we can never lose sight of the fact that Turnus has received his incurable wound and that, in spite of initial moments of prowess on a battlefield essentially empty of opposition, he will ultimately become Aeneas' victim, the last and greatest sacrifice demanded in token of the final disappearance of resistance and the seeming inauguration of a new era of peace. Like the sacrifice of Palinurus, the death of Turnus looks two ways — to the defeat of Italy and hence subordination of all Italian elements to Trojan domination; and to an amalgamation which, as Jupiter vows, will lead to an unparalleled accumulation of power and extent of dominion. Though he elsewhere pays brilliant homage to the future that is Rome, in Book XII the poet neither allows nor wants us to experience this glory as he concentrates the wrath of Jupiter, and his minion Aeneas, and the force of destiny on the figure of Turnus.

It is true, as has often been argued, that in these last books Aeneas is in some ways modeled on Achilles,[19] but the end of XII destroys anything beyond the most superficial likeness. There is no *Iliad* XXIV when Achilles can reconcile the satiety of hatred which his heroism deems vital with a return to the uses of humanity. The progress of empire, as Virgil puts it before the reader, is attributed only to madness, vengeance, and death. The slaying of Turnus is the ultimate, all-embracing tragedy of the *Aeneid*.

The transition from the beginning of the final battle to the actual moment of supplication and death is also partially carried out through reference to *Georgic* III. Several details are especially salient. Of the episodes which intervene in *Georgic* III between the description of breeding and of the plague, two seem to have appealed particularly to Virgil. One is the splendid portrayal of the deadly viper, that bitter pest of cattle, which leads immediately into the pessimistic ending and was utilized in good measure as the basis of the snake imagery in *Aeneid* II. The other, which is likewise redolent of the potentiality of death, is Virgil's passing fascination with the Scythians who eke out their lives overwhelmed with ice and snow. When Virgil describes the breaking of Turnus' sword (lines 739–41) —

> . . . postquam arma dei ad Volcania ventum est,
> mortalis mucro glacies ceu futtilis ictu
> dissiluit; fulva resplendent fragmina harena.

When his blade met the armor of Vulcan, the mortal sword was shattered like brittle ice. The fragments sparkle on the yellow sand . . . —

he may be thinking back to the dire effects of the chilling cold on life among the Scythians (*G.* III, 363–65):

> aeraque dissiliunt vulgo, vestesque rigescunt
> indutae, caeduntque securibus umida vina,
> et totae solidam in glaciem vertere lacunae . . .

Everywhere brass splits, clothes freeze on the wearer. They cut the liquid wine with axes, and whole lakes turn into solid ice.

The possibility gains point from the subsequent elucidation of how the barbarians hunt under such conditions (*G.* III, 371–75):

> hos non immissis canibus, non cassibus ullis
> puniceaeve agitant pavidos formidine pennae,
> sed frustra oppositum trudentis pectore montem
> comminus obtruncant ferro graviterque rudentis
> caedunt et magno laeti clamore reportant.

They do not hunt these deer with hounds let loose or with any nets, nor do they herd them frightened through fear of the crimson feathers; but with the sword they cut them down at close quarters, as they push in vain with their chests against the mass before them and bellow pitifully. Then with loud shouts of joy they bring them home.

We have stressed above the impressive detail of the *puniceae pennae* and its importance. That the image comes from *Georgic* III and is utilized again by the poet at the very moment when the frozen hand of death is about to put a firm grip upon Turnus, lends it further force. In the simile of XII, 749ff, the stag can still move. There, too, some of the vitality of the passage is borrowed from a brief reference to the breeding of hunting dogs which follows forthwith in *Georgic* III. But it is not long before the sight of the *Dira* brings the chill breath of doom to Turnus (lines 867–68):

illi membra novus solvit formidine torpor,
arrectaeque horrore comae et vox faucibus haesit.

A strange numbness caused by fear unknits his frame. His hair stood
up in terror and his utterance clung to his throat.

And this picture is elaborated in turn at the very moment of his
collapse when the poet says that his blood stood frozen stiff from
the chill (*gelidus concrevit frigore sanguis*, line 905). In the
third *Georgic* the death of the cattle from the cold leads the
poet's mind swiftly to the plague which overwhelms the whole
world of nature (lines 368–70):

intereunt pecudes, stant circumfusa pruinis
corpora magna boum, confertoque agmine cervi
torpent mole nova et summis vix cornibus exstant.

The cattle die. The great bodies of the oxen stand surrounded with
frost. Stags herded together grow numb from the strange mass and the
tips of their horns scarcely rise above it.

For Turnus the chill of death and the disease sent by Jupiter in
the form of the Fury are one and the same thing.

This winged monster, who stirred up Turnus in VII and now
sides with Aeneas to kill him, has much in common with Somnus, the winged messenger of Neptune's doom to Palinurus.
"Mene huic confidere monstro?" — "Am I to put faith in that
monster?" — Palinurus asks of the disguised Sleep, little knowing
that he is the slave of the prodigious ocean come to force the confidence the pilot rejects. When Juturna cries (line 874) *"talin
possum me opponere monstro?"* — "Can I confront such a monster?" — she is looking directly at the monster itself, sent like a
poisoned arrow to batter in the guise of an owl against the shield
of the hapless warrior.

Turnus faces and accepts the unavoidable — faces it alone.
For this is the time when Juturna, who cannot oppose the dam-
nation of Jupiter, must desert her brother. The *Dira* brings with
it the last and perhaps most pathetic of the many references in

Book XII associating Turnus with Dido. Line 871, which immediately precedes Juturna's sad speech of renunciation —

> unguibus ora soror foedans et pectora pugnis

the sister tearing at her face with her nails and beating her breast —

comes word for word from that instant (IV, 673) at which Anna realizes the suicide of her sister and its meaning in the wider context of history (IV, 682–83):

> "exstinxti te meque, soror, populumque patresque
> Sidonios urbemque tuam."

"My sister, you have destroyed yourself and me, the people, the Sidonian senate and your city."

That this remains unsaid in XII does not prevent the last moments of Turnus from having a particularly moving gravity and power. Virgil borrows constantly — but with his usual care and variation — from *Iliad* XXII as Hector flees beneath the walls of Troy and succumbs to the wrath of Achilles. Above all, he re-creates the atmosphere of dream and fantasy so pervasive in *Aeneid* II and so overpowering in *Iliad* XXII. In the latter, both heroes are unconscious of the real world which surrounds and complements their superhuman clash, the world of towers and springs, city and plain. But the dream is really Hector's alone, for the dream is death (*Iliad* XXII, 199–201):

Just as in a dream a man cannot pursue someone who flees from him; the one is not able to escape, neither is the other capable of pursuit: thus Achilles was unable to overtake Hector as he ran, nor was Hector able to escape.

Turnus' fate is also a dream, this time nearer the moment of death itself (lines 908–14):

> ac velut in somnis, oculos ubi languida pressit
> nocte quies, nequiquam avidos extendere cursus
> velle videmur et in mediis conatibus aegri
> succidimus; non lingua valet, non corpore notae

sufficiunt vires nec vox aut verba sequuntur:
sic Turno, quacumque viam virtute petivit,
successum dea dira negat.

As in dreams, when by night languid sleep weighs down the eye, we seem to desire in vain to pursue our eager course and in the midst of the endeavor fainting we fail; the tongue has no strength, the body does not provide its usual power; neither voice nor words follow: thus, wherever he valiantly sought escape, the dread goddess denied Turnus success.

But at his moment of death he gains a peculiar vengeance. There is no weeping, no hymn of praise and sorrow, such as accompanied Hector's demise, nor is there any attempt to mitigate Aeneas' wrath or to draw him once again back into the world of the living, as Homer does for Achilles in *Iliad* XXIV. What there is is the madness of Aeneas as he views the belt of Pallas (lines 945–49):

ille, oculis postquam saevi monimenta doloris
exuviasque hausit, furiis accensus et ira
terribilis: "tune hinc spoliis indute meorum
eripiare mihi? Pallas te hoc vulnere, Pallas
immolat et poenam scelerato ex sanguine sumit."

He, after he had drunk in with his eyes the trophy, that memorial of his fierce grief, burning with rage and fearful in his wrath: "Art thou, clad in the spoils of one I loved, to be torn hence from me? Pallas it is, Pallas who slaughters you with this wound and exacts vengeance from your tainted blood."

And with his words we turn once more and for the last time to the opening lines of the epic — to Juno as she ponders the reasons for her anger and bitter griefs (*causae irarum saevique dolores*), and plots a new series of trials for the Trojan hero which last until this very moment.

When the epic opened it was Aeneas' turn to shudder with cold as the winds, the first pawns of Juno's anger, threatened imminent death (*solvuntur frigore membra*: I, 92). Now, as the poem reaches its climax, it is one of Virgil's most bitter and cogent ironies that he uses this very phrase at the exact moment

Aeneas becomes the personification of avenging wrath and brings death to Turnus.[20] The wheel has come full circle. It should cause little wonder when Juno seems to surrender so readily to Jupiter's plea that she give over her anger in contemplation of future Roman magnificence. For, according to the poet's wishes, it is she, not Aeneas, nor the grandeur for which Augustus seems to stand, who wins the greatest victory as the soul of Turnus passes with a resentful moan to the shades below.

NOTES

INDEX OF PASSAGES

GENERAL INDEX

ABBREVIATIONS OF JOURNALS USED IN THE NOTES

AJP	*American Journal of Philology*
Am. Lit.	*American Literature*
CJ	*Classical Journal*
CP	*Classical Philology*
CQ	*Classical Quarterly*
CR	*Classical Review*
CW	*Classical Weekly — Classical World*
ÉtCl.	*Les Études classiques*
G&R	*Greece and Rome*
HSCP	*Harvard Studies in Classical Philology*
JHS	*Journal of Hellenic Studies*
JRS	*Journal of Roman Studies*
Jahr. Arch.	*Jahrbuch des Deutschen Archäologischen Instituts*
Jahr. für class. Phil.	*Jahrbuch für classische Philologie*
RhM	*Rheinisches Museum für Philologie*
SbHeid	*Sitzungsberichte der Heidelberger Akademie der Wissenschaften, Philos.-Hist. Klasse*
TAPA	*Transactions and Proceedings of the American Philological Association*

*   *   *   *

The abbreviation *RE* refers to the Pauly-Wissowa-Kroll *Realencyclopädie der classischen Altertumswissenschaft.*

NOTES

Chapter 1   *Aeneid* Book II: Madness and Flight

1. I am much indebted in the pages which follow to the admirable analysis of the imagery of Book II by Bernard M. W. Knox, "The Serpent and the Flame: The Imagery of the Second Book of the Aeneid," *AJP* 71 (1950) 379–400. For supplementary bibliographical information, see G. Duckworth, "Recent Work on Vergil (1940–1956)," *CW* 51 (1958) 153.

2. On the wooden horse in general, see W. F. J. Knight, "The Wooden Horse," *CP* 25 (1930) 358–66, and "Epilegomena to 'The Wooden Horse'," *CP* 26 (1931) 412–20.

The idea of the horse as a womb is traditional, as is that of pregnancy, and is Roman as well as Greek (see, e.g., Ennius frag. sc. 76V³). See R. G. Austin, "Virgil and the Wooden Horse," *JRS* 49 (1959) 17ff. The word *ingens* (especially in conjunction with the word *cavernas*) also has connotations of pregnancy (see *Aen.* III,390 = VIII,43). The "life" of the horse is perhaps the most exciting ambiguity evident throughout the description. Cf. Knox (above, n. 1), esp. 384–85, n. 12.

3. There are many parellels for the nautical ambiguities suggested. I mention a few random examples. On *uterus* as "hold," see Tac. *Ann.* II, 6, and on *cavernae* as the ribs of a ship see Lucr. II, 553 (and Bailey's note thereto for further instances). For *latus* as the side of a ship, see *Aen.* I, 105, and Hor. *c.* I, 14, 4. Further instances of the latter may be found in *de Or.* III, 180. On *cavernae* in this sense see Servius on II, 19.

Servius quotes instances of the use of *aedifico* and *texo* in connection with shipbuilding in his note on line 16. For the latter word one might add Ennius frag. sc. 66V³ (and cf. the use of *textrum* in *Ann.* frag. 477V³ which comes from a note of Servius on *Aen.* XI, 326, commenting once again on the same use of *texo*.).

4. The idea gains point when compared with *Aen.* I, 419–20:

> iamque ascendebant collem, qui plurimus urbi
> imminet adversasque aspectat desuper arces.

And now they climbed the hill that rises loftily over the city and looks down on the buildings that confront it.

The horse looks on the city from above, not only because it is placed on the *arx* but also purely on grounds of its own size. Likewise, for reasons of its height and bulk, and only secondarily for the threat it poses, it is *minans*, threatening (line 240, with which cf. *Aen*. I, 162; II, 628, and elsewhere).

5. And uses of *latebrae* and *insidiae* parallel to *dolum* (line 44) may be found at lines 36, 38, 55, 65, and, secondarily, 195.

6. The motif of the breaking open of the city walls is a cumulative one beginning with line 27 (*panduntur portae*), receiving strong emphasis at line 234, and leading finally to line 266 as, with the gates opened (*portis patentibus*), the occupants of the horse meet happily with their brethren newly arrived from Tenedos. This same image recurs a moment later when we learn that the wiles of the Greeks have now become clear (*Danaumque patescunt insidiae*). Like the city gates and then the *latebrae* within the horse's belly, everything has been opened when at last the deceits of the Greeks become clear to all.

On the breaching of the walls, see W. F. J. Knight, "The Wooden Horse at the Gate of Troy," *CJ* 28 (1933) 254–62 and G. Duckworth, "Magical Circles and the Fall of Troy," *CJ* 40 (1944) 99–103. The horse glides in on slippery wheels (*rotarum lapsus*, lines 235–36). The fact that one of the two other cases where Virgil uses *rotae* with a combination of *labor* occurs at *Aen*. I, 147, may not be completely coincidental. Incongruous as a comparison between the huge lumbering horse and Neptune's speeding water chariot may at first seem, the latent metaphor of a ship associated with the horse (especially when taken in conjunction with the snake imagery to be discussed shortly) may be offered as a partial reconciliation. The horse is much more speedy and supple certainly than the Trojans suspect. To convey this quality of litheness through ambiguity must then be considered a specific part of the poet's intent.

A detailed analysis of how the ship imagery is developed is in itself interesting. I present a few of the ambiguities. *Lapsus rotarum* must be taken literally as a poetic figure meaning only wheels, but the notion of gliding and floating which the phrase suggests passes into the verb *inlabitur* (line 240). *Labor* is used of a ship at least twice by Virgil (*Aen*. VIII, 91, and X, 687). Likewise *funis* could be considered the cable by which a ship is hauled or moored, as well as the bridle of a horse, and is so used regularly by the poet (e.g. *G*. I, 457; *Aen*. III, 266 and 639; IV, 575; V, 773; VIII, 708). *Vinculum* has also the same meaning (cf. *Aen*. I, 168; IX, 118; X, 233). The horse glides swiftly as a ship, on its overland course.

For possible connections between the wooden horse and imagery of ships in the literary tradition inherited by Virgil see Austin (above, n. 2) 22–23.

7. The verb *reddo*, which the poet uses, in line 260, of the horse opening its belly, can also be used of a ship unloading passengers. Servius, in his note on the line, is reminded of such a usage in Horace *c*. I, 3, 7.

8. On the place of the storm in the larger perspective of the epic and especially on its position in Bk. I balanced by the Allecto episode in VII, see V. Pöschl, *Die Dichtkunst Virgils* (Innsbruck 1950) chap. 1, *passim*.

9. Virgil has in mind, during this whole passage, a splendid description by Lucretius (VI, 189–203) of winds churning up storm clouds. J. Henry (*Aeneidea* I, pp. 266–67) sensed in these lines the inherent metaphor of horses, which can be elaborated at length. With the whole passage cf. *G.* III, 179ff, where, to turn the tables, horses are compared with winds. In *G.* III, 196–201, the vocabulary reflects closely the description of the storm the winds create in *Aen.* I.

On the verb *incutio*, see commentators on Lucretius I, 13 and 923–24; VI, 772. If Heinsius' conjecture is correct, there is an excellent example of its connection with whipping in *Aen.* XI, 727–28, where Jupiter urges Tarchon into battle:

Tyrrhenum genitor Tarchonem in proelia saeva
suscitat et stimulis haud mollibus incutit iras.

The father rouses Tyrrhenian Tarchon to fierce battle and goads his wrath with no gentle spur.

Ennius, *Ann.* frag. 512V³, also uses the final phrase, as quoted by Servius on I, 69. Cf. the use of *concutio* in *Aen.* XI, 451ff, where the poet makes subtle use of the metaphor of horses to describe the youth clamoring for arms. See also *Aen.* V, 146–47; VI, 100–1; VIII, 3. The difficulties of the phrase *fecundum concute pectus*, in VII, 338, may also be at least partially explained thereby. We also find there emphasis on the unruly *iuventus* as in XI, 451ff, a motif inherited from the *ignobile vulgus* of I, 149.

For *fremo* cf., e.g., Lucretius V, 1076 and 1316ff, and *Aen.* XI, 496, 599, 607.

10. The phrase *pectora mulcens* occurs in a passage of Lucretius where he describes a vain attempt to soothe the hearts of war-horses, terrified by the sudden appearance of lions (V, 1317).

11. The final lines of *Georgic* I offer a kindred example of how Virgil's mind, when seeking to elaborate thoughts centered on potential destruction, turned to a charioteer helplessly following his raging steeds (lines 510–14):

vicinae ruptis inter se legibus urbes
arma ferunt; saevit toto Mars impius orbe;
ut cum carceribus sese effudere quadrigae,
addunt in spatio, et frustra retinacula tendens
fertur equis auriga neque audit currus habenas.

Neighboring cities, their covenants broken, bear arms against each other.

Impious Mars rages the whole world over, as when chariots pour forth from behind the gates and speed one after another along the course, and the charioteer is borne along by his steeds, pulling back on the reins in vain, and the chariot heeds not the curb.

Impius Mars is simply a particular manifestation of *impius Furor* whose connection with the winds and the wooden horse will be discussed shortly. The simile is prepared for in line 510 with the phrase *ruptis legibus*. Laws keep men happy and living together in peace. When they are broken, all evils pour forth, as when the gates are opened at a chariot race and, in turn, the horses tear along out of control. S. P. Bovie ("Imagery of Ascent-Descent in Vergil's *Georgics*," *AJP* 77 [1956] 337–58) finds in the simile the final picture of Italy's decline into civil war.

12. *Aen.* VI, 734. For other uses of *carcer* in connection with horses cf. Ennius, *Ann.* frag. 85V³ and 484V³; Lucretius II, 263–64, and IV, 990; Hor. *s.* I, 1, 114; *G.* I, 512 (quoted above) and III, 104; *Aen.* V, 145.

13. Cf. the phrase *clauso carcere* in line 141. Horace (*e.* I, 14, 9) uses the metaphor of *claustra* to describe the barriers, mental and in a sense physical, which keep him tied down in Rome and away from his beloved villa.

14. The imagery is reminiscent of XII, 441ff, to be discussed later. Cf. the similar use of *ruunt* to describe headlong racers in *G.* III, 104 (= *Aen.* V, 145).

15. One need not elaborate the mythological link between Neptune and the origin of horses (see *G.* III, 122). A survey of certain specialized aspects of the mythology of horses is offered by A. B. Cook, "Animal Worship in the Mycenaean Age," *JHS* 14 (1894) 81–169 (esp. pt. v: "The Cult of the Horse," pp. 138–50). See also J. E. Harrison *Prolegomena*, pp. 179 and 387–88, and G. M. A. Hanfmann "ΛΥΔΙΑΚΑ," *HSCP* 63 (1958) 76–79.

For a further ambiguous use of *cuspis* as trident, see Ovid *M.* XII, 580, and with this situation in *Aen.* I cf. Lucan II, 456–57.

The equation between horses and violence is made explicit by the poet on more than one occasion. The clearest example is Anchises' interpretation of the omen of the four horses, the first creatures sighted as the Trojans near the eastern shore of Italy (*Aen.* III, 537–43). Likewise, in *Aen.* I, 444, a horse serves as the symbol of the warlike propensities of the Carthaginians as well as the *signum* of their state. But more often than not the metaphor is a hidden one. For example, it is latent in a reference such as Jupiter's to Italy as a land teeming with empire and raging with war (*gravidam imperiis belloque frementem*: IV, 229). In connection with this line, Conington rightly refers to X, 87:

"quid gravidam bellis urbem et corda aspera temptas?"

"Why do you meddle with violent hearts and a city pregnant with war?" Finally in G. III, 275, the poet describes how mares become pregnant by the wind, a detail which is in part a further rationalization of the welter of mythological references pointing to the close connection between horses and winds.

On the religious association of horses with death, see L. Malten, "Das Pferd im Totenglauben," *Jahr. Arch.* 29 (1914), 180–255.

16. Virgil utilizes the word *cuspis* to depict Laocoön's instrument in line 230. The parallelism between the two events is surely also a proof (Henry to the contrary) that the point of the spear-trident was used by Aeolus, not the butt end, to release the winds. Of the many verbal correspondences between the two episodes it is perhaps sufficient to note here the repetition of *latus*, of the adjective *cavus*, and the verb *impello* (I, 82; II, 55). Austin (above, n. 2) p. 18 and n. 5, has recently shown that the detail of Laocoön's spear-throw is probably an addition of Virgil's own to the legend of the horse. If so, the parallel with the events in Bk. I takes on still further meaning in any elucidation of the unique in Virgil's imagination.

17. Cf. Bk. II, 51. *Laxus* is also used similarly in G. II, 364. In fact, both *laxo* and *laxus* are commonly associated with certain aspects of sailing (cf., e.g., *Aen.* III, 267; VI, 412; VIII, 708).

The noun *compages* occurs three times in the *Aeneid*: here to describe the ship; in I, 293, associated with the doors of the building in which *Furor* is imprisoned; and in II, 51, as part of the construction of the wooden horse. The difference between the first two of these three instances can be viewed in terms of a tension between *artus* and *laxus*. See Lucr. IV, 1113 and 1205; VI, 1071 (with which cf. line 1016 in the same book). In IV, 1205, Lucretius seems to treat *compages* as synonymous with *nodi* — knots — which also help tie down *Furor* in *Aen.* I, 296.

18. The verb *includo* appears in II at lines 19 and 258. *Clauso carcere* is used of the winds at I, 141. The concealing of the men in the horse (II, 18–19: *furtim includunt*) finds its parallel in Jupiter's hiding of the winds (I, 60: *abdidit*).

19. G. II, 216; III, 544.

20. In this episode, too, there are parallels with the storm in I (e.g., with line 205, cf. I, 84–86; with line 212, cf. I, 82).

21. For a more detailed exposition of the "snake" imagery in Bk. II, see B. M. W. Knox (above, n. 1) *passim*.

22. Lines 236–37 — *et stuppea vincula collo / intendunt* (and they stretch cords of rope around its neck) — have a special importance of their own. For *vincula* can be not only the horse's bridle (there is a good metaphorical example in Val. Max. II, 9, 5), but the tether that

keeps it properly stabled (see the use of *vincla* in *Aen.* XI, 492). The irony of the passage lies in the words *stuppea* (how far will mere hemp endure against such a creature!) and *funem* (line 239) which, though serving to draw the horse into the city, looks ahead but a few lines to the rope by means of which the hidden Greeks descend from the horse's paunch.

Other ambiguities applied to the horse — its double nature as both alive and dead, and its hyperbolic quality as mountain and ship — are also present here. *Vincula* are the chains which hold a prisoner within his cell (the word is used in I, 54, of the bonds with which Aeolus controls his horse-winds) but they are likewise the cables which hold a ship to its mooring (see, e.g., *Aen.* I, 168).

For this reason there may be more to the phrase *rotarum lapsus* than first meets the eye. We have noted elsewhere a possible connection between *inlabitur* (line 240) and the gliding of a ship (see above, n. 6). It is also possible that the phrase *rotarum lapsus* as used by Virgil is simply a poetic euphemism for the ὁλκοί or κύλινδροι which were used as rollers to draw a ship overland. Cf. Gomme on Thuc. III.15.1. A χαμουλκός was apparently the same thing (cf. Amm. Marc. XVII, 4, 14). The φάλαγγες (Lat. *phalangae*) were also rollers used for the same purpose. See Kiessling-Heinze on Hor. *c.* I,4,2, and the definition and references in Lewis and Short.

23. The idea of the horse "leaping" into the city, used by Ennius in his *Alexander* (frag. *sc.* 76V³), is adopted by Deiphobus in his description of the fall of Troy (VI, 515–16) —

> cum fatalis equus saltu super ardua venit
> Pergama et armatum peditem gravis attulit alvo . . .

when the fatal horse with a leap climbed over the heights of Pergamum and, its belly teeming, brought in armed might.

The equating of Sinon with the horse in lines 328–30, at last explicit and deliberate, gains further point when compared to *G.* III, 499, where the phrase *victor equus*, words used separately in the *Aeneid*, is applied to a triumphant steed alone.

24. See the perceptive remarks by B. Fenik, "Parallelism of Theme and Imagery in *Aeneid* II and IV," *AJP* 80 (1959) 7–8.

25. On the differences in plot between this episode and the *Doloneia* of *Iliad* X, and on the quality of the episode as a whole, see A. Cartault, *L'Art de Virgile dans l'Énéide* (Paris 1926) 666–675.

26. Cf. also the use of *cupido* in VI, 721.

27. Cf., e.g., IX, 320ff, with VI, 26off.

28. With lines 440–41 cf. lines 379–80.

Chapter 2 *Aeneid* Book V: Game and Reality

1. Servius, ed. Thilo and Hagen (Leipzig 1881), on V, 1 ("cuius pars maior ex Homero sumpta est: nam omnia quae hic commemorat, exhibentur circa tumulum Patrocli"). He goes on in the same sentence: "nisi quod illic curule exercetur, hic navale certamen" ("except that in Homer there is a contest with chariots, in Virgil a naval battle").

2. J. Huizinga, *Homo Ludens: A Study of the Play Element in Culture* (Boston 1955) chap. 1, *passim*.

3. Cf., e.g., 89 and 609, and n. 11 below.

4. *Respexi*: II, 741. Cf. also *G.* IV, 491 — Orpheus looking back at Eurydice.

5. We are fortunate in having a fresh commentary devoted to Bk. V alone (P. Vergili Maronis, *Aeneidos, Liber Quintus*, ed. R. D. Williams, Oxford, 1960), hereafter referred to as "Williams." For a supplementary up-to-date bibliography of literature on Bk. V, see G. Duckworth, "Recent Work on Vergil (1940–56)," *CW* 51 (1958) 154–55.

6. Servius proposes two meanings for the word *olli*, "aut tunc: aut illi," but the parallel with Bk. III seems to eliminate any possibility of an adverb here.

7. For other parallels, cf. *astitit* (line 10) with *consedit* (line 841), and with the phrase *noctem hiememque ferens* (line 11) cf. *somnia tristia portans* (line 840). Somnus, of course, takes Palinurus' wonted position *puppi alta* (lines 12 and 841). The verb *incumbo* is also repeated in lines 15 and 858 (cf. its menacing implications in line 325). With the phrase *supra caput astitit* cf. IV, 702, where Iris stands over the dying Dido.

8. Since, as detailed above, the boat race offers other close parallels with Palinurus' situation, the book is unified in typically Virgilian fashion, with the opening lines proposing the themes and imagery which dominate the whole. In similar fashion, the initial description of the labyrinth in Bk. VI may reflect at least partially the course of Aeneas' underworld journey. Professor Pöschl has pointed out to me in conversation that there may consequently be a deliberate parallel between Daedalus-Icarus and Augustus-Marcellus. For a recent moderate approach to the sculpture of Daedalus and its role in Bk. VI, see P. J. Enk, "De labyrinthi imagine in foribus templi Cumani insculpta (Vergilii Aen. VI 27)," *Mnemosyne*, ser. 4, 11 (1958) 322–30.

9. Though the fire imagery changes from baleful to productive during the course of Bk. II itself, there is only a partial resolution of the snake imagery. Doubtless this sensation of latent danger is meant to continue over into the scene around Anchises' tomb.

10. There are other details which associate Aeneas' action in Bk. V with Laocoön; e.g., Laocoön comes to make his speech, protesting the

acceptance of the Trojan horse, accompanied by a great crowd (*magna comitante caterva*: II, 40) in exactly the same manner as Aeneas arrives at his father's tomb (V, 76).

11. The most striking feature of the snake itself is its brightness and sheen (lines 87–89):

> caeruleae cui terga notae maculosus et auro
> squamam incendebat fulgor, ceu nubibus arcus
> mille iacit varios adverso sole colores.

Its back was spotted with dark markings and its scales blazed with gold's bright gleam, as a rainbow in the sun's slanting rays throws out a thousand varied hues from the clouds.

Here also the description suggests hidden violence, since the vivid imagery takes the reader out of this specific context and looks to the figure of Iris. She it was who had appeared during Dido's death and who comes once again in the course of Bk. V, this time on a mission of destruction. To the relief of Dido's tortured spirit she had arrived (IV, 701)

> mille trahens varios adverso sole colores.

bringing a thousand varied hues in the sun's slanting rays.

In Bk. V she makes her way (line 609),

> . . . viam celerans per mille coloribus arcum . . .

speeding a path through a rainbow of a thousand colors,

to fulfill Juno's command to burn the ships. Departing as she had come (line 658),

> ingentemque fuga secuit sub nubibus arcum.

she cut in her flight a huge rainbow beneath the clouds.

The parallels between her appearance and that of the snake cause further hesitation about the beneficent quality of the omen at Anchises' tomb. Propitious as the snake may seem to Aeneas for the moment, the two objects which regularly come from a shrine in Virgil are oracles and fire. Usually it is holy fire, as in the case of II, 297, but here the vivid gleam which the snake throws off (we note especially the word *incendebat*) seems to point in sinister fashion toward the future. It is from the inner hearts (*focis penetralibus*, lines 660) that the women snatch the flaming brands with which to fire the fleet. Iris, the very agent whereby this is accomplished, already gleams in the supposedly harmless snake, just as in IV she had prefigured the light which was soon to burn brightly from Dido's pyre.

Just as there are numerous connections between Iris and the snake, so both are in turn linked imagistically with the appearance of Somnus (cf., e.g., line 657 with line 861).

12. The boat race is, of course, the major addition and change from Homer's games in *Iliad* XXIII, taking the place of Homer's chariot race. Even so, most critics, among them W. F. Jackson Knight (*Roman Vergil*: London 1944) 84, find it somehow lacking.

On the games in general see W. H. Willis, "Athletic Contests in the Epic," *TAPA* 72 (1941) 392–417, and E. Mehl's appendix ("Die Leichenspiele in der Äneis als turngeschichtliche Quelle") to K. Büchner's essay on *P. Vergilius Maro*, *RE* 8 A, 1487–93. On the relationship between Virgil and Homer, see R. Heinze, *Virgils Epische Technik* (Stuttgart 1957) 145–70; H. W. Prescott, *The Development of Virgil's Art* (Chicago 1927) 206–25; and the brief discussion of Williams, pp. xiii–xvi.

13. See *P. Vergili Maronis Opera*, with commentary by J. Conington, II (ed. 4, rev. by H. Nettleship, London, 1884), on line 160 ("'Medio' is not explained by the commentators, but it seems to mean 'half-way' . . .") or Williams ("medio: 'at the half-way stage'"). Cf. the use of *medium* in line 1.

14. One other similarity between Menoetes and Palinurus deserves elaboration. Gyas orders Menoetes to cling to the rocks (lines 164–65)

> . . . sed caeca Menoetes
> saxa timens proram pelagi detorquet ad undas.

but Menoetes, fearing the hidden rocks, twists the prow toward the open sea.

He is rebuked, we recall, and a moment later thrown overboard. Palinurus, pilot in the adventures of real life, behaves in much the same fashion when confronted with the perils of Charybdis (III, 561–62):

> . . . primusque rudentem
> contorsit laevas proram Palinurus ad undas . . .

First Palinurus turned the groaning prow to the waves on the left.

If the actual facts are disparate (a turn to port saves the fleet of Aeneas, but would have been the unsafe, albeit daring, thing in the case of Gyas' ship), the nautical instincts are in each case similar. The fate of Menoetes awaits Palinurus, even though doom is postponed through all of Bk. III because the pilot is still necessary. Lines 555–59 of III, which describe the rocks and waves of the dangerous passage, look to the *caeca saxa*, the dark rocks of the goal, which Menoetes means to avoid. But ultimately they anticipate the loud rocks (*rauca saxa*) of the Sirens which offer the closest brush with death by sea that the now pilotless Aeneas experiences. That Virgil was specifically looking back to Bk. III at this point in the boat race is shown by the many other reflections (e.g., III, 560, is echoed in V, 189–90).

15. Cf. also V, 224, with VI, 353.

16. Of the similarities in treatment between the two episodes, the recollection of line 270 in line 858 is perhaps the most interesting. Sergestus barely escapes while Palinurus dies, tearing the helm with him (cf. the uses of *vix* in lines 270, 847, 857).

Jackson Knight's possible interpretation of Palinurus as "the steering will deranged by passion" (*Roman Vergil*, 165) seems more applicable to Sergestus than to Aeneas' helmsman. Then again Sergestus ought to be considered, from the parallels between the section of the boat race which centers on him and the journey past the Sirens, the comic counterpart of the Aeneas who might have gone aground on the Sirens' rocks, had *furor* got the better of him. Whatever the case may be, the human element certainly enters into Sergestus' downfall in the same way that madness triumphs over moderation in the epic's final lines.

17. This motif of frustration, which may find its Virgilian origin in the story of Orpheus and Eurydice, is central to Bk. V. See n. 16 above for the uses of *vix*. *Nequiquam* may be found in lines 276 and 860; *frustra* in 27 and 221.

18. The use of *saxo* is more likely locative than instrumental.

19. One other point in this episode deserves notice. The crucial juncture of the race takes place when the men are tired, almost at the very goal itself (*sub ipsam / finem*, lines 327–28). This holds true in the boat race (*ipso in fine*, line 225) and is implied in the boxing contest (line 463) where Aeneas imposes the end upon the tired Dares. This combination of nearness to goal, weariness, and even mishap just before the very end, is common between the games and the actual journey of Bk. V. The theme is first expressed in Aeneas' ambiguous statement of line 29, urging the men to make for the harbor of Acestes so he might land the tired ships (*fessas demittere navis*). Yet, as Conington-Nettleship point out, this use of *demittere* in the sense of "land" is unparalleled. But the adjective *fessus* looks to the whole expedition itself (line 41), especially to the women (*fessas matres*, line 715; and cf. line 717) whom Aeneas leaves behind in Sicily. Hence the irony of the phrase *demittere navis*, as "land" but also as "let go" almost in the sense of "destroy," for the tiredness of the women manifests itself in the burning of the ships, themselves also weary of wandering.

20. The deadly accuracy is not left unmentioned either, however, for he once left the champion Butes stretched *moribundum* (line 374) on the sand.

21. The phraseology of line 465 is drawn from G. IV, 488, at the point where the lovers had almost successfully escaped when a sudden

madness seized Orpheus (*cum subita incautum dementia cepit amantem*).

22. The foot race and boxing contests look not so much to events within Bk. V as to the ultimate and most important conflict of the whole poem, the clash between Aeneas and Turnus in XII. Here what was done during the games of V in a spirit of sportive rivalry now recurs, overhung with impending death. The battle between the two heroes is indeed almost a parody of an athletic contest, fought out first by a duel with weapons, then on the race course, and finally by a violent display of strength, the last two paralleling the middle contests of Bk. V. Virgil deliberately conveys this tone, for at one crucial point in the proceedings he states (XII, 764–65):

> . . . neque enim levia aut ludicra petuntur
> praemia, sed Turni de vita et sanguine certant.

Nor are the prizes they seek light or sportive, but they vie for the life blood of Turnus.

After much time spent in futile chase, Aeneas challenges Turnus (line 890):

> "non cursu, saevis certandum est comminus armis."

"We must fight, not as in a race, but in the hand-to-hand combat of fierce arms."

But it is to the foot race that Virgil dedicates the majority of lines within the description of the last encounter. Aeneas decides the setting for the games in Bk. V as he makes his way (lines 287–89)

> gramineum in campum, quem collibus undique curvis
> cingebant silvae, mediaque in valle theatri
> circus erat . . .

toward a grassy spot, which woods on the circling slopes girded on all sides, where, in the valley's midst, was the circuit of a theater.

In Bk. XII, by contrast, the Trojans and Latins give way to open up a place for the preliminary clashes, and around and through this space Turnus flees in the hope of escaping from Aeneas. But he cannot (lines 744–45),

> undique enim densa Teucri inclusere corona
> atque hinc vasta palus, hinc ardua moenia cingunt.

for on all sides Trojans hemmed him in with thick crowds, and here a broad swamp, there the high walls, surround him.

The sea race anticipates the necessity of Palinurus' death. Here, in the reality of the final clash with all idea of game far behind, luck once more triumphs over innocence as Turnus falls victim to the future course of Rome.

The motif of the race is especially important, and R. W. Cruttwell, *Virgil's Mind at Work* (Oxford 1946) 87–88, interprets it as a serious counterpart of the *lusus Troiae*, primarily because of the labyrinth image. The comparison is intriguing but, as interpreted above, the labyrinth simile seems equally to lead to Bk. VI. The many parallels between Bks. V and XII (e.g., V, 230, and XII, 49; V, 456, and XII, 501; V, 458, and XII, 553) deserve separate elaboration.

23. We might also note that Euryrion brought down (*deiecit*, line 542) the bird from the lofty heavens and Somnus cast down (*proiecit*, line 859) Palinurus from the side of the ship.

24. J. Henry, *Aeneidea* (Dublin 1881) III, 127–34, on V, 520–26.

25. And, ironically, it is Polites' son, named Priam for his grandfather, who is one of the leaders of the troop of boys (line 564). Cf. also *Aen.* VI, 308 (= *G.* IV, 477).

26. See n. 8 above, but cf. the just strictures of R. A. Brooks, "Discolor Aura. Reflections on the Golden Bough." *AJP* 74 (1953) 261, n. 2.

27. The simile may also look to the past for a moment. Throughout the *Aeneid* we are never allowed to forget Dido. She reappears in VI, the cold spirit of revenge. Ironically, it is a robe of Dido's weaving with which Aeneas drapes the bier of Pallas in XI, 73–75. The death scenes of Camilla and Turnus are in large measure re-enactments of Dido's downfall. Here the horse on which Iulus rides is one which Dido gave as a memento and pledge of her love (*sui monimentum et pignus amoris*). Gave to whom? Perhaps to Aeneas, but more likely it is the very animal little Iulus rides in Bk. IV. As we learn early in VI, the misguided love of Pasiphae resulted in the Minotaur, product of an evil love (*Veneris monimenta nefandae*). It is possible that Virgil's mind jumped from one scene to the other through the liaison of the labyrinth image in Bk. V.

28. The poet leaves *in medio* (VIII, 675) ambiguous. Does he mean in the middle of the ocean where the dolphins are playing or in the shield's center, at the place of the utmost importance? Since doubt remains, both interpretations should be accepted. The first is stressed here only for present purposes.

29. Cf. line 674, where the irony is fully apparent. Much of the imagery is borrowed from *de Rerum Natura* II, 40ff.

30. In fact, if beauty of movement is the order of the day, the similes sometimes appear to give the lie even to that. In the labyrinth picture, the traces of the path are broken by misleading deceit (*ancipitem dolum*), which is synonymous with the deceptive *error*. To denote wandering and lack of purpose seems to be the latent but real motive of the simile and, though the picture of the dolphins which follows lends a lightness and

gaiety to Daedalus' toilsome maze, there still remains an aura of insecurity which disrupts the initial precision. Finally, the parade begins to give way to a more realistic picture of the commotion of a field of battle (*fugas et proelia*, line 593); yet all still remains within the context of a *lusus*.

31. The poet may have combined the metaphors of torch and bit here. For *excutio* and the imagery of the bit, cf. VI, 78–79, 100–101 (see above, chap. I, n. 9).

32. Henry (above, n. 24) III, 199, in his succinct commentary on line 815, defines the episode as "the superstition of the scape-goat, or expiation by transference." The idea of pacification through human sacrifice, and then by images, is frequent enough to need no discussion here. See, e.g., Frazer's elucidation of the ceremony of the Argei in *Fasti* V, 621ff (Publii Ovidii Nasonis *Fastorum Libri Sex*, ed. Sir J. G. Frazer [London, 1929], IV, 74–109). Part VI of the original *Golden Bough*, entitled "The Scapegoat," is also a mine of information.

33. Lines 763–64 and 777–78 anticipate the action of Neptune.

34. The most perceptive piece of recent criticism on the figure of Palinurus is to be found in the epilogue of Cyril Connolly's *The Unquiet Grave* (New York 1957), 134–47.

35. This image is anticipated in Anchises' description of night in line 738 — *torquet medios Nox umida cursus* (dewy night turns in middle course). Night literally races through the sky, but the image of "twisting" is also inherent in the boat race (lines 165, 177), as, of course, is the *meta* (lines 129, 159, 171).

36. Aside from book II, other examples of a similar setting may be found at VI, 520ff, and IX, 236ff. Although he attempts to fight off Somnus, Palinurus' position in line 857 becomes much like that of the sailors in lines 836–37.

37. It is thus that Sinon, the master of trickery, pretends that he was decked out in II, 132–33:

> "Iamque dies infanda aderat; mihi sacra parari
> et salsae fruges et circum tempora vittae."

"And now the dread day was at hand, the sacred rites were prepared for me, salted meal, and fillets about my temples."

He builds his false story on the supposed demand that the prophet of Apollo makes for human sacrifice in order to speed the Greeks on their way across the sea — another Iphigenia, as it were — for the return home. And just as the journey of the Greeks is the opposite of what Sinon claims it will be, so Laocoön is the actual victim in place of the crafty Sinon. Both Palinurus and Laocoön die even though their positions in life were as close as possible to the god of the sea. The adventure of Sinon is a travesty on their sacrifice.

38. On Twain, see Leo Marx, "The Pilot and the Passenger: Landscape Conventions and the Style of *Huckleberry Finn*," *Am. Lit.* 28 (1956) 129–46. And we remember that Ishmael learns of life and evil from Ahab and the sea, escaping in the end by means of a coffin.

Not that Aeneas is hereafter without a guide. Palinurus, who offers allegiance to sea and stars, gives place to the Sibyl, the perfect leader through the period of life-in-death. In Bk. VI, the past with its years of wandering yields to the historical Roman future, water to land, uncertainty to at least some assurance regarding what is to come, individual heroism to involvement in a national destiny. Only at the epic's conclusion is the story refocused on the personal and private hatred of Aeneas and Turnus. The almost-Roman Sibyl knows of the past and future, the world of the dead and that of the living. She comprehends that both must be a part of the heroism of Aeneas; that from the dead alone will come reassurance of the validity of future history. Yet, even before the end of VI, she, too, disappears suddenly without mention, being no longer of assistance once death has lent stability to life. From now on Aeneas is the ruler of his own destiny.

In Bk. VI, as in II, Aeneas' emotional involvement (which in the end postulates suffering and loss) and the symbol of his experience are separated. In II, fallen Troy is, metaphorically, the headless corpse of Priam, reinterpreted by the simile of the aged ash gradually hewn to bits, but the emotional loss is the disappearance of Creusa. In the subsequent two books, emotion and symbol are combined in the figures of Anchises and Dido. Palinurus, too, falls into this pattern. Once more the past is "torn" from Aeneas, emotionally, in the person of the helmsman himself, symbolically in the useless boat, mutilated by the pilot in his fall. When we turn to VI, the separation is once more clear, between golden bough and Sibyl. Of the Sibyl as guide, we have spoken above. The golden bough parallels her — and this stage in the life of Aeneas — symbolically, for, being alive and yet dead, it looks both to past and future, and serves to betoken the hero's progress through a world of which he is only momentarily a part. Like Palinurus, it, too, is torn away (V, 858; VI, 143), clinging (*cunctans*: V, 856; VI, 211), both to be and to fulfill a *munus* (cf. VI, 142, 629, 637), this time to Persephone, the world of the dead, not Neptune, the interlude of journeying now past. The world of the dead must also be propitiated for a misuse of its legitimate purposes, just as the god of the sea demands an offering when his usefulness is over.

One need add only briefly that the change from Palinurus to Sibyl as guide is, in a sense, akin to that change Dante experiences when Virgil, personification of philosophy without revelation, must give up his position to Beatrice at the top of *Purgatorio*, for she alone, as theology, can lead him into and through *Paradiso*.

39. Looked at from another point of view, the death of Palinurus

means the end of all anti-Roman sentiments in the epic and prepares the stage for the gradual evolution of *Romanitas* which comes in the seven books that follow. Everything connected with the sea was viewed with general suspicion by Roman authors. They were essentially a land people, as opposed to the Greeks, and though in this case land means war, nevertheless it was more important that the *casus* and *errores* of the sea give way before the stability of the Italian land and people.

40. For Priam the imagery of the trunk, as we saw in the previous chapter, is artistically elaborated in the simile of II, 626ff, which contains many overtones of an aged and wounded old man.

On a possible connection between the loss of the tiller and a similar event in the epic of Gilgamesh, see W. F. Jackson Knight, *Cumaean Gates* (Oxford 1936) 25 and 41.

41. Aeneas' loss of his pilot before reaching his destination, whether physical or spiritual, is parallel to Marlow's loss of his native helmsman in the journey up the river to find Kurtz, in Conrad's *Heart of Darkness*. (See Lillian Feder, "Marlow's Descent into Hell," *Nineteenth-Century Fiction* 9 [March, 1955] 280–92). An even closer connection exists with Conrad's *The Secret Sharer*, where growth into self-knowledge comes about by the appearance and disappearance of another self — coming like a "headless corpse" and going like a hat, bobbing up and down in the ocean's swell.

42. The later connection with Lavinia is one forged more by the fire of fate than of passion, and Aeneas' sorrow at the death of Pallas smacks as much of Augustus' relationship with Marcellus as of any sudden feelings of sympathy on the hero's part.

43. On the apparent parallels between Palinurus and Elpenor, see Williams, pp. 198–99 (on lines 827f) with his references. The problem of the inconsistencies between the descriptions of Palinurus in Bks. V and VI has been well discussed by Jackson Knight (*Roman Vergil*, 291–92) and P. Jacob, "L'épisode de Palinure," *ÉtCl* 20 (1952) 163–67.

44. *Odyssey* XII, 154–200. This book as a whole was much in Virgil's mind as he wrote Bk. V (e.g., the model of lines 8–11 is *Od.* XII, 403–6).

45. See J. R. T. Pollard, "Muses and Sirens," *CR* n.s. 2 (1952) 60–63.

Chapter 3   *Aeneid* Book VIII: History's Dream

1. For a bibliography of recent work on Bk. VIII see G. Duckworth, *CW* 51 (1958) 157–58. Articles he cites of particular importance will be noted again below. Lacking a commentary devoted specifically to VIII, one turns constantly for guidance to the last edition of Conington-Nettleship. The thoughts of W. Warde Fowler (*Aeneas at the Site of*

Rome: Oxford 1917) are always stimulating. R. Heinze (*Virgils Epische Technik*: Stuttgart 1957) has no specific section devoted to VIII, but his occasional remarks (e.g. pp. 364ff) should be noted.

2. See D. L. Drew, *The Allegory of the Aeneid* (Oxford 1927) 6–41.

3. See especially lines 348, 364ff.

4. See J. R. Bacon, "Aeneas in Wonderland: A Study of Aeneid VIII," *CR* 53 (1939) 97–104.

5. See F. Bömer, "Studien zum VIII. Buche der Aeneis," *RhM* 92 (1944) 319–69.

6. See above, chap. 1, n. 15. Horses are a prime part of Turnus' equipment for the final clash in XII and add to the violence which its opening lines attribute to him. It is interesting to note that in XII, 84, one of the prime qualifications of his horses is that they surpass the snows in whiteness (*candore nives anteirent*), the chief characteristic of the warrior horses Anchises observes on the Italian shore (*candore nivali*: III, 538). For an explanation of the color of these horses, see R. D. Williams (P. Vergili Maronis *Aeneidos, Liber Tertius*: Oxford 1962) on III, 537.

7. Servius (on VIII, 19), with his usual tendency to exaggerate Virgil's indebtedness to his models, states that the simile is word for word from Apollonius Rhodius. Those interested not only in Virgil's specific verbal changes but also in examining how a difference of context can completely alter the imaginative effect of any given lines will find Virgil's source in *Argonautica* III, 755ff. Though Virgil gives himself many times elsewhere the occasion to use this simile (lines 20–21, as observed above, are repeated from IV, 285–86, and similar expressions often appear, e.g., at X, 680), only here does he do so as a splendid transition vehicle from one sphere of existence to another that is thoroughly different.

8. The escape from reality into one's own private pastoral world is a common enough occurrence in Latin literature, especially in the poetry of Horace. See Viktor Pöschl, "Horaz und die Politik" (*SbHeid*, 4 abh., 1956) 14 and 17ff.

9. *Tumeo* and *tumidus* are twice used in Bk. II (lines 381, 472) in connection with snakes. The latter context finds Pyrrhus as a swollen serpent lurking underground, ready to burst forth in new strength at the coming of spring. In II, wrath and violence are constantly developed through images of potentiality, to be magnified, not suppressed, as in VIII.

10. See, e.g., IV, 393 and VI, 468.

11. In relation to the word *pietas* it should be observed that suddenly in VIII, 84, Aeneas is called *pius* again, just as he is about to perform the due sacrifice of the pig to Juno.

12. The only person killed during the storm of Bk. I is the pilot Orontes. Aeneas himself had watched the wave strike his ship (cf. I,

113–17, with the various descriptions of Palinurus in Bks. V and VI) and when Achates reports to his leader on the survival of the fleet he notes (I, 583–85):

> "omnia tuta vides, classem sociosque receptos.
> unus abest, medio in fluctu quem vidimus ipsi
> summersum; dictis respondent cetera matris."

"You see that everything is safe, fleet and comrades restored. One alone is missing, whom we ourselves saw sinking in mid-ocean. All else fits the words of your mother."

Palinurus fulfills the same role, much expanded and at a much more critical moment which demands his death alone.

13. Though the last four lines of this quotation are repeated in VIII (the only change being from *is*, III, 393, to *hic*, VIII, 46), the first could well be said to summarize the introductory mood of VIII. *Sollicito* recalls the trials of the outside world while *secreti* establishes the isolation of the hero on the river bank. The same word is applied to Aeneas in VIII, 610, as he receives the shield in the remote valley by Caere's cool stream.

14. As in the case of the Cacus legend, Virgil's account of the omen of the pig is a good illustration of how he varies tradition for his own purposes. The equation of the thirty pigs with the number of years before Alba Longa was to be founded appears in Varro (*Rust.* 2.4; *Ling.* 5.144). Fabius Pictor apparently mentioned the pig (Diodorus frag. 7.5). In Dionysius' account (I, 55ff) the pig led Aeneas from Laurentum to the site of Lavinium. No pig at all is mentioned by Livy. On the place of this prodigy in the legend of Aeneas see F. Cauer "Die römische Aeneassage," *Jahrb. f. cl. Phil. Suppl.* 15 (Leipzig 1887); J. Perret, *Les Origins de la légende troyenne de Rome* (Paris 1942), esp. 322, 333, 525.

The confused aspect of the traditions brings Mr. Jackson Knight to remark (*Roman Vergil*, p. 110) ". . . in particular, Vergil does not make the sow lead the Trojans, and he seems not to have finally decided exactly what he meant the sow to signify."

15. Those wishing for an analysis where the Jungian archetypal connection between birth and water is elaborated can turn to Otto Rank *The Myth of the Birth of the Hero* (New York 1959). A close analogy exists with Cantos I and II of *Purgatorio* where Dante is described in terms of his newborn soul, setting sail across the waters to the shore of purgation. The water rush, which must be plucked at the end of Canto I, looks to the golden bough for some of its attributes (it springs up again as soon as torn off) but also to the mother pig, as symbol of birth into a land where innocence is regained.

In placing this particular moment of Aeneas' career into the total perspective of his heroic achievement (and more generally still into the paradigm of epic as a whole), I have gained much insight from Heinrich

Zimmer, *The King and the Corpse* (New York 1960) and Joseph Campbell, *The Hero with a Thousand Faces* (New York 1956). Campbell comments on the *Aeneid* on pp. 30–31. But in placing total emphasis on the revelation of destiny to the hero in the sixth book, he neglects the actual initiation of Aeneas in Bk. VIII into a real world which, paradoxically, must be left in order to be regained (and never is by the titular hero himself). The two books bear the same relation to each other as the episode of Tiresias does to that of the Phaeacians in the *Odyssey* — the one pronouncing the future from the land of the dead, the other offering, with its images of fire and leaves, nakedness and stream, the potentiality of rebirth into the perfection of marriage and stable rule.

16. For a more detailed examination of the sinister implications underlying Aeneas' arrival at the mouth of the Tiber see K. J. Reckford, "Latent Tragedy in *Aeneid* VII, 1–285," *AJP* 82 (1961) 254ff. The sources of the legend are well discussed by H. Boas, *Aeneas' Arrival in Latium* (Amsterdam 1938) 53ff.

17. Note the descriptive parallels between VI, 297–301, and VIII, 31–34; VI, 407–412ff, and VIII, 155ff.

18. When Evander cries, upon first seeing Aeneas (lines 154–55),

> . . . "ut te, fortissime Teucrum,
> accipio agnoscoque libens! . . ."

"How willingly I accept and recognize you, bravest of Trojans!"

he is still using a vocabulary associated with the sudden appearance of an omen. Cf. Tolumnius' interpretation of the omen of the birds in XII, 259–60:

> "hoc erat, hoc, votis" inquit "quod saepe petivi.
> accipio agnoscoque deos . . ."

"This was the very thing," he says, "which I often begged for in my prayers. I accept and recognize the gods."

19. *Purgatorio* XXVIII. A suggestion of the same contrast between life and death that exists in *Aeneid* VI and VIII is inherent in the differences between the *selva oscura*, in which Dante begins his journey, and the divine forest of the Earthly Paradise. It is not only the latter's overwhelming beauty which Dante stresses but — and we think once more to *Aeneid* VIII — the fact that innocence is an important component of its Golden Age. As Matilda describes it (XXVIII, 142–44):

> "Qui fu innocente l'umana radice;
> qui primavera è sempre, ed ogni frutto;
> nèttare è questo di che ciascun dice."

20. On the Cacus-Hercules interlude see more recently H. Schnepf, "Das Herculesabenteuer in Virgils Aeneid (viii 184f)," *Gymnasium* 66

(1959) 250–68, and his notes for an adequate bibliography of past interpretations. Schnepf seeks mainly to find parallels between Hercules and Augustus.

21. The word *monstrum* appears at II, 245; III, 658, and VIII, 198. *Molis* is used at II, 32, 150, 185; III, 656, and VIII, 199.

It has often been said, correctly, and most recently by R. D. Williams (above, n. 6, p. 17), that the Polyphemus episode fits only poorly with the basic thematic material of Bk. III, having no direct connection either with Aeneas or the future of Rome. Nevertheless, though an isolated figure in his context, he fits well into one of the symbolic patterns which Virgil delights in elaborating, of violence, gigantic and strong, suppressed or on the loose.

22. It is possible that the use of *super* in line 245 and *desuper* (line 249), as Hercules prepares to leap down into the cave of Cacus, may anticipate the position of Apollo at the battle of Actium (lines 704–5):

> Actius haec cernens arcum intendebat Apollo
> desuper . . .

As he watched these things, Apollo of Actium stretched his bow from above.

23. A possible direct connection between Cacus and the underworld is discussed by J. Kroll, *Gott und Hölle* (Studien der Bibliothek Warburg: Leipzig 1932), esp. 389–98. The violence of Cacus and the doom of Pallas both help break down the spell of idealism which surrounds Evander's pastoral haven. On the presence of death in the pastoral world see E. Panofsky "Et in Arcadia Ego: Poussin and the Elegiac Tradition," in *Meaning in the Visual Arts* (New York 1955).

Aeneas' journey up the Tiber is in many respects similar to that of Marlow up the jungle river in Conrad's *Heart of Darkness* (see above, chap. 2, n. 41). Even though Aeneas is escaping for a moment from the world of reality into an ideal realm, he still finds that it was a land once lorded over by Cacus, who has much in common with Kurtz, the object of Marlow's up-river search ("Those round knobs were not ornamental but symbolic; they were expressive and puzzling, striking and disturbing — food for thought and also for vultures if there had been any looking down from the sky; but at all events for such ants as were industrious enough to ascend the pole. They would have been even more impressive, those heads on the stakes, if their faces had not been turned to the house."). Aeneas learns of the power of blackness, as well as of the strength of pastoral idealism, from the source of Rome.

24. For the use of the grove elsewhere in the *Aeneid* to introduce important episodes one need only refer to Bk. I (the *lucus* in the midst of Dido's city, I, 441–50ff) and to the dark wood which introduces Aeneas and the Sibyl to the underworld. On the grove and its relation to what he calls an emblem, or threshold symbol, which often takes the form of

an initiatory adventure, see E. Honig, *Dark Conceit: The Making of Allegory* (Cambridge, Mass., 1960) 71. He defines his terms on p. 72: "The emblem outlines a concise picture in brief focus. The threshold symbol generally frames a brief preparatory action of the hero and is the thematic center for the whole episode."

If the calming of the Tiber, and its quasi-allegorical connection with the wrath of Juno, and the pig are the emblems, the Cacus-Hercules clash is what Honig would call the "threshold symbol," save that Aeneas does not participate in the action but merely absorbs its implications through the dramatic narrative of Evander. This episode is the symbolic, mythic prototype adventure which precedes the tensions of the shield (distant future) and the war with Mezentius and Turnus, which is soon to come. To its importance as microcosm of the future, Virgil adds emphasis by incorporating it into the ritual progress of Aeneas which betokens initiation into the heroism of Hercules, with his suppression of evil, and also into the necessity for heroism (which in the case of Hercules is still tinged with *furor*) to subsume its more violent qualities to the pastoral humility of Evander.

After he satisfies the demand of Pallas and passes into the world of Evander, the hero should be exposed to an adventure. In this case the challenger is Cacus, the challenged is Hercules, who stands as partial symbolic model for Aeneas. Only upon leaving the site of Rome does the actual confrontation of Aeneas with war take place, even though symbolically it is anticipated here. The clash of Hercules and Cacus is the meeting, in a world which is still dreamlike and unreal, of Aeneas (Evander deliberately equates him with Hercules) with his antagonist. The events depicted on the shield, culminating in the battle of Actium, are the modern Roman equivalent of what to Aeneas is the past. Aeneas, though initiated into the dream paradigm both of Rome's pastoral ancestry and of the necessity for good to clash with evil through heroism, is halfway in between. But the world is still a dream, the hero still ignorant of his model, as he remains, even at the book's end, contemplating the shield with amazement and complete lack of understanding. What now becomes most important is his decision, forced by the *signum* of Venus, to face the unknown future, to leave the world of the past, of dream and escape, and confront the present. This means the horrors and bloodshed of war and, specifically, as he learns from the sign sent from his mother, the death of Pallas which projects upon the present suffering of Aeneas the future tragedy of Marcellus and reaffirms the need for sacrifice to attempt to gain a peace which will never be his.

25. A brief discussion of these lines is given by M. Taylor, "Primitivism in Virgil," *AJP* 76 (1955) 276.

26. In line 371, *minis* picks up *minis* in line 40; *tumultu* recalls the same word in line 4.

27. Cf. line 410 (*sopitos suscitat ignis*) with Aeneas' gesture in lines

542–43 (*Herculeis sopitas ignibus aras / excitat* — he awakens the sleeping altars with fire to Hercules).

28. See V. Pöschl, "Das Zeichen der Venus and die Gestalt des Aeneas," *Festschrift Regenbogen* (Heidelberg 1952) 135ff.

29. On line 631 Servius comments "sane totus hic locus Ennianus est" — clearly this whole passage is Ennian. See the enlightening note of E. Warmington in his edition of Ennius *Ann.* frag. 71 (= 68V³) (London 1935) p. 27. n. *b.* In emphasizing the Ennian phraseology, however, he minimizes the influence of the Lucretian context, which seems to me of paramount importance. I hope to analyze in detail at a later time the influence of *Annales* I on *Aeneid* VIII.

30. Virgil uses the same word here, *fingere*, as he does in line 365, to describe Evander's command to Aeneas to fashion himself according to the likeness of a god, and in line 726 to depict the actual molding of the shield. All three usages are closely allied and typify different levels of *Aeneid* VIII.

Chapter 4   *Aeneid* Book XII: Tragic Victory

1. On Book XII as a whole I have benefited from the commentary by W. S. Maguinness (London 1953) and the analyses of W. Warde Fowler in *The Death of Turnus* (Oxford 1919). On the figure of Turnus, Pöschl's treatment is of the greatest value (*Die Dichtkunst* 153–227). For a summary and discussion of recent views, see G. Duckworth, "Fate and Free Will in Vergil's *Aeneid*," *CJ* 51 (1955–56) 357–64, and "Turnus and Duryodhana," *TAPA* 92 (1961) esp. 81–88. The last scene of the book has been much debated (see notably A. Thornton, "The Last Scene of the *Aeneid*," *G&R* 22 [1953] 82–84; Lillian Feder, "Vergil's Tragic Theme," *CJ* 49 [1953–54] 197–209).

2. The need to retain the Helen passage, with Servius and against the manuscript authority, has now been thoroughly established. See most recently N. L. Hatch, "The Time Element in Interpretation of *Aeneid* 2. 575–76 and 585–87," *CP* 54 (1959) 255–57; R. G. Austin, "Virgil, *Aeneid* 2. 567–88," *CQ* n.s. 11 (1961) 185–98.

3. Cf. VII, 362; X, 774; XI, 484.

4. Those interested in tracing any possible link between Turnus and Paris might consider the fact that Virgil probably found the source for line 9 —

> haud secus accenso gliscit violentia Turno.

In like manner swells the wrath of fiery Turnus —

in a brief mention of the Trojan war by Lucretius (I, 474–75) telling how

> ignis Alexandri Phrygio sub pectore gliscens
> clara accendisset saevi certamina belli. . .

the fire, swelling beneath the Trojan heart of Paris, set aflame the blazing battles of a fierce war.

Love leads to war, and Turnus, thinking of war, finds its cause in love.

5. The contrast between red and white is a common one in Latin poetry. See Fordyce on Catullus 61. 9f and 187. On *purpureus* as a color associated with death as well as life, see Williams on *Aen.* V, 79. For a splendid discussion of the terror an author's use of the color red often produces see M. Bodkin *Archetypal Patterns in Poetry* (Oxford 1934) 44–45. That the shedding of blood is a necessary concomitant of this marriage is one of the central themes of Bk. VII (lines 318–19; 554–56), anticipating these very lines in XII.

6. This may also explain why so much of the vocabulary of the opening lines is repeated after this simile. *Turbat* (line 70) recalls *turbidus* (line 10); *figit* (line 70) picks up *fixum* (line 7); *ardet* (line 71) reflects *ardet* (line 3) and *arma* (line 71) recalls *arma* (line 6).

The verbal connection between line 70 —

> illum turbat amor figitque in virgine vultus.

Love sets him in turmoil; he fixes his gaze on the maiden. —

and IV, 4–5 —

> . . . haerent infixi pectore vultus
> verbaque . . .

His features and words remain embedded in her breast — is a further link between Dido and Turnus.

7. Punic lions were apparently noted for ferocity, which adds to the effect of the physical vigor that the wounded beast seems to possess. The phrase *Poenos leones* appears in *Ecl.* V, 27, where the implication is that even the fiercest animals weep at the death of Daphnis.

8. The wound of love is intimately connected with war and forms part of Turnus' crucial relationship to Latinus and his city. With the death of Turnus dies all opposition to the new order. Hence, through his love for Lavinia, he takes more and more the city's part, and his downfall is even more closely linked with the ruin of his city than is Dido's. The link never becomes as explicit as the symbolic relationship between Priam, the aged ash, and the gods ruining Troy. Nevertheless, in the death of Amata (as much a figure for Dido as Turnus himself) and in Aeneas' attempt to burn out the city, we have the last in a series which begins with the middle section of Bk. II and progresses through the whole of Bk. IV, where the metaphorical fire of love soon becomes destructive as it not only consumes her body, but also, through the subtlety of imagery, offers Aeneas as the destroyer and plunderer of woman and city alike. Finally, the encircling of Dido (*cingere*: I, 673), an image

appropriate to maddened beast as well as besieged city, asserts its full implications only in the death of Turnus, defender of his dying city, lover of its heiress, and raging animal at last brought to bay.

9. See Maguinness (above, n. 1) on XII, 158.

10. Cf. lines 334 and 366 with 455.

11. The verb *insequitur* is also used at II, 530, and XII, 466. One might add that Latinus, called *praedives* in XI, 213, rich as Priam had once been, is also soon to lose his own city.

The simile itself is apparently original with Virgil. Those interested in tracing its genesis should turn not only to *Aen.* II but also to *G.* IV, 16–17, where, speaking of Procne and of swallows in general, the poet says:

> omnia nam late vastant ipsasque volantis
> ore ferunt dulcem nidis immitibus escam.

For they lay everything waste far and wide, and carry home in their mouths the winged bees themselves as a sweet morsel for their pitiless nestlings.

The last line surely inspired *Aen.* XII, 475. It is probably true to say also that one further detail in the simile, the *umida stagna* (lines 476–77), comes directly from the *virentia stagna* of *G.* IV, 18.

12. The simile seems to typify a latent irony in much of the book's imagery by which metaphors ordinarily associated with violent, but sometimes productive, nature are utilized to describe the horrors of war. Lines 283–84 offer a good example where we learn how

> . . . it toto turbida caelo
> tempestas telorum ac ferreus ingruit imber, . . .

a swirling tempest of spears goes through the whole sky and iron rain falls.

We note also the mention of bloody dew (*rores sanguineos*) in lines 339–40, an image the poet also uses to describe the heads of Amycus and Diores dripping with blood (*rorantia sanguine*, line 512).

13. With XII, 625ff, cf. II, 387. In each case what appears the first road to victory ends only in defeat, soon or late.

14. It is worthy of note that the three verbs of the simile, *fremit*, *gaudet*, and *attollens*, are all associated with Turnus in the opening lines of the book. He rouses his spirit (*attollit animos*, line 4), and, in his character as wounded lion, *gaudetque comantis / excutiens cervice toros* (lines 6–7) and finally *fremit ore cruento* (line 8). What in the initial moments of the book characterizes Turnus' emotion is here taken over by Aeneas — not, however, as a wounded lion, destined to die, but in the guise of mountains, tall and sturdy, whose inner strength is fate, not necessarily the stability of personal assurance.

15. I have found mention of the love-death motif in *G.* III most re-

cently in the remarks of J. Bayet in Fondation Hardt *Entretiens* II (Geneva 1956) 160.

16. Cf. II, 19; VIII, 225, and so forth.

17. It is possible that the image Virgil means to suggest at lines 481ff (which undergoes such an ironic metamorphosis here) is that of the labyrinth, at the center of which remains the monster to be killed. It is a universal poetic archetype (see Northrop Frye *Anatomy of Criticism* [Princeton 1957] 150, 190f) whose implications for Virgil, *Aen.* VI, have been discussed by Jackson Knight in *Cumaean Gates.*

18. The simile which vivifies the Fury's descent compares her to an arrow (lines 856–59):

> non secus ac nervo per nubem impulsa sagitta,
> armatam saevi Parthus quam felle veneni,
> Parthus sive Cydon, telum immedicabile, torsit,
> stridens et celeris incognita transilit umbras: . . .

like an arrow, driven by the cord through the clouds, an arrow armed with the venom of cruel poison, which a Parthian has shot, a Parthian or perhaps a Cretan. Whistling and unseen, it leaps through the swift shadows.

Virgil seems to stress the word *immedicabile* and to recall through it two things, first the imagery of line 46 describing Turnus' illness, secondly the fact that Venus came to her son in the role of healer (*medicans,* line 418). Turnus' sickness and death is as predetermined as Aeneas' cure. The *telum* is but the deadly personification of the original weapon (line 8) by which the lion was wounded.

The simile, by its emphasis on the unseen and unexpected (*nubem, incognita, umbras*), plays its share in developing the atmosphere of dream and darkness which pervades these final lines.

19. On the connection between Aeneas and Achilles, see L. A. Mac-Kay, "Achilles as Model for Aeneas," *TAPA* 88 (1957) 11–16, and W. S. Anderson, "Vergil's Second *Iliad,*" *ibid.* 17–30.

20. This is only one of many connections between the present suffering of Turnus' death and past trials of Aeneas. Line 868, for instance, which describes the terrors of Turnus seeing the *Dira* —

> arrectaeque horrore comae et vox faucibus haesit.

His hair stood up in terror and his utterance clung to his throat —

is borrowed as a whole from IV, 280, and in part from II, 774. In the former, Aeneas confronts the vision of Mercury, demanding that he leave Dido and Carthage. The latter recalls the moment of Creusa's appearance to the distraught Aeneas seeking for her in the ruins of Troy. It is Turnus who must now go through the dream-world of madness that Aeneas had confronted in II; only his wandering results in death, not escape.

INDEX OF PASSAGES

GENERAL INDEX

Pig, allegory of, 111–115, 118–121, 126, 143, 149
Pöschl, V., viii
Polites, 27, 36, 86, 172, 177, 188
Polyphemus, 131
Porta Carmentalis, 135
Posidon, 121, 122; *see also* Neptune
Pregnancy, 3, 5, 7, 9, 12, 14, 15, 20
Prescott, H., viii
Priam, 3, 18, 24, 28, 29, 33, 36–39, 41, 46, 51, 52, 68, 86, 98, 99, 129, 172, 173, 175, 177, 181, 188
Prison, imagery of, 10, 11, 14, 17, 35, 156, 187
Proserpina, 42
Pyrgo, 89
Pyrrhus, 27, 33, 34, 36–39, 86, 172, 175, 177, 188

Red and white, imagery of, 158–160, 188, 197
Rending, imagery of, 37, 97, 98
Rome, viii, xii, xiii, 17, 37, 47, 48, 57, 58, 63, 80, 85, 91, 99, 104–107, 109, 111, 113, 115, 117, 121, 123, 128–132, 134–136, 141, 145, 147–152, 157, 175, 179, 190–193, 196, 201
Romulus and Remus, 120, 148
Rutulians, 49, 50, 52, 59–61

Saces, 166, 180
Sacrifice, 65, 67, 74, 81–83, 92, 93, 97, 99, 112–118, 120, 144, 149, 164, 165, 192, 196; Laocoön as, 24, 25, 27, 37; Nisus as, 81; Pallas as, 144; Sinon as, 18–21
Saturn, 105, 106, 134
Scythians, 196, 197
Sea, as *monstrum*, 71, 96, 165
Sergestus, 77–80
Servius, 59, 64–65
Sibyl, 4, 28, 30, 31, 37, 42, 44, 46, 50, 51, 56, 64, 74, 95, 117–120, 125, 126, 128, 129, 146, 158, 191
Sicily, 72, 92
Silvanus, 145, 147
Sinon, 3–5, 7, 8, 17–23, 25, 27, 30, 35, 129

Sirens, 77–79, 95, 102, 103
Sleep (Somnus), 71, 72, 76, 78, 79, 82, 84, 85, 94–97, 101, 198; and snake imagery, 26
Snakes, snake imagery, 5, 7, 17, 19, 20, 22–27, 34, 37, 40, 41, 51, 66, 67, 72, 73, 80, 81, 84, 96, 129, 165, 177, 196
Spear, 6, 12, 13, 133
Storm, xi, 8, 14, 16, 58, 66, 70–72, 114, 115, 146, 171
Styx, 44, 50, 120, 126, 128, 129, 147
Swan, 166

Tartarus, 28, 56, 57, 59, 146, 150
Tenedos, 5, 20, 23–25, 73
Thunderclap (*fragor*), 144
Tiber, xi, 21, 48, 62, 101, 105, 108–110, 115, 117–129, 141, 143, 145, 147, 149, 159, 160; and image of birth, 126; and Juno's anger, 112–118, 120, 126; as river of life, 128
Tiresias, 100
Tisiphone, 195
Trident (*cuspis*), 13
Trojans, 4, 5, 18, 19, 25–27, 30, 49, 53, 60, 70, 96, 105, 114, 116, 117, 124, 125, 128, 142, 152, 165, 166, 189, 190, 196
Troy, 3, 7, 8, 15, 16, 18–20, 24, 26–29, 31, 32, 37–41, 43, 45–48, 50, 51, 64, 68, 69, 74, 91, 96, 99, 102, 109–111, 125, 129, 130, 134, 142, 144, 173, 175, 176, 181, 191, 192, 199
Turning-point: *meta*, 75, 95; *scopulus*, 77–79
Turnus, x–xiii, 48, 52, 60–63, 89, 90, 105–108, 124, 144, Chapter 4 *passim*; as lion, 52, 62, 63, 153, 154, 157, 169, 187, 188; as stag, 63, 157, 160, 188, 189; as tiger, 61, 62, 153; as wolf, 60, 62, 153
Twain, Mark, 98

Ulysses, 18, 21; *see also* Odysseus
Underworld, xi, 4, 28, 30–34, 36, 44–48, 56, 59, 74, 92, 97, 99, 100, 118, 125, 127, 144, 147, 191